STORMING HEAVEN

ALSO BY LATELY THOMAS

The Mayor Who Mastered New York
The First President Johnson
The Vanishing Evangelist
A Debonair Scoundrel
Sam Ward: King of the Lobby
Delmonico's: A Century of Splendor
Between Two Empires

"I ruled like a queen in my kingdom."

Aimee Semple McPherson, aged forty-nine. Photograph taken in 1939.

STORMING

❧HEAVEN❧

*The Lives and Turmoils
of Minnie Kennedy and
Aimee Semple McPherson*

LATELY THOMAS

WILLIAM MORROW AND COMPANY, INC., NEW YORK

19 70

Second Printing, November 1970

Printed in the United States of America by
Quinn & Boden Company, Inc., Rahway, N.J.

Library of Congress Catalog Card Number 74-118057

TO

FAITH AND FABLE

Contents

Grateful acknowledgment is made to the following for permission to reproduce the photographs appearing on the designated pages: Pacific & Atlantic Photos, Inc., pages 46, 47, 57, 93, 179, 185; International News Photos, pages 52, 245; *Los Angeles Times,* pages 215, 310, 342, 345; The Associated Press, pages 181, 323, 328. Except as thus acknowledged, all pictures in this volume are from the collection of the author.

AUTHOR'S NOTE

Several years ago there was published an account of the bizarre disappearance, in 1926, of Aimee Semple McPherson, the most scintillant evangelist of her day, while swimming in the Pacific Ocean off a Los Angeles beach, and of her materialization five weeks later in the desert in Mexico.

Under the title *The Vanishing Evangelist: The Aimee Semple McPherson Kidnaping Affair*, that book recounted in suspenseful detail the months-long turmoil that followed Mrs. McPherson's explanation of those related occurrences—a turmoil that convulsed Los Angeles, divided the state of California, and enthralled millions of onlookers who watched the unfolding extravaganza through the medium of the press and radio.

That turmoil brought Sister Aimee and her redoubtable mother, Mrs. Minnie Kennedy, to the startled attention of a far-flung public and into international renown; and for long afterward curiosity regarding these two women, remarkable by whatever standards they might be judged, remained at a high pitch.

At the time of preparing *The Vanishing Evangelist*, the author's intention was to carry the story of Mrs. McPherson and Mrs. Kennedy through its later stages, which were no less interesting, not to say extraordinary, than had been the events of 1926.

Circumstances militated against the immediate carrying out of this design. Now, in this book, the subsequent careers of mother and daughter are recounted for the first time.

Because some knowledge of the 1926 affair is indispensable for understanding much that occurred later, the essential portions of that story have been incorporated in the present narrative. For fuller treatment of the episode's intriguing complexities the reader is referred to the earlier work.

L. T.

"Tell them the lamentable tale of me . . ."
—*Richard II*

"The Child of God"

⁓

"Like Rachel and like Leah, which two
did build the house of Israel . . ."
—*Ruth* 4:11

It was on the afternoon of Tuesday, May 18, 1926, that Aimee Semple McPherson, premiere woman evangelist of her era, waved to her secretary, Emma Schaffer, from where she was disporting like a porpoise several hundred feet out in the sea off Ocean Park, California, and then disappeared—virtually before the eyes of the Bible-reading, devoted Emma. The furor set off by this startling feat could not have been greater had the President of the United States soared into space without visible means of propulsion. The headlines screamed—and they would keep on screaming for eight months to come, as mystery piled on mystery and wonders succeeded wonders, until millions of onlookers grew dizzy from watching the dissolving mirages. Only the whole was not a mirage, it was poignantly, some said scandalously, real.

The reasons for the sensation lay buried in the personality and past of Aimee Semple McPherson. Neither of these was commonplace. Born on a Canadian farm, she was the only child of a one-time Salvation Army lassie and a lackadaisical Methodist farmer, James Kennedy. Her mother, born Minnie Pierce in 1871, had been confided by *her* mother, a "shouting Methodist" of the old stamp, as a deathbed bequest to the wife of a Salvation Army officer in Lindsay, Ontario. Minnie's girlhood was spent amid the martial piety and practical service of the Army, and *her* daughter's introduction to ecstatic religious expression, in turn, would be to the braying of brass and the hallelujahs of joyful penitents.

It would be the lifelong boast of Minnie Kennedy that she had prayed her daughter into being. This she meant literally. The story that she told, and that her daughter would repeat many times in public and in print, was that Minnie while still in her teens was forced by some unidentified illness to leave her Salvation Army guardians and return to Canada. There, apparently shortly afterward, she became the wife of James Kennedy, whose farm lay about five miles outside the town of Ingersoll, in Ontario. Kennedy was forty-eight; his bride, fifteen. Jim Kennedy was hard-working, patient, and taciturn, all qualities of which he would have need in the years ahead.

Her premature divorcement from the freedom and excitements of Salvation Army life was resented by young Minnie Kennedy; and the extent of her resentment would be set forth graphically by her daughter, when the latter came to write her autobiography, *This Is That,* in the following words:

"Then it was, while weak in body, depressed in spirit, and mourning over the loss of a mother's sympathetic hand, that she married, hoping to be able to continue her work for God, but amidst the strenuous and unaccustomed duties of heavy farm work, she was compelled to acknowledge that she was caught in the devil's net, and helpless so far as active service was concerned, and must largely devote herself to the manifold duties of farm and home. . . . Shorn of her usefulness, fettered by circumstances, she did truly grind in the prison house."

Whether, in spite of this candid wording, James Kennedy ever saw himself as accessory to Satan's schemes is not recorded. What is known is that all her life long Minnie Kennedy would mistrust men and their motives—and say so.

Grieving sore (as her daughter related the story), Minnie took refuge in prayer, Bible reading, and complaining. She kept up a tenuous connection with the Salvation Army barracks in Ingersoll, making twice-weekly trips into town to take part in the meetings and help in the Sunday school. In time she attained the rank of junior sergeant major (Sunday school superintendent, according to her daughter), a title that young Aimee would consider having a splendid ring. Usually Minnie pedaled the five miles to town on her bicycle, though in a pinch she would tramp the distance rather than miss a session. Occasionally, when a horse could be spared from the farm work, she would go by buggy or cutter. Kennedy did not share his wife's religious tastes; he had once sung in the Methodist choir, but that period of active fervor had gone by. Nevertheless, he was tolerant of his young wife's vagaries.

One day (runs the tale) Minnie, feeling forlornly that she had exchanged her true calling for a barren marriage, turned to her Bible for comfort, and came again upon the familiar story of Hannah and Samuel. Hannah, also, had been trapped in a cheerless marriage; but sensing that a child might be the means of her salvation, she had prayed for such a sign of divine favor. In answer, Samuel was born.

On an impulse, Minnie Kennedy knelt and prayed in emulation of Hannah of old, but with a difference; for whereas Hannah had prayed for a man child, Minnie begged for "a little baby girl"—one who, she said, would make up for her own faintheartedness and backsliding by taking her place in the religious life that she herself had so rashly abandoned.

Such was the tale, and the sequel, it was said, was the birth, on October 9, 1890, in the farmhouse with the scrollwork under the eaves, of a girl child, as requested. The baby was named Aimee Elizabeth, and the family would call her Betty.

When she was three weeks old, Minnie bundled her against the cold and carried her to the barracks in Ingersoll; reportedly the infant cooed contentedly throughout the service. At six weeks of age, Aimee was promoted to a chair on the platform and was solemnly dedicated to the work of the Lord.

The Kennedy home was permeated with religious atmosphere. Instead of lullabies, Minnie crooned hymns to her baby; and as Aimee grew older, in place of fairy tales Minnie told her wonderful Bible stories—Daniel in the lions' den, the prodigal son, Ruth and the gleaning—and by the time she was five, little Betty could recite whole chapters out of the Old and New Testaments for the edification of visitors. Minnie noted with approval that she was quick to learn, and not shy.

There is no doubt that the child's character was indicated at an early age. She was courageous, headstrong, affectionate, and sunny-tempered. Dolls did not interest her; she preferred live playmates, and had many—a pigeon, a cat, a bullfrog that she kept under her bed, and a romping Newfoundland dog. Even as a tiny girl she rode the farm horses without fear, and she could throw a stone farther and harder than any boy her age.

Her urge toward leadership seemed to be instinctive. On her first day at the crossroads school, she was taunted by the other children about her Salvation Army connection. In those days the Salvation Army was not the revered institution it would later become; it was looked down upon, even despised, by the regular churches and churchgoers. Aimee was the only child with a Salvation Army background in the school.

Instead of fighting her tormentors, she discovered a cheese box that would do for a drum, tied a red rag to a stick for a "Blood and Fire" banner, and started marching around the school yard, thumping and singing at the top of her voice. One by one the other children, unable to resist the lure of a parade, fell in behind her, and the taunting ceased. In this crisis, as in greater ones to come, Aimee's courage and her active imagination served her well.

From grammar school Aimee progressed to the Ingersoll Academy, or high school. She was apt in the classroom, but more apt at every kind of athletic sport. She stood well with the other students, winning a popularity contest the prize for which was a trip down the St. Lawrence River.

Her adolescence was more turbulent than was that of her more placid schoolmates. She was intense in her quest for knowledge, and especially, as youth always is, in her search for fundamental truths— truths on which she could base her faith unquestioningly. To doubt or waver or be in uncertainty would always be agony for Aimee: she required to *know*. No halfway answers would satisfy her; she demanded positive statements and would take nothing less.

It was inevitable that religious doubts should arise during this period of normal stress, and she dramatized this turmoil as she would dramatize everything. So intense was her power of imagining, some-times the line could hardly be discerned where the reality ended and perfervid imaginings took over.

The school's geography book provided a concrete stumbling block when it introduced her sketchily to the theory of evolution. This shocked Aimee, for it ran counter to everything she had been taught regarding the literal truth of Biblical statements. She questioned her

Aimee Elizabeth Kennedy, Canadian farm child, aged ten, in her tippet, proudly holding her Salvation Army tambourine.

teachers and got vague answers. Then she tackled her parents, demanding that they cite proofs showing that the Bible was right in saying the earth was created in six days, and the textbook was wrong in saying that it was formed over a span of millions of years. Both could not be true, and if the Bible was wrong on that point, might it not be wrong on every other point? What could one trust? Was everything she had learned at home meaningless? Was there even a God at all? All the fervor of her sixteen years was poured into her doubts.

Reassurance was to come, and when it did, it would come in terms of drama. Minnie, dismayed by her daughter's skepticism, argued and pleaded, without effect. One night, after an anguished session, she ordered Aimee to go to her room and think over her wickedness. The excited girl ran upstairs, and without pausing to light the lamp, flung the window wide open and crouched down before it with elbows on the sill and gazed out at the wintry scene. The sky was clear and brilliant with countless stars, and she thought—could it be possible that there was no divine, directing will behind their immensity? She felt bursting with the need to *know*. Which could she believe—the Bible or the textbook? The peaceful scene seemed to offer no answer. In her words:

"The white mantle of snow which covered the fields and the trees glistened in the clear, frosty air, and—my! how big that moon looked up there, and how ten million stars seemed to wink and blink and twinkle! I drew a comforter round me and sat on, unmindful of the cold, looking up at the Milky Way, the Big Dipper. . . . Surely there *must* be a God up there back of them all. . . . It was all so big, so high, so above the reach and ken of mortal man—surely a DIVINE hand must hold and control this wonderful solar system. . . . Suddenly, without stopping to think, I threw both arms impulsively out of the window, and reaching toward heaven, cried:

" 'Oh God—if there be a God—reveal yourself to me!' "

In reality, she realized, her cry had been only a whisper; "but just that whisper from an honest, longing heart" brought a response, and in a moment, mysteriously but certainly, she felt that her doubts had been melted away, she need doubt no longer.

Mother Kennedy learned about this solemn baptism of truth belatedly. More trials were in store for Minnie, for at the moment she saw no change in her child's increasing worldliness. Aimee was caught reading novels; she was seen in the town's little moving-picture theater—both actions regarded as sinful in Minnie's prim theology. Then Aimee took up dancing. It started when a girl seized her during choir practice in the basement of the Methodist church, and whirled her around to the tune of "Nearer My God to Thee"— "in perfect waltz time."

Minnie scolded and forbade, but Aimee would have her way, and she succeeded in badgering her mother into buying her a new dress and dancing slippers to attend a school prom.

Minnie really took a stern line, however, when she discovered that her daughter was taking up with Pentecostalists—"Holy Rollers," they were called—who preached the "baptism of the Holy Spirit" and "speaking in tongues" and other "extreme things." They had established a mission in an empty store in Ingersoll, and the whole town was gossiping about the way they "fell under the power," rolled on the floor, and otherwise acted disgracefully. Thinking it would be a lark, Aimee asked her indulgent father to take her to one of the services. Jim Kennedy probably was curious himself, and giggling Aimee thought it would be "loads of fun."

So, the next afternoon, without informing Minnie, they slipped into the mission while a service was in progress and took seats in the back of the hall, where they trusted they would not be noticed. When Aimee saw the town milkman shake and quiver "under the power," then fall to the floor and lie stretched out "praising the Lord," she tittered uneasily. But a real shock came when a tall young man arose on the platform and read from his Bible—Acts II, verses 38 and 39:

"Then Peter said unto them, repent and be baptized every one of you in the name of Jesus Christ for the remission of sins, and ye shall receive the gift of the Holy Ghost. For the promise is unto you, and to your children, and to all that are afar off, even as many as the Lord our God shall call."

Aimee sat up. The speaker was six feet two inches tall, with blue eyes and unruly brown hair; one curl kept falling down into his eyes no matter how often he brushed it back.

"Repent! Repent!" he cried. Repent of worldly ways—of dancing, and movies, and novel reading, and ragtime music—the very pleasures Aimee had given herself to. People who were wrapped up in that sort of thing were on their way to perdition, the preacher said, and unless they repented, and that right speedily, they would be damned eternally.

To Aimee it seemed that these words were being hurled at *her*. Nobody had ever addressed her in such a manner before; on the contrary, as an only child she had been rather petted and told "how smart and good I was." She cowered and was swept by the strangest sensations when the speaker, closing his eyes, stretched out his hands directly toward her and began to speak in tongues, in sounds and words that she could not understand. To her it seemed "the voice of God thundering . . . awful words of conviction and condemnation. . . . It seemed as though God had said to me—'YOU are a poor, lost, miserable, hell-deserving sinner!'"

Shaken and trembling, she whimpered to her father to take her away from there.

The name of the young preacher was Robert Semple, and he was a boilermaker by trade in the town of Stratford, and by avocation a Pentecostal exhorter.

For the next three days Aimee lived in an agony of fear, convinced that she stood in imminent peril of hell fire unless the Lord deigned to save her. She prayed with all the force of her nature for redemption. The climax came on the third day, as she was driving home alone from school:

"I could stand it no longer. The lowering skies above, the trees, the fields, the very road beneath me seemed to look down on me with displeasure, and I could see written everywhere—

"'Poor, lost, miserable, hell-deserving sinner!'

"Utterly at the end of myself—not stopping to think what preachers or entertainment committees or anyone else would think—I threw up my hands, and all alone in that country road, I screamed aloud toward the heavens:

"'Oh, Lord God, be merciful to me, a sinner!'

"Many people," she would say later, "smile now as I testify of that awful terror that seized upon my soul, but the eternal welfare of my soul was at stake—for me it was going to be life or death, heaven or hell forever."

Throughout her life it would be the same—all or nothing, life or death, heaven or hell, now and forever.

"Immediately the most wonderful change took place," her narrative resumed. "Darkness passed away and light entered. The sky was filled with brightness, the trees, the fields, and the little snow birds flitting to and fro were praising the Lord and smiling upon me. So conscious was I of the pardoning blood of Jesus that I seemed to feel it flowing over me. I discovered that my face was bathed in tears, which dropped on my hands as I held the reins. . . . Song after song burst from my lips. I shouted aloud and praised God all the way home. I had been redeemed!" *

But Aimee was not satisfied with simple redemption: she felt that she must strive for the "baptism of fire" that the Pentecostals talked about, and she set about invoking it characteristically—with hammer and tongs. Cutting school, she spent hours in the home of a Pentecostal sister, praying desperately. At school she stole down to the locker room in the basement, and was found there praying with defiant disregard for appearances.

About all this her mother remained in the dark until a Salvation Army officer drove out to the farm to remonstrate with Minnie over her failure to control her daughter.

"We don't mind other people going to that mission," Minnie was lectured, "but we really are surprised and think you do wrong in letting your daughter go—you being connected with the work for so many years."

When Aimee reached home that evening, her mother was on the warpath. Minnie laid down the law: let Aimee sneak out of school just once more, to consort with those "Holy Rollers," and that would be the end of school for her; she would be kept home altogether.

"I will not have you talked about!" Minnie stormed.

Being talked about was rather agreeable to Aimee; still, she hesitated to defy her mother outright. On the way to town the next morning, however, she kept thinking how wonderful it would be if something should happen, some miracle, perhaps, that would let her get the fire baptism with a clear conscience.

Something did happen. A blizzard swept over the countryside, halting trains, blocking roads, and bringing down telephone wires. By evening Aimee could not get home, and could not communicate

* Compare this with John Wesley's account of his experience of personal salvation at the age of thirty-four: "On May 24, 1738, at a meeting in Aldersgate, Luther's 'Preface to the Epistle to the Romans' was being read. At about a quarter before nine, while he (Luther) was describing the change which God works in the heart through faith in Christ, I felt my heart strangely warmed. I felt I did trust in Christ, Christ alone, for salvation; and an assurance was given me that He had taken away *my* sins, even *mine*, and saved me from the law of sin and death."

with her mother. Hugging herself, she raced to the home of the Pentecostal sister, where she was sure of shelter. Realizing that the time was short, she spent all that evening, which was Friday, in earnest prayer, but without avail. Early Saturday morning, before anyone else was up, she stole down to the icy cold parlor, and kneeling beside the Morris chair she renewed her bombardment of heaven. And then the response came. Quivering with a strange agitation, she slid gently to the floor, where she lay "stretched out under the power of God" and, in her words, feeling as though "caught up and floating upon billowy clouds of glory. . . . Suddenly, out of my inmost being, flowed rivers of praise in other tongues as the Spirit gave me utterance." She was "speaking in tongues."

By the next morning, Sunday, the storm had abated and telephone lines had been repaired. But Aimee did not call her mother; instead, she hurried to the mission, and there again "went down to the floor under the power." A scandalized onlooker ran out and telephoned to Mother Kennedy, advising her that she had better come to town and see to her daughter, who was "lying on the floor . . . before all the people, chattering like a monkey."

Minnie frantically called Aimee to the telephone, but all she could get out of the child was gibberish; Aimee was still "under the power." Hitching up the cutter, Minnie drove into town and gathered up her errant daughter. All the way home she scolded and wept; but although Aimee felt remorseful, she had no sensation of regret, and she responded to her mother's reproaches by defiantly singing hymns.

At the farm, Aimee was marched up to her father and ordered to tell him how abominably she had behaved. He held his head and moaned; and after Aimee had been sent to her room, Jim told his wife with a certain amount of prescience:

"It is perfectly useless to argue with her, for no matter what we say, she only thinks she is being persecuted and will hold to it all the more tenaciously."

After that, events moved swiftly. Aimee was set in her determination to be a Pentecostalist, and Minnie gave up hope of ever seeing her daughter in a Salvation Army uniform. Robert Semple came back to Ingersoll, and soon Aimee told her mother that she and Semple were going to be married and go as missionaries to China.

The wedding took place under the apple trees in a Pentecostal "saint's" backyard, and Minnie and Jim Kennedy saw the couple off at the depot. As the train pulled out, Minnie waved her handkerchief bravely, while Aimee, leaning out of the car window, pointed upward, bidding her mother "look to Jesus." Neither woman expected to see the other again in this world. Aimee was seventeen.

Adoring bride at seventeen. Aimee with her husband, Robert Semple, Pentecostalist preacher. They went to China.

So the shock was severe when, a little more than a year later, Minnie received a cablegram from Hong Kong saying that Robert Semple was dead, and Aimee herself was dangerously ill, alone and penniless in a foreign land, with a weeks-old baby. The child, a girl, had been born after her father's death, and Aimee had named her wistfully Roberta Star Semple.

Minnie cabled money to enable Aimee and her baby to come home. Minnie was back in Salvation Army work temporarily, and the reunion took place in New York. Aimee was not at all her old self; she seemed crushed, defeated by her tragedy. Robert Semple was the only man to whom she ever gave herself entirely, submerging her will in his, and with the deprivation of that strong support she grew faint, confused, and listless. Minnie tried to arouse her, tried to persuade her to come back to the farm and start over again, but Aimee shrank from meeting the glances of people around Ingersoll and reading the doubt in their eyes as to whether the Lord had really sanctioned that gadding off to China. A coolness developed between the two women, and when Minnie went back to Canada, Aimee stayed in the East, drifting from mission to mission, dispirited, destitute, and self-reproachful over her inability to provide proper care for her baby.

Then came news that she had married again, her husband Harold Simpson McPherson, a decent but uninspiring wholesale grocery clerk. The couple had gone to live with McPherson's parents in Providence, Rhode Island.

In later life Aimee would admit honestly that her motive in marrying Harold McPherson had been to give her child a home. For a while she made a valiant but futile attempt to transform herself into a suburban housewife. Nothing could have been less feasible, and the struggle told on her vitality. She became subject to neurotic crises the causes of which she could only dimly discern. Sometimes she would be plunged into profound depression, and hour after hour sobbed, "Jesus! Jesus! Jesus!" Just that one word. Inevitably there was domestic discord. McPherson, who had expected to enjoy the placid satisfactions of a home, found himself saddled with a wife incapable of such fulfillment. He could not understand her "tantrums." A son was born, whom Aimee, with a fond glance toward Canada and the farm, named Rolf Kennedy McPherson. But the psychic struggle continued, until twice she fell gravely ill with a complexity of illnesses. Compelled to undergo surgery, she sank to the verge of death. Minnie Kennedy was summoned, and kneeling by the bedside she pledged her love and loyalty anew.

In her own mind, and this was not all delirium, Aimee believed that she had been saved at the very brink by the submission of her will to divine direction—a step she had resisted until then. As usual, she dramatized this mystic intercession. "Go preach the Word!" had been the summons ringing in her ears, she said, and she had sobbed that she could not, did not know how, lacked the strength, had home and family obligations—all the obvious evasions. The voice had kept on, she still resisting, until one night, about two o'clock in the morning, she heard a nurse murmur, "She's going," and "everything went black."

Then, in her words, "before losing consciousness, as I hovered between life and death, came the voice of the Lord, so loud that it startled me:

" 'NOW—WILL—YOU—GO?'

"And I knew it was 'go,' one way or the other. . . . And with my little remaining strength, I managed to gasp:

" 'Yes—Lord—I'll—go.'

"And go I did! . . . In two weeks . . . I was up and well, though weak in body. I have hardly known an ache or pain from that day to this."

The effect when she told this mystical summons and surrender from her pulpit, in later years, was thrilling and convincing. Nothing was more fundamental to her belief than the reality of this long-resisted, and then absolute, submission to God's will. And she would wind up the story with the shout:

"Oh, don't you ever tell me that a woman can not be called to preach the Gospel! If any man ever went through one hundredth part of the hell on earth that I lived in, those months when out of God's will and work, they would never say that again!"

II

Aimee's first step toward obeying that irresistible call was practical: she wired to her mother for money. When it arrived, selecting a night when her husband was not at home, she wrapped up the children, threw her possessions into two suitcases, and left Harold

McPherson's home forever. Recriminations would follow, but she had set her course and nothing could deflect her.

Leaving Roberta and Rolf with their grandmother at the farm, Aimee immersed herself in the ardors of a Pentecostal camp meeting nearby, and almost immediately felt that she had been received back into God's grace. Then she accepted an invitation to preach to an apathetic half-dozen "saints" in a village close at hand. From that inauspicious start she forged ahead steadily—learning as she went, cheerfully enduring hardship, privation, and often public disapproval, laughing at her mishaps, and surmounting obstacles with courage and ingenuity. She had no regularly organized support, at first knew nothing about the details of evangelism, and while living from hand to mouth, made mistakes; but she seldom made the same mistake twice.

With the proceeds of her first collection—$65—she bought a tent and was swindled; the canvas was so rotten and moth-eaten it could not be pitched. But Aimee set to work with a sailmaker's needle and palm and, helped by a few sympathetic women, stitched and patched the crazy affair until it could be made to "do." With her next ready cash she replaced it with a better tent, and then that with a better one still, and so on, and each replacement was more commodious and of better professional quality.

Harold McPherson made several attempts to barnstorm with her, but he could not endure the hand-to-mouth, rootless existence, and he resented Aimee's tight control of their purse. The final angry parting came, he said, when she sailed out of town, at the close of one revival, without leaving him the price of a railroad ticket to get to their next meeting place.

The message she brought to the rustics and later to the millhands of the North and the fishermen of the South was one of uninhibited joyfulness joined with religious exultation. Farmers in overalls drove miles to her meetings, sometimes conducted in the light of barn lanterns strung between the trees, with the porch steps of a house serving as her mourners' bench. No matter what the handicaps, she "made do," cheerfully, promptly, and energetically. She became skilled in the lore of the "big tops," knew grades and weights of duck and drill, and could drive tent stakes and stretch guy ropes with the handiness of a circus roustabout. She was her own advance agent, business manager, and star of the show. She bossed the volunteer helpers who were attracted to her in each town, arranged transportation, scattered handbills announcing her revivals, argued with unobliging police and fire inspectors, ordered the printing and paid the light bills, and after each grueling day's work slept on an army cot under canvas that tore loose in the wind and leaked when it rained. Her meals were prepared on a smoking oil stove and eaten off benches or crates or whatever was handy. And she thrived on the work and loved the gypsy life.

She acquired a "Gospel car"—an automobile with eye-catching slogans splashed along its sides—"Jesus Is Coming Soon—Make Ready," and "Where Will You Spend Eternity?" She met prejudice with smiling good humor. People living near the place of her holding-forth might complain about the noise and seek to have the police eject her. Coreligionists might frown on the spectacle of a woman preacher—had not St. Paul ordained that women should keep silent

Aimee and Harold S. McPherson, in the days of her first barnstorming as an itinerant evangelist. McPherson couldn't abide the life.

in the churches? She met opposition with firmness and goodwill. When a police captain refused to give her meetings protection against a gang of rowdies, she drove her Gospel car up to the stationhouse and prayed for his better understanding. It turned out that the captain stood in need of prayer, for shortly thereafter he fell dead at his desk.

For two years Aimee journeyed up and down the Atlantic seaboard, from Maine to Key West, calling the poor, the neglected, the obscure, and the oppressed to accept salvation on her terms of joyfulness. Her sincerity, dynamic personality, and inborn ability to sway crowds brought her increasing recognition. But the life was hard. Often she went hungry, and on one occasion she fought against a hurricane all night, making the rounds of her canvas, driving in the tent stakes with a maul as fast as the gale ripped them out. She was jeered by unbelievers, scorned by the "respectables," rebuffed by churchmen; but through the toil and turmoil she persisted, and by the time of the First World War she was pushing into the higher ranks of itinerant evangelists.

The hardships of those early days of vagabond existence, the penury borne cheerfully, the artless persistency and naïve faith displayed by Aimee herself and the drifting enthusiasts who attached themselves to her as to a nature stronger than their own, was conveyed poignantly by Aimee in a report of her trip from Tampa to Miami, just before Christmas, during her second winter in Florida. She wrote:

"When we left Tampa the car was filled with tracts and from the west to the east coast of Florida . . . we faithfully distributed our literature until within a few miles of our destination, when all had been given out. . . . Our car being heavily loaded this trip, we did not carry a sleeping tent, and learned a little of what Jesus meant when he said, '*The birds have nests, and the foxes have holes, but the Son of man has not where to lay His head!*' The first night we spent in the car; the second night was spent wrapped in a blanket by the camp fire on the prairie near Okeechobee. . . . The third night was spent in a fisherman's shanty near Palm Beach. . . . The next night was spent in a little railway depot to keep out of the driving rain.

"All the homes around us had their Christmas trees and fine dinners, but as our tents had not yet arrived, and we did not wish to spend the Lord's money on a room, we built a palm-leaf shanty on the beach, and hung our simple Christmas gifts on a little tree growing near. We kneeled down around it and read the story of Jesus' birth, and after prayer opened our little tokens."

Another incident of that winter would have a strange echo years afterward. One day as Aimee was struggling to pitch her tent in a vacant lot, pounding in stakes with a maul, a car stopped on the highway and a woman got out. This woman had been brought up in the Salvation Army, although she was not connected with the work then. The signs scattered around indicated that the wielder of the maul was an evangelist, and in sheer admiration of such fortitude and determination, she emptied her purse into Aimee's hand, and with a "God bless you," jumped into her car and drove away, without inquiring the evangelist's name. The name of the woman in the car was Rheba Crawford, and years later the paths of these two would cross, with tragic consequences.

As Aimee's success increased, so did the calls on her time and energy. Business details irritated her; her gift was for preaching, inspiring, converting, and in regard to that she could seldom be faulted. But for business she had neither head nor inclination. She was a poor judge of character and was easily imposed upon. Her income was erratic and her outgo was total. Dubious hangers-on attached themselves to her caravan, and she allowed them to remain, although they gave some of her transactions a questionable air. Money dribbled through her fingers, and trying to make ends meet and manage every department of her enterprise so drained her energies that during the winter of 1917–1918 she feared she would fail. She told the readers of the little magazine she was publishing, the *Bridal Call:*

"I am very weak in body, and have to hang on to God for strength at each meeting. . . . I am alone, playing, leading, singing, preaching, and praying at the altar, besides having the *Bridal Call* to prepare; it is only the power of God that can sustain me. . . . Please pray for me, saints, that I do not fail God."

When collapse threatened, Aimee turned to the source of help that never yet had failed, her mother. Minnie Kennedy was in the north, with Roberta, while little Rolf shared the rigors of his mother's life. James Kennedy had died, and Minnie had left the Canadian farm for good. When a series of telegrams arrived from Aimee in

Key West, begging her mother to come to her rescue, Minnie responded. She had been receiving glowing reports of wonderful successes from her daughter; but she knew Aimee's propensity for seeing things not as they were, but as she wished them to be. So Minnie traveled south with an open mind. But having arrived, and having assessed the situation, she decided to take hold and save Aimee from an ignominious retreat. Minnie's forte, although she had not developed it yet, was business management, and she set to ruthlessly to rid the enterprise of the drones and parasites, bring order into the financial chaos, and get her daughter on the road again. Soon Aimee was telling her *Bridal Call* subscribers:

"Mother has been with me from that day. . . . She has never shirked a duty nor one of the responsibilities laid upon her by the work, lifting from my shoulders the entire burden of the correspondence, caring for the . . . *Bridal Call* subscriptions, overseeing the care of the children, packing, traveling, and a score of other duties, and I have been left free to give myself continually to prayer, the ministry of the Word, and writing. She has ever been the source of cheer and inspiration."

An understanding was reached between the two women, nothing in writing but a tacit agreement, that thenceforward they would pool their resources, sharing equally in the labors and the rewards of the undertaking.

Heading north with renewed zest, in the summer of 1918 Aimee preached prominently at a Pentecostal revival in Philadelphia, and then in the towns roundabout through the autumn. That fall the nation was gripped by the terrible epidemic of Spanish influenza, and Roberta was stricken while her mother was preaching in Yonkers. Aimee suffered agonies of self-reproach as she watched her daughter grow weaker, lying in a cheerless boardinghouse; and as the crisis passed and recovery set in, she resolved to take her family to a milder climate, where the children might go to school and develop under healthier conditions.

Minnie, although she was approaching fifty, was game for making a fresh start. Preparations were begun; the battered Gospel car was traded for an open Oldsmobile, to which the flaunting slogans were transferred. And in October of 1918 the little group rolled out of New York, headed for California. Besides Aimee and her mother,

The Gospel car in which Aimee and her mother crossed the continent in 1918. Photo taken several months later, during a California revival. Aimee in center, flanked by her children, Rolf and Roberta, Minnie Kennedy at right holding guitar.

there were the children, and a grim-visaged, pince-nezed Pentecostal "saint" known as Sister Baer. The car was piled high with luggage, camping equipment, and tracts to scatter along the way. Aimee did the driving.

To cross the continent by automobile in 1918—and in the midst of the wartime dislocation of all travel facilities—required daring. The stamina of Aimee's party would be taxed to the utmost. They could expect to cope with breakdowns, punctures, storms, mountain trails, trackless desert, floods, and bitter cold. At night, if they were not fortunate enough to find shelter with some wayside friend, they huddled under a makeshift tent rigged out from the side of the car; the canvas leaked in the rain, and sometimes by morning was frozen stiff. More than once they crept through flooded river bottoms, hub-deep in water. But they pushed on pluckily, and on Armistice Day rolled into Tulsa, Oklahoma. Warned of snow in the northern mountain passes beyond, from that point they followed a southern course, and just before Christmas Day they entered Los Angeles. As they rolled along the city's sun-drenched boulevards, lined with stately palms, Aimee mentally echoed the command laid upon Joshua before the walls of Jericho:

"Shout; for the Lord hath given you the city."

This was her stage.

III

Aimee liked to remind people that she had arrived in Los Angeles with ten dollars and a tambourine—and four years later opened Angelus Temple, built, equipped, and paid for.

She started her first revival in the city one week after her arrival. This was in Victoria Hall Mission, a dingy upstairs meeting room at 125 South Spring Street, under the auspices of the Assemblies of God—a Pentecostal sect preaching and teaching the four basic tenets of what she later called her Foursquare Gospel, which she said had been revealed to her in a vision.* So much zip did she put into the proceedings that for three successive Sundays she also filled Philharmonic Auditorium, the largest hall in the city. She never quite recovered from her awe at the rental fee—a hundred dollars for three hours' use—a stupendous sum to her in those days, and all more than covered by the collections.

Then, almost before one could say how it had come about, she was able to move her family into their first real home, on Orange Grove Drive just off West Adams Boulevard, on what was then the western fringe of the city. The two-story bungalow had been provided free of cost, the lot, all construction materials and labor donated by enthusiastic converts. This was the first real property Aimee owned, and she named the place "The House That God Built," praising God for His thoughtfulness in providing La Cienega school for the children just half a block away.

Leaving Rolf and Roberta there with their grandmother, she hit the trail eastward again. This time she traveled in Pullman cars, and in city after city where she spoke—Denver, St. Louis, Dayton, Washington, Montreal—her audiences overflowed. So much prominence began to bring her to the notice of the press, but the general public heard little about her until her healing sessions provided sensations. Anointing the sick and praying for their recovery with the laying on of hands was Pentecostalist doctrine, and Aimee conformed. In fact, she told glowingly of a broken, or badly lacerated, ankle that had been

---

* Regeneration, Divine Healing, the Second Coming of Christ, and the Baptism of the Holy Ghost.

Aimee Semple McPherson as she arrived in Los Angeles just before Christmas, 1918. She was twenty-nine.

healed by prayer instantaneously, as her own personal experience of divine healing power.

Her first invocations of this healing power were tentative, for she could not understand what caused the results. That it was some force beyond her control she was sure, and anything she could not control made her uneasy. The source of the power that produced seemingly miraculous "cures" she identified as Jesus, the force being transmitted through her as a mere instrument or conveyer.

"Jesus is the healer," she would say; "I am only the office girl who opens the door and says 'Come in.'"

But the healing sessions attracted public attention, especially when near-riots occurred among the throngs of crippled and afflicted persons who clamored to come under the touch of her hand. In San Diego, a

Aimee and her children before "The House That God Built," her first home in Los Angeles, donated to her within four months of her arrival in California.

city filled with valetudinarians, the crush became so great that the civic authorities turned over Balboa Park for her use. For two days, from early morning until dusk, she anointed and prayed for the sick as they passed before her, until she was carried back to her hotel, fainting from exhaustion. In Denver, where she filled the Civic Auditorium, seating sixteen thousand, by proclamation of the mayor church bells were rung and factory whistles were blown, bidding the people kneel in the streets, in stores and offices, and pray for the greater success of Mrs. McPherson's healing sessions.

Aimee's boundless vitality and her sincerity (for sincerity it was) were infectious. She had adopted a uniform for the platform, a simple

Roberta and Rolf as children were part of their mother's stage properties, as in this 1919 picture that was distributed by the thousands in
Aimee's appeals for support.

ROBERTA AND ROLF WITH THEIR MAMMA
send you their love and will you please pray for them?

SMILES? YES, BUT TEARS ARE NEAR! AMERICA, WE LOVE YOU! NOW WE ARE ABOARD SHIP SAILING FOR THE OTHER SIDE OF THE WORLD. GOD BE WITH YOU TILL WE MEET AGAIN

Sailing for Australia in August 1922 on evangelistic mission. From left, Minnie Kennedy, Roberta Semple, Sister Aimee, Rolf McPherson.

white dress resembling a nurse's, with a military-type blue cape, and as "the little lady in white" she became well known in revivalist circles from coast to coast. She had called her mother back into the field to cope with the myriad backstage details, and both women toiled heroically.

Only in Los Angeles was Sister McPherson comparatively obscure; her triumphs were elsewhere. Mother and daughter early decided, however, on their need of a permanent base in the city, and Angelus Temple was the result.

Aimee would tell the story of the temple's building countless times;

to her it was a miracle, a glorious testimonial to God's blessing on her work.

By scrimping and frugality, Minnie Kennedy had saved about five thousand dollars from their earnings; this was their only capital. With this they bought the lot on Echo Park, and hired scrapers and horses to dig the foundation, trusting to a beneficent Heaven, and their own tireless efforts, to furnish the money needed to carry on the project.

Aimee barnstormed the country, telling about her vision of a center of evangelism in the West, where all creeds could gather. She was prolific in devising sales gimmicks that would somehow identify the donor with the enterprise personally. The temple was to be fireproof, constructed of reinforced concrete, and she sold little bags of cement for five dollars apiece. Instead of speaking of "shareholders" in the undertaking, she talked about "chairholders," and dramatized the title by selling miniature, theater-type folding chairs—the kind she intended to install in the temple instead of pews—for twenty-five dollars each. Purchasers were promised that their seats would be numbered and reserved for them until a certain time before each service. One hundred thousand dollars was raised from the sale of four thousand of these chairs.

Donations for everything that would go into the temple were avidly solicited. A tribe of gypsies whom Aimee had befriended gave one of the great stained-glass windows. Aimee would thrill audiences by telling how, the first time she and her mother saw the lot for sale at Echo Park, they had determined to buy it, and then and there, right on the "For Sale" sign, Aimee had sketched the plan of the tabernacle she saw in her mind's eye. The lot was shaped like a slice of pie, the curved edge toward Echo Park and the sides running back to a point. At this apex or point Aimee placed the pulpit, with the seats fanning out from it, the aisles and ramps converging at that spot.

In Denver her enthusiasm raised seventy thousand dollars for the project, and forty thousand in St. Louis. And little by little Angelus Temple arose, virtually unregarded by the people of Los Angeles.

Their attention was drawn dramatically to the unheralded development on New Year's Day, 1923, when, before droves of contributors who had come from afar, Sister McPherson solemnly consecrated the structure to "the cause of inter-denominational and world-wide evangelism," as a plaque on the entrance pillar stated.*

Lush descriptions of the sumptuous house of worship were carried in the newspapers—the concrete dome, said to be the largest of its type in the world (it was not), with its outer surface sparkling from crushed sea shells mixed in the cement, and its interior curve painted to give the illusion of a perpetual blue sky; the seating capacity of five thousand; the furnishings, the carpets, hangings, and array of pictorial windows; the two balconies, the sweeping ramps, the stage and baptismal pool with painted backdrop representing the banks of the river Jordan; the organ, the Steinway grand piano; the list ran on and on. The newspapers estimated the cost at hundreds of thousands of dollars, if not a million or more, and Minnie Kennedy was happy to tell reporters that there was not one penny of debt on it, from dome to basement.

Erecting such a place of worship was an astonishing feat, and filling it, and keeping it filled, called for further prodigious efforts. Aimee threw all her virtuosity into accomplishing this, and accomplish it she did, by means that some deplored and some praised, but the effectiveness of which nobody could deny. The religion she preached she called the Foursquare Gospel, and it was a nonstop outburst of joy, joy, joy. There was no dismalness at Angelus Temple; no mourners' bench, no wailing over sin, no depressing emphasis upon damnation and hell fire. The glimpses of lurid wickedness that she introduced sparingly into her panorama of hope and comfort now and assured bliss hereafter served as subtle excitants; they titivated but did not terrify. They were the spice in the otherwise too cloying cake, the topping on the tutti-frutti, the fine print on the tickets she scattered profusely, though not gratuitously, to all who yearned to ride the Happy Road to Heaven.

The first year at the temple would be recalled as a perpetual camp meeting, a time of excitement and glorious confusion, and of activities improvised from day to day. Sister put everybody to work. When she saw someone who might be useful, she reached out and pulled him in. To make everyone share in the sense of achievement, she devised things for everybody to do. There was a choir of nearly a

---

* And still states (1970).

Aimee as godmother to gypsy children in 1923, the year Angelus Temple opened. Sister Aimee is holding the baby, baptized John Stephen Marino, and little Robert Semple Marino sits alongside. The mother, Rosie Marino, left, and aunt, Princess Mary, belonged to a Mexican tribe devoted to Sister.

hundred, under the direction of youthful Gladwyn Nichols, brought in from the Salvation Army. There were subsidiary choral groups, and a band of thirty-six. There was the sisterhood, and the sewing circles that stitched layettes for needy mothers. There was the brotherhood that found jobs for men just out of prison. There was the commissary, which answered appeals for food, clothing, rent money,

Aimee took to the streets to fill Angelus Temple. Here, in a new car, she invites the sidewalk crowd. In car Emma Schaffer, Aimee's secretary, sits between the children.

or other assistance with practical promptness at any hour of the day or night, investigating later. There was soon to be the Bible school, an imposing building next door, with a full teaching staff. There were nurseries to take charge of infants during the services, and ushers, and pages, and music arrangers, and writers, and typists, to help mail out the *Bridal Call*, now much expanded, and to publish a new church magazine, the *Crusader*. Even the general public was included in the humming activity at Angelus Temple; Aimee pioneered the correct time service, cordially inviting people to call the temple, day or night, and be told the correct time cheerfully.

When radio broadcasting came in, Aimee acquired her own station, KFSG (Kall Four Square Gospel), and by its means extended her influence for a thousand miles over the entire West.

The feature closest to Aimee's heart was the Prayer Tower, where men and women knelt in two-hour relays, the women by day and the men by night, offering perpetual prayer. From the day the temple opened, prayer arose from this room without interruption, and this Aimee called the real force, the "dynamo of power," that kept Angelus Temple functioning.

Whatever was topical was grist for Aimee's mill. When the Los Angeles Fire Department made her an honorary battalion chief she preached in her uniform, urging higher pay for policemen and firemen.

In 1923 Aimee recorded "canned sermonettes" to spread her message. Reporters described her as "buxom" and "motherly" at this period, no hint of glamor.

In everything relating to self-advertising, Sister McPherson displayed a sureness of touch that bordered on genius. That many of her publicity stunts lacked dignity did not bother her; she saw the results as sufficient justification: while conservative churches were empty, her temple was filled. Her tastes, sentimental and garish, matched those of the multitude. A technique that was all her own was her use of "illustrated sermons"—tableaux, pantomimes, and scenes acted out on a fully equipped stage, with footlights, scenery, props, and all the paraphernalia of the theater, to dramatize her text and point the moral in terms as broad and unmistakable as a newspaper cartoon. Forbidden by their creed to attend the theater, her devotees derived from these spectacles all the satisfactions of theater-going with none of the sin.

Gradually the institution at Echo Park shed some of the aspects of nonsectarianism and adopted the form of a separately organized congregation. This brought it into collision with regularly organized

When she was stopped for speeding, Aimee came on the platform with motorcycle, dressed in traffic policewoman's uniform, and preached on "Stop! You are breaking God's law!"

churches, and some of the more evangelically minded clergymen who at first had approved and encouraged her withdrew their support. A few grumbled that Sister McPherson was raiding their memberships, and a handful openly denounced her as a fraud and a menace. When this criticism became pronounced, she resigned from the city's ministerial association, which she had joined at the outset, in the same spirit in which she joined the Los Angeles Chamber of

Sister Aimee and an assistant pastor baptizing a convert in her baptismal pool at the back of the stage in Angelus Temple. The backdrop represented the River Jordan, flowers strewed the edge, and the water was heated and (in the early days) perfumed with rose petals, until other preachers laughed her out of it.

Commerce; from the latter she did not resign. But this antagonism, much talked about generally, seemed only to enhance Sister Aimee's allure; certainly no competing congregation had a pastor as magnetic, resourceful, or entertaining as the siren of Echo Park. The temple's enrolled membership grew and grew, until it was said to exceed ten thousand—claimed to be the largest single Christian congregation in the world. And Aimee, as she put it herself in all modesty, "ruled like a queen in her kingdom."

Throughout this surge of triumphal progress, Mother Kennedy held in her firm grasp the temple's financial and temporal affairs. Minnie, too, was blossoming, but in her case the flowers of her developing character were acrid and repellent to some of those around her. A farmwife, forced by stark necessity to pinch pennies, tenacious as a peasant of her possessions, she had had no training that would seem to equip her for administering a complex enterprise like Angelus Temple. She, who had never handled large sums of money, now received and paid out thousands regularly; the temple's weekly pay-roll alone ran into four figures. She was called upon to deal with important questions of property rights and acquisition, of banking, and of internal discipline. For Minnie, in addition to being the business head of the temple, was also its sergeant-at-arms. In this capacity she was ruthless, and even in her blander moments she could be disagreeable.

The crowds that flocked to Angelus Temple during the first months were a cut below those that Aimee had been drawing in other cities. Los Angeles, then as now, was notoriously filled with misfits and oddities, and undesirables strongly tinctured the first temple throngs. There were neurotics, girl chasers, drifters, and those whom Minnie referred to disdainfully as "nuts." To Aimee, all audiences were alike, simply crowds to work upon; but her mother sensed the danger of tolerating questionable characters, and set to work systematically to weed them out. She wasted no tact on the operation, and under her drastic purge the level of temple adherents slowly improved. Aimee, burdened with her own immense labors, supported her mother's measures, while managing to escape the odium they incurred.

The temple staff grumbled at Minnie's tightfisted economies. For a while she refused to have a switchboard installed, but had two pay telephones put in the lobby and told the department heads to use them—and their own nickels. She watched the petty outgo as sharply as she did the larger expenses, and challenged every suspicious item. She kept the books. She took charge of the collections and banked them. And she exercised absolute powers of censorship over the membership to purge it of "riffraff," "dead beats," and "upstarts" who questioned her authority. No strong-willed individual except herself was to get a foothold in her domain, if she could prevent it. People who were "too independent" were routed out.

Naturally, there were some who rebelled against the autocratic rule of Minnie, and in August, 1923, only eight months after the temple was consecrated, the first definite surge of revolt was felt. A formally typed complaint was handed to Aimee. It filled three pages, and although signed simply "The Committee," its authors were known. In a formidable list of grievances, Minnie Kennedy was accused of commercializing the temple and refusing to give any account of monies received or paid out. The complainants, it was said, had joined Angelus Temple under the impression that they were joining a church, whereas no church organization existed; all property was held in Mother Kennedy's name, and there was no board of trustees or other responsible group to supervise the temple's affairs. If Mother wished to excommunicate a member, she simply tore up his or her membership card, without notification or opportunity of appeal. The "chairholders," who had been told that they were acquiring rights to the space occupied by their seats "from the floor up through the dome to Heaven," had discovered that they had no proprietary rights at all. Sister McPherson was petitioned to take over control of the temple in fact, relieve her mother, transfer title to the property to a board of trustees, and assume full management authority herself.

The complainants did not accuse Aimee of any dereliction; her conduct was declared to be "kind, loving, and Christ-like . . . beyond reproof or comparison in these days," while Minnie, by contrast, was termed "pernicious, hurtful, antagonistic, unchristian, unjust, and nagging," and her discipline was castigated as "unnecessarily severe." Furthermore, she had gathered around her "a corps of helpers who are of her same temperament . . . ill-bred, uncivil, snappy, overbearing, and unchristian in their attitude toward the public, the members, and those trying to be of service in the church."

In recognition of Minnie's "splendid handling of the financial affairs thus far of the Temple," it was suggested that she bow out gracefully and receive a cash payment of twenty-five thousand dollars. If she were not removed somehow, the complaint wound up, and if the other reforms were not instituted, the matter would be referred to the district attorney and "facts and witnesses are being gathered for the preparation of the action to be filed"—action that would open the whole situation to the press, and result in "much notorious publicity and a great hindrance to our work."

The Committee got nowhere with their threat. The temple's business affairs had been organized on a secure legal basis, in which the membership had no part, and Mother Kennedy made short work of the Committee by tearing up their membership cards. The dissidents found themselves in Echo Park, ruefully contemplating the temple's facade, lined with what Aimee called her "crystal doors," although to others they looked like ordinary millwork. Aimee backed her

Nothing that would contribute to Aimee's impact upon the public was overlooked. In 1925 she took off in an open airplane to attend a convention of radio executives in San Francisco.

mother solidly in the matter, fully appreciating that without Mother there would be no Angelus Temple. But this indication of unrest in the ranks was indicative of a condition that grew to be endemic at Echo Park—and that did not bother Aimee and Minnie in the least.

When the Santa Ana branch of the temple broke away, angered by Mrs. Kennedy's refusal to surrender title to their building after they had paid for it, Aimee again backed her mother against the insurgents.

"Why should I give away property that I have, so to speak, raised with my own voice?" she demanded.

The matter went to court, and Aimee and Minnie engaged a lawyer, a former judge named W. H. Thomas, and the action was stalled until the complainants gave up in disgust. Meanwhile, Minnie had stripped the church bare, down to the communion set. Aimee laughed and said that the communion set had simply been removed to be cleaned; but, cleaned or not, it was not returned, and title to the property, valued at about three thousand dollars, was retained by the temple pair. Judge Thomas was handed his fee by a judge of the superior court, Carlos S. Hardy, who relayed a protest from the temple women about its size. Thomas was struck that it was the first time he had ever been handed a fee by a judge, but the check was a temple check and he accepted it.

Title to Angelus Temple and all other church property was held jointly by Aimee Semple McPherson and Minnie Kennedy in their own names at this period. A nonprofit religious corporation, the Echo Park Evangelistic Association, had been formed to carry on the activities of the church. Of this corporation Aimee was president, Minnie Kennedy was vice-president, and Aimee's devotedly sub-servient secretary, Emma Schaffer, was secretary.

Late in 1925, a deed of trust was signed by both Aimee and Minnie transferring their property to the Echo Park Evangelistic Association. This deed was not recorded until after 1926, but it made little difference practically, since the association in effect was another name for mother and daughter.

Plainly there were several aspects to the phenomenon at Echo Park, and more than one side to its leader.

Gladwyn Nichols, head of the temple's music department, and his wife had encountered Sister McPherson for the first time in San Francisco in 1919, when she was conducting religious services in a former saloon there, renamed Glad Tidings Tabernacle. Both the Nicholses were captivated by her dynamism, by her femininity, and her remarkable preaching. Her power of projection was unique: when she described a scene, she placed her hearers in it; when she spoke of Jesus, it was with such intensity that the audience became half-persuaded he was in their midst, possibly sitting in the front row, as rapt as themselves.

A couple of years later, Aimee's widening circle of religious admirers was startled and pained when Harold McPherson sued for divorce in Rhode Island. Aimee handled the touchy matter with reticence and dignity. On legal advice, she protected herself by filing counter-suit in California. Both actions charged desertion. Although Mrs. McPherson was still relatively obscure in Los Angeles, the news-papers there were sufficiently intrigued by the anomaly of a woman preacher vaguely adhering to a sect that frowned absolutely on divorce, herself seeking a marital separation, to send reporters for an interview. Aimee told them that her husband had deserted her two years previously (the year she moved to California), because "his ways were not of the church but of the world." She had brought her action reluctantly, she said, merely in self-defense.

The press did not pursue the matter, and when McPherson's case came to trial in the East no opposition was offered. He testified that his wife was of a roving, restless disposition, and had compelled him to move frequently. Describing their disagreements, he said that during one quarrel she had threatened to kill him and herself. Supporting witnesses were his mother, Mrs. Annie McPherson, who said that her son's wife was "a difficult woman to live with," and a boarder in the elder Mrs. McPherson's home, who stated that McPherson had set up "three homes to my knowledge" to humor his wife, and "finally gave up the attempt to please her.

"Mrs. McPherson was more interested in her evangelistic career than anything else," this witness said. "She had a fiery temper and made life unendurable for her husband. She could throw herself into a fit at any time."

McPherson was awarded a divorce and given custody of their son Rolf for two days each week. However, he did not avail himself of the right for a reason which he stated in a bitter interview five years later:

"I would rather give up the pleasure of seeing my own son than put up with even the slightest connection with my former wife."

In the same interview he said that she had a "dual personality"— brilliant and alluring on the platform, but given to "wildcat habits" at home.

Minnie Kennedy herself was often baffled by her daughter's dual nature. Years afterward she would say frankly:

"On the platform Sister is wholly spiritual, magnetic, and beautiful, truly a child of God. Off the stand she has human traits, the same as others."

As 1926 dawned Aimee Semple McPherson was at the peak of her achievements, a power in Los Angeles. But unknown to her flock, to herself, or to the world at large, she stood on the verge of a demonstration of those "human traits" that would shake her empire to its foundations.

Surrealism on the Sands

"And shall these labors and these honors die? . . .
—*Henry VI, Part 2*

Mother Kennedy not only watched the money, she watched her daughter. She knew how impulsive, rash, and headstrong Aimee could be. In business matters Minnie believed her daughter could be overreached by any schemer and that she was too generous to be entrusted with the handling of money. There were times when Minnie looked on her remarkable child as something younger than Aimee's thirty-five years of age, and Aimee herself encouraged the attitude by her habit of compliance. She was not combative by nature, disliked quarreling, and avoided disputes. Besides, she appreciated that in her own sphere Minnie Kennedy was usually right. Only in regard to her behavior on the platform was Aimee fully independent, and in that department Minnie conceded that Aimee's judgment was absolutely correct. But as time went on, it seemed to Mother that her daughter was too confident and was growing careless of appearances.

There was one matter that gave Mother uneasiness more than any other. Sister kept a telephone beside her pulpit chair and during the services would receive calls, perhaps during an anthem or a solo. By this means she also kept in touch with the radio broadcasting studio on an upper floor of the temple, to check on how the service was coming over the microphone.

The engineer in charge of station KFSG was Kenneth Gladstone Ormiston, a pleasant chap in his thirties. He was married and had a little son. Although he walked with a noticeable limp, he was attractive, had a quick sense of humor, and was lively company. He was not particularly religious and not a temple adherent, and he treated

In 1924 Aimee acquired her own radio station, KFSG (Kall Foursquare Gospel). It was the third radio station in Los Angeles and the engineer in charge was Kenneth G. Ormiston. This photograph of Sister Aimee and Ormiston is the only known photograph of them together. It was published in Aimee's church magazine on the occasion of the first broadcast.

his employer like a woman, not like a religious symbol, being not at all awed by her exalted position. This Aimee found refreshing. Living as she did in the worshipful atmosphere of her followers and the temple workers, she sometimes found the adulation cloying. With Ormiston she could unbend, be jolly, tell a joke and laugh at the jokes of others. She formed the habit of chatting with Ormiston over the platform telephone during broadcast services, sometimes giggling at his comments on the proceedings.

Unfortunately, the acoustics of Angelus Temple were so nearly perfect that these irreverent exchanges could be overheard in the balcony. Minnie began to receive criticisms of Aimee's behavior, and she remonstrated with her, warning that she stood in a vulnerable position; her familiarity might easily be misconstrued, especially since Kenneth Ormiston was a married man, and Sister herself was divorced.

"Somebody," said Minnie, "will be saying you have a case on him, or that he has a case on you."

Aimee pouted and kept up her intercom chatting.

Sometimes, perhaps during a prayer meeting that did not require Sister's presence, a little group of friends would gather in the radio control booth and listen to the proceedings, now and then laughing at Ormiston's droll remarks about what was coming over. Judge and Mrs. Hardy enjoyed these sessions, and Gladwyn Nichols, or others of the select inner circle of temple intimates, might join in. And Minnie became more and more distressed by this association with the radioman. She also learned that Ormiston's wife was accusing him of carrying on with the temple's pastor.

Whenever Minnie missed Aimee, she knew where to find her— in the radio control room, often alone with Ormiston. When Mother tracked her there and lectured her on her disregard of appearances, Aimee would pout and slump in her chair like a scolded child, or shrug and flounce away. Scenting danger (for a scandal would be ruinous to their enterprise), Minnie began to make things uncomfortable for Ormiston, hoping he would quit; she suspected that Aimee would not consent to his being fired. And fretting over the situation did not improve Minnie's temper.

Aimee herself gradually became edgy. For years she had been pouring out energy, carrying a load of work that would have crushed most women, with never a letup. She did not complain, but the strain was telling, her nerves were fraying, and she resented her mother's interference.

One of her staunchest adherents, Rudolf Dunbar, who served as choir chaplain, observed her tenseness and urged her to take a respite from her responsibilities, or she risked a breakdown. Dunbar was a prosperous insurance executive with offices in Chicago and Los Angeles.

Aimee protested that she could not be spared; who would keep the temple running? Dunbar suggested that Paul Rader, an evangelist who was having much success in Chicago, might be induced to fill in as substitute preacher for a while; in fact, he volunteered to get

Rader's consent. And this he did, personally guaranteeing Rader's expenses and salary.

Such officiousness did not sit well with Mother Kennedy. For the time being, however, she said nothing, merely eyed Dunbar balefully. When the arrangements were completed, then the temple members were told that Sister was going on a vacation trip to the Holy Land, and collections were taken up to defray the cost of her traveling in the finest style. An affectionate farewell demonstration at the railroad station also was planned.

Minnie, who felt she had been working as long and as hard as her daughter, was disappointed when Aimee failed to suggest taking her along, but she consoled herself with the thought that the Lord wanted her to remain at her post.

About this time Ormiston threw up his job and disappeared. His wife came to the temple demanding to know where he had gone; and Minnie was relieved that she had no information to give; she really had no notion where Ormiston might be. Since he had left home once before and had come back, she advised Mrs. Ormiston to wait patiently.

On January 11, 1926, Aimee set out on what for her was to be a great adventure. Thousands of her followers gathered at the railroad station to give her a rousing send-off. The temple band played, Paul Rader prayed on the observation-car platform, and Minnie wept with pride as Sister, trim in a blue tailored suit, a bundle of American Beauty roses cradled in her arm, waved good-bye and shouted benedictions. Roberta Semple was traveling with her, and their first stop was to be in Northern Ireland, where Roberta was to visit her father's parents, the James Semples, in their village home near Belfast.

Back at the temple, Mother gathered up the reins with a resentful eye on Rudolf Dunbar. The way he had stage-managed Sister's departure displeased her, and she told Gladwyn Nichols:

"He is a businessman. We don't want his kind around here. Get rid of him."

The upshot was that things were made so uncomfortable for Dunbar that he took the hint and withdrew.

By that time Mother Kennedy was suffering a succession of shocks. First it was a report that a scandal sheet in Hollywood was preparing

Mae Waldron, Temple secretary, who appeared as a witness in the 1926 hearing against Aimee and her mother and in later embroilments between Aimee and Minnie Kennedy.

to publish an article saying that Kenneth Ormiston was traveling with Mrs. McPherson in Europe, and definitely not to the Holy Land. Emma Schaffer brought the report to Mother; Emma's face was blanched with fright. Minnie asked her where she had heard the story, and Emma said it had been brought to the temple by a young stenographer, Mae Waldron.

Minnie summoned Miss Waldron (whose married name was Emmil) and taking her out on the sidewalk in front of the temple, so as to elude eavesdroppers, demanded how she had found out about the intended scandal article. Mae said that she lived in Hollywood, and the rumor was widespread there. Minnie ordered her not to say a word to anybody else. Then she cabled to Thomas Cook Sons, the travel agents who had arranged Aimee's tour, instructing them to put a guard on Sister. The agents cabled back that they were complying. Next Minnie cabled directly to her daughter, warning her of the storm blowing up at home.

Just where Aimee received this cablegram Minnie did not know, but she believed it was somewhere in Italy. In any event, Aimee turned around, went back to Ireland, and collected Roberta there; the two then went on to Palestine together.

Meanwhile, Minnie was trying frantically to locate Ormiston. If she could find him and get him to reappear briefly at the temple and perhaps speak over KFSG so that his voice would be recognized, the scandal would be scotched. But no trace of the radioman was found. Adding to Mother's alarm was a fresh visit paid to the temple by Ormiston's wife, who, livid with jealousy, said she had just come from her lawyer and was preparing to file suit for divorce, naming Mrs. McPherson. Minnie was terrified, and tried her best to talk the woman out of her intention, but without success.

Just then, fortunately, the boy who had been handling the radio controls since Ormiston's departure came in excitedly and said the elusive Kenneth had just telephoned from Washington state, to report the temple's broadcast coming in clearly. Minnie at once sent him money, asking him to come to the temple. Upon that, Mrs. Ormiston, without explanation, dropped her plan and sailed home to her parents in Australia.

Ormiston did show up at Angelus Temple as requested and was seen around Echo Park for several days and spoke over the radio. Then he vanished again, and Minnie congratulated herself that she had nipped that threat to the temple in time. Nevertheless the strange concatenation of events worried her; she suspected that things were going on about which she had not been told, and she looked forward anxiously to her daughter's return.

The news from abroad seemed to be reassuring. Sister McPherson preached by invitation several times in England, and on Easter Sunday filled the Royal Albert Hall, the largest auditorium in the British Isles. It was a personal triumph for her, though Minnie considered the "love offering" tendered by the sponsors of the meeting— five hundred dollars—hardly an adequate remuneration.

It was Saturday, April 24, when Aimee and Roberta finally returned to Los Angeles. They were welcomed at the station by twelve thousand deliriously happy temple followers and by another five thousand at Echo Park. Judge Hardy and the city's acting mayor extended an official welcome-home, and Aimee treated them and her radio listeners to a glowing report on her experiences abroad. After that the temple pastor slipped quickly back into the routine of daily activities that had claimed her before her vacation.

But hardly had Aimee unpacked her trunks of souvenirs (including a van-load of costumes for use in her illustrated sermons) before Minnie Kennedy realized that a change had come over her hitherto docile daughter. Whereas in their discussions of temple affairs they had always spoken of "we," now Aimee said "I." In response to her mother's questions she grew sarcastic and vague. And she demanded money, real money, saying it was due her and she was determined to get it. Heretofore Minnie had given Sister twenty-five dollars a week for pin money arguing that Aimee had little use for cash, for the temple maintained charge accounts at the city's best stores and specialty shops, and she was free to use them. Minnie always wanted her to look well turned out and begrudged no outlay for that purpose. Why Aimee should want substantial sums of money in her possession her mother could not understand. Yet, after thinking it over and deciding that her daughter was entitled to her share of everything, she agreed that Sister should receive the collection taken on the first Sunday of every month, the money being turned over to her directly, without even being counted, and no subsequent accounting being asked. How much this collection amounted to nobody at the temple knew, but since thousands of dollars were taken in weekly, and Sister's monthly love offering was noticeably plentiful, the sum must be considerable. Aimee got it all and gave no explanation as to what she did with it. Minnie refrained from prying, suspecting that she would not be told the truth anyway.

Soon after Aimee's return, Minnie encountered Ormiston again and asked what he was doing; she had no wish to see him around the temple and hoped he would make himself scarce. He replied negligently that he was "working around," and staying "out at the beach."

About the same time Aimee developed a passion for swimming in the ocean and made almost daily trips to Ocean Park. She was an ardent swimmer, and Minnie was uneasy about these jaunts, having a dread of the water herself; but Aimee laughed at her fears. Sister's companion on these seaside trips was her gaunt secretary, Emma

Schaffer, who also was frightened of the water but would have promptly submitted to drowning if necessary to save Sister.

May 18 was a day of bright sunshine, light breezes, and a warm sea. Shortly after noon Aimee told her mother that she was going to the beach and invited her to come along. Minnie had accounts to run through and declined. Aimee drove away in her expensive Kissel car with Emma Schaffer. Emma, who did not drive, always sat in the back seat when Sister took the wheel.

A few hours later came appalling news: Sister had gone into the water and had not come out. Search had been made, but there was not a clue to her fate.

At the first word, all Minnie's horror of the water welled up and she gasped:

"Drowned!"

Thus began the hectic drama that, stretching into weeks and then into months, Minnie would look back upon with stunned incredulity, marveling that she had had the capacity to live through it all.

II

When Mother Kennedy tried to retrace her steps in that maze she seemed to lose her way in a fog of unreality. But it had been all too real, agonizingly real at the moment. That was the terrible part of it—*it had been real*. Some of the questions that had bothered her during those months she would never be able to answer to her satisfaction.

The reporters had been the first to put questions. Swarming in, they had poked into everything, even pushing into Aimee's bedroom in search for "clues." They seemed to imply that Minnie knew something she wasn't telling, although she had no doubt whatever that her daughter was dead. Aimee had been seen for the last time far out in the water, hadn't she? Maybe it was foul play, or maybe a rip tide, or some monster of the deep. Minnie had an imperfect comprehension of marine life, but she pointed out that other people had drowned under similar circumstances and no to-do had been made about it. The thing that intrigued the press and the police and virtually everybody was that no body could be found. When every means proved futile, from deep-sea divers to airplanes scanning the

An airplane joins the search for Sister's body off Ocean Park beach in May, 1926. A crowd gathered at a rumor that a corpse had been found, but it was a dead seal.

surface of the water miles from land, Minnie could only conclude that her child had been wafted up to Heaven bodily, in some mysterious manifestation of divine grace. The Bible said that had happened to Elijah, and Aimee had always preached that the day of miracles was not past.

Minnie had a multitude of things to think about in this terrible crisis. All the burden of Angelus Temple suddenly devolved upon her, and her task it was to hold the organization together until it could surmount the shock. The followers were hysterical, without Sister they were lost, and Mother's firm hand was needed to steady them. The temple remained, and Minnie's duty was to see that it did not collapse. Personal grief must give way to larger interests, even though she herself reeled under the catastrophe.

It was the newspapers that kept raising questions. They printed rumors that Sister had been seen here, there, everywhere, from Canada to Mexico. Minnie was not impressed. The letters had poured in, spirit messages, advice from mediums, demands for ransom, blackmail threats—all the world seemed bent on getting into the act, and Minnie had been driven distracted, following up false leads and fending off cranks. All the plausible letters she turned over to the police, she explained, and since they, also, were convinced that Sister was drowned, why shouldn't her own mother feel the same way? To allay the excitement and bring matters to a close, Mother announced positively, standing beside Sister's vacant pulpit chair:

"Aimee is dead. Whatever you read in the newspapers, unless it is about the finding of the body, do not be alarmed."

To Roberta, who was fascinated by the newsboys yelling their "extras" outside the temple doors, Minnie said:

"Just remember always, Roberta, your mother's body is in the sea—but her spirit is with the Lord, shouting victory."

The press first brought Ormiston's name into the mystery, and "Find Ormiston!" became the cry. Minnie still was not impressed. And how silly the uproar had become when the radioman suddenly

Minnie Kennedy conveys her prayerful hope of success to a deep-sea diver about to search underneath the pier to seek her daughter's body.

appeared and offered any help he could give toward establishing her daughter's fate. But there had been no help he could give, and after convincing the police of that he had dropped out of sight again.

In a final effort to silence the rumors, Minnie then offered a reward of twenty-five thousand dollars to "the person or persons who will bring my daughter, Aimee Semple McPherson, to the Angelus Temple unharmed and as well as she left us on Tuesday, May the 18th instant."

"If only the public could see the situation in its sane and sensible light!" Minnie moaned. "It's a shame that all these unfounded reports should gain circulation!"

Captain Herman Kline, head of the Los Angeles police detective bureau, assured the press that no theory was tenable except accidental drowning; he could discover no evidence pointing to anything else. Still the crank letters continued to rain on Mother Kennedy.

"What shall I do? Oh, what shall I do?" she beseeched her helpers, and they could offer no helpful advice.

A memorial service was held, drawing crowds, and Mother assured the throng:

"We do not believe Sister's body will ever be recovered. Her young body was too precious to Jesus."

A memorial collection was taken at this rededication of faith, the newspapers reporting that it netted some $40,000.

Preposterous, retorted Minnie, and calling Brother J. W. Arthur to the platform, she had him read from the ledger the exact sums received, in cash and pledges: $4,690.56 cash, and $29,500 in pledges payable in one year, making a grand total of $34,190.56. That was a long way from $40,000, Minnie sighed wanly.

Brother Arthur proved an unfailing source of strength throughout the ordeal. He was a Canadian, too; after running a country store in a bleak hamlet in North Dakota, he had turned Methodist preacher and migrated to California, where he had been cured by Sister Aimee, he stated, of a stomach cancer. Thenceforward his life and all his energies would be devoted to Angelus Temple and the two women who had brought it into being.

The great memorial service had been held on Sunday, June 20, after Sister had been gone more than a month. But even that formal farewell failed to clear the air, to Mother's continued distress, and she begged those around to pray for her.

On the following Tuesday the letter that would become famous as the "Avengers" letter was put into Minnie's hands, according to her telling of the sequence. According to post office records, it had been left at the temple by special delivery mail the previous Saturday. Written in a rambling jargon, half underworld lingo and half a hortatory style like Sister's own, it stated that Aimee had been kidnaped and was being held for half a million dollars' ransom; and if this was not paid she would be sold into white slavery in Mexico. A strand of greasy hair resembling the evangelist's was enclosed for identification.

That night Minnie placed this letter on the pillow beside her head, and morning found her still trying to puzzle out what it could mean. Was this another false lead? Was it just an attempt to get money out of the temple? The hair looked like Aimee's, and there were things in the letter that apparently only Aimee would know, but could Minnie be sure?

While she was still mulling the enigma, the telephone rang. It was Captain Kline calling; he said he had just received "another of those identification clues." He didn't take much stock in this one, but Mrs. Kennedy's daughter was said to have been found alive in Douglas, Arizona.

Then a call directly from Douglas came through, and while Captain Kline listened in, Minnie lifted the receiver and said tentatively, "Hello?"

Back came a voice that she recognized as her daughter's. Aimee began to babble, and Minnie broke in sharply with, "Don't talk!"

Later that morning, accompanied by Roberta and Rolf and escorted by a deputation of newspaper reporters and investigators from the district attorney's office, Mother set out for Douglas. When she got there, she found that Aimee had "talked her head off."

The story that Aimee was telling anyone who would listen (and it seemed that the whole world wanted to hear it) was one of abduction, torture, and a thrilling escape and flight through the desert. No *Perils of Pauline* moving-picture serial contained more hair-raising adventures than Sister's account of where she had been and what had happened during the five weeks of her disappearance.

She had been kidnaped, she said, lured by a story of a dying infant to an automobile parked near the beach, pushed into the car, and smothered with a cloth saturated with some sickly smelling anesthetic

This is how Aimee demonstrated for the press and Temple officials how she succeeded in cutting her bonds on the jagged edge of a tin can and escaped kidnapers.

like chloroform. A blanket thrown over her head had muffled her cries, and she lost consciousness. When she came to, the next morning, she was lying bound on a cot in a house that she guessed was near Calexico; the window was boarded up so she could not see out. Her abductors were a heavy-set, burly man named Steve, a woman called Rose, and a sallow, "hollow-chested" companion sometimes called Frank. She was told she was being held for ransom, and when she refused to cooperate by communicating with her mother, they threatened and tortured her, Steve holding a lighted cigar on her hand. Still she resisted.

Eventually, she said, she had been tied hand and foot, placed in an automobile, and transported to a shack in the desert. It was an adobe shack somewhere in Mexico south of Douglas; she could not be more precise in locating it. From there her abductors had dispatched the "Avengers" letter demanding five hundred thousand dollars and enclosing the lock of hair for identification. If that should not suffice, they suggested that they might cut off a scarred finger that Minnie would recognize and send that.

The day before her reappearance, Aimee went on, during the absence of Rose, who had gone to buy groceries, she had managed to roll off the cot where she lay pinioned and, working her way to a discarded tin can, had sawed through her bonds on its jagged edge. Climbing out the window (the door was closed), she had fled into the desert, staggering on blindly all afternoon and into the night, until at last she saw the lights of the saloons in Agua Prieta, a town just across the line from Douglas. There she had collapsed, had been revived, and had been brought into Douglas.

While Aimee repeated for her mother this harrowing tale, Minnie sat staring in amazement, grasping her daughter's hand.

"I can't realize it," Minnie told reporters. "It is like a blow, the shock just numbs me. It seems like a dream, just like she was resurrected from the dead."

Then tears came to her eyes, and she moaned:

"Here is Sister a wreck! She will probably never be the same!" And as an afterthought: "I can't help but feel that our years of hard work will be hurt as a result of what has happened. We were always so careful and conservative! It is so unfortunate it had to be Sister! If I had been at the beach, this would never have happened."

But the evangelist's return to Los Angeles had been triumphal— crowds all along the way, cheers, hallelujahs, "votes of confidence" by the raising of hands. From the train Sister was carried through a deliriously clamoring throng in a flower-decked chair, and her entrance into Angelus Temple was like a resurrection indeed. Amid the joyful commotion, Minnie hoped and trusted: her daughter was no ordinary woman, as her whole career attested, and extraordinary things could happen to her. So Minnie was incensed when, even amid the rejoicings, the newspapers expressed disbelief in her daughter's lurid tale.

They printed speculation, dwelling on the many discrepancies. After Aimee had struggled through cruel desert heat the better part of a day and a night, according to her reckoning, her garments showed no perspiration stains. Although the terrain she said she had traversed bristled with cactus and flinty stones, her clothing was not torn and her shoes were only lightly scuffed; grass stains were visible on the instep. At the hospital her physical condition was checked thoroughly and seemed normal. She was not noticeably sunburned,

Aimee's triumphant return to Los Angeles from Douglas, Arizona, June 26, 1926. Thousands cheered as she was carried off the train in a flower-decked chair.

and upon reaching Agua Prieta she had been satisfied by a single glass of water (one witness said two) although the commonest symptom after exposure for hours to the desert sun is an insane craving for water.

Minnie thought it outrageous that such trivia should be brought up. She asked Aimee about them, and Aimee repeated that her story was true in every detail. Minnie accepted her word; the welfare of the temple and her own sanity required it. No matter what happened, she would stand by her daughter as she always had, and Angelus Temple was not going to be snuffed out by malicious slanders.

Aimee was annoyed when the reporters persisted in questioning her. Of course her story was true, she declared; she had told it just as it happened, and her followers believed her.

"My story is true!" she repeated again and again. "Why should I lie? What motive would I have? What would I have to gain?"

But suspicion would not down, and there were those who felt she might have much to gain. Suppose a ransom had been paid, and it developed that there were no kidnapers? The supposition opened

Aimee preaching in Angelus Temple on the day of her return. "My story is true!" she repeated. At right stands her secretary, Emma Schaffer, who had been the only person present when Aimee disappeared.

up a vista of possibilities. At least, Aimee Semple McPherson was being advertised as she never had been before; to millions of people who had never previously heard of her, the evangelist's name was becoming a household word. Already she was a national question mark.

That her word should be doubted at first affronted and then shocked her. Her followers accepted it as they accepted the Gospel, she pointed out; they had firmer faith in Sister's word than they would have had in any less authentically vouched-for revelation from above. "If an angel from heaven should come down and tell my people that Sister is not a child of God, they wouldn't believe it," she declared angrily. Doubt of her veracity challenged her very self, and she would not let it pass. People did not believe her? Well, she would make them accept her word. And that became the keynote of the next several months of ordeal for Minnie Kennedy and that wonderful, headstrong, willful daughter of hers.

Looking back, Minnie would smile at her simplicity. When a

reporter had asked whether she would be willing to go before a grand jury, she had replied, why, of course, although she did not then even know what a grand jury was.

"I imagined," she would recall with a chuckle, "that it was a body of men, with men like Lincoln and Washington, that was organized to protect people in trouble."

She learned her error swiftly. Both she and Aimee were questioned before the grand jury, and Minnie grew circumspect in her replies when it dawned on her that she was not there to be protected at all. She told the jury the truth, namely, that when her daughter disappeared, she believed she was drowned, and nothing had shaken that belief until she heard Aimee's voice on the telephone, from Douglas. Whenever the district attorney, Asa Keyes, touched on temple finances, he found Minnie armed at all points. There was no mortgage on the temple, she corrected him, and the only insurance policy that had ever been carried on her daughter's life had been canceled after her return from Europe in the spring. The suggestion that there had been bad feeling between the two temple leaders Minnie blandly rejected. Her relations with her daughter were "splendid," she said, though she admitted that "I boss her around considerably and try to keep her from getting into trouble." Their common care, she said tartly—adding that it had been the care of the people who had given money to erect the temple—was that their work should never fall into the hands of "any bunch of men," and "I have stood by that."

Asked who would get the money if the temple were sold, Mother replied stoutly:

"It could not be sold. It is for the work of the Lord and could not be sold."

The grand jury reported that it had found no evidence to indict anybody, kidnapers or others. Aimee greeted the announcement as a vindication, stating:

"California, Arizona, and Mexico have been searched, not for the criminals, but for evidence against the evangelist. . . . There is no such evidence. Mrs. McPherson's story, related time and again, to officials and others, remains as firm and unshaken as the first time it was told."

Minnie hoped the unfortunate affair could now be forgotten. But instead had come all that sensational talk about a cottage at the seaside resort, Carmel—about a man and a woman who had occupied the place furtively for ten days during the period of Sister's absence; about identifications, first of Ormiston as the man, then of Sister as the woman; about searches and seizures of Bibles and grocery slips and radio sets and spice cans and whatnot; about murky encounters in the night and an elusive blue Chrysler coupe, and on and on. The more the disclosures tumbled out, the more stubbornly did Sister repeat her story. And the crowning indignity had been Minnie's arrest on charges of conspiracy to perpetrate a hoax, corrupt public morals, interfere with the law, and so on. Aimee, and to Mother's despair, Kenneth Ormiston, although nowhere in sight, were accused jointly with her.

Surely no mother was ever subjected to greater humiliation on a willful daughter's account than was Minnie when she was brought to the Hall of Justice to be bailed out like a criminal. The hard stares of courthouse loafers cut her like knives. Aimee, too ill to appear, stricken by real enough ailments, escaped that public indignity, but not her mother.

Then had come the interminable court hearing to determine whether they must stand trial. Day after day Minnie heard the evidence as it piled up against her daughter, and betrayed none of her feelings. She still had faith; but she was endowed with sturdy common sense, and try as she might, she simply could not but see the gross implausibilities. She was not, like Aimee, gifted with an imagination that could conceive a thing to be the way she wanted it to be, and then ignore the contradiction with apparent sincerity. Minnie would not reject her child's story entirely; but she questioned. And she did become convinced that Aimee had not told her the whole truth.

Daily during the hearings the set of Minnie's lips tightened and the penetrating gaze of her small gray eyes became more stony. She blushed when that whirligig of lying, the so-called "hoax woman," Mrs. Wiseman-Sielaff, nonchalantly described confidential sessions at Angelus Temple during which, she said, she had been coached by Mrs. McPherson to impersonate her and had collected money for imaginary trips and expenses (here Minnie blushed), only to be exposed at the very moment when she was endeavoring to persuade the newspapers that she (or perhaps her sister—it was never quite clear) had been the occupant of the cottage at Carmel with

Ormiston. The "hoax woman" had been added to the roster of defendants in the case, a fact which increased the indignity to Minnie. Aimee passed off Mrs. Wiseman-Sielaff's damaging testimony by saying that since the silly, conscienceless creature had managed to fool the district attorney with her ridiculous story (hadn't she been in an insane asylum once?), it was not to be wondered that she had been able to fool "two inexperienced, trusting women."

Except for the staunch support of friends, both in the temple and outside its ranks, Mother Kennedy could never have borne up. Judge Hardy had been a veritable buckler and shield. From their early days in the city, he had befriended them and had helped them with temple affairs, although he had not become a member; a Baptist, he stayed true to his church. But he had spoken many times over KFSG and had helped to organize the temple's young people's group, the Crusaders. As a friend—not of course as a lawyer, for judges were debarred from practicing law during their tenure—he had steered Aimee and Minnie past the quicksands lurking in property deeds and mortgage bonds, fields in which both women's knowledge was scant. Judge Hardy had even quietly instituted searches for evidence to corroborate Mrs. McPherson's kidnaping story, without success, however; but more than once he had publicly indicated his skepticism that the district attorney really wanted to clear up the mystery at all. Sister and Minnie had been grateful for the judge's loyalty, and had expressed their gratitude tangibly in the form of a check for twenty-five hundred dollars, to enable the judge and his wife to take a trip to Alaska.

Toward the close of the hearing the "little blue trunk" had added a fresh sensation, when photographs of the feminine finery it contained showed a remarkable similarity to clothing known to have belonged to Sister. The trunk had been seized in New York, where it had been left by a "Ralph Stringer," who was definitely identified as Ormiston. The contents included scented negligees, morning, evening, and night gowns, custom-made shoes from a Los Angeles shop that Aimee patronized, and, it was said, the very black satin slippers that an alert Carmel witness had spotted on the feet of the woman in the cottage by the sea.

Aimee ridiculed the find. "Probably a circus performer's costumes," she scoffed. Minnie had her own ideas.

Mother Kennedy arrested, September 17, 1926. Surrounded by staring reporters, detectives, and "courthouse loafers," Mother suffered in silence.

At the start of the hearing Aimee had urged her followers to stay away from the courtroom, and begged them, if they loved her, to read nothing about the case in the newspapers or listen to any accounts over the radio except her own. These she broadcast nightly, giving her own version of what had occurred during that day. Often the district attorney's staff cringed as their actions were travestied by the evangelist, who used all her powers of mimicry to discredit witnesses, impugn the prosecutor's motives, and act out the courtroom drama in terms of ridicule.

On November 3, the hearing judge handed down his ruling. Without passing on the ultimate guilt or innocence of the four defendants—Aimee, Minnie, Ormiston (still missing), and that dupe or duper, Mrs. Wiseman-Sielaff—the judge decided that "after a full examination of the entire evidence, there is sufficient cause to believe the defendants guilty." All were held for trial.

When the curt decision was read, Aimee sat stunned. Then she sprang up, protesting her innocence.

Minnie Kennedy slowly, deliberately, smiled.

III

Months before that nerve-racking day, a blind lawyer, R. A. McKinley, had injected himself into the case in a dubious manner, and during the course of interviews with the temple leaders, his sharpened hearing had detected an undercurrent of antagonism between the two women.

McKinley had first come forward with a queer story about having been approached by two men who claimed to be Sister McPherson's abductors; they wanted him to act as go-between in collecting a ransom, selecting him because he was blind and could not shadow or pursue them. This reported overture had been while Sister was still missing, and later McKinley had met the evangelist and her mother several times at Angelus Temple, where Aimee had urged him to try to procure some tangible proof of the truth of her story. Particularly she wanted him to make fresh contact with the kidnapers and find and identify the adobe shack in Mexico from which she said she had escaped. The most diligent hunt by United States and Mexican authorities had failed to discover anything like the shack she described.

McKinley had "strung them along," meanwhile collecting money. At one point, curious to see how far Mrs. McPherson would commit herself, he had shown her a snapshot of a man which she immediately identified, in the presence of her mother, as the kidnaper Steve.

"Mother, that looks like the man that was Steve!" were her words.

Minnie was skeptical. She studied the print and said all she could make out was one ear; couldn't they have an enlargement?

Actually the photograph had been taken in McKinley's own office. Calling in a waterfront character named Joe Watts, the attorney's secretary, Bernice Morris, had drawn long sideburns on his cheeks with a makeup pencil, smudged his face to make him look swarthy, blackened his eyebrows with mascara, pulled his hat well down over his eyes, and then snapped him with her Brownie camera.

McKinley returned from that interview astonished.

"You never could have told me—never in the world could you have told me before tonight," he blurted to the secretary, "that the old lady wasn't in this business! Now I believe, as sure as God makes

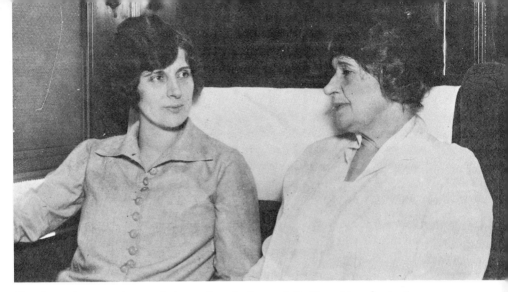

On the train returning to Arizona in vain hope of finding Aimee's shack, signs of tension between Mother Kennedy and her daughter began to appear.

me live, that she is absolutely innocent! Aimee is trying to fool her mother more than anybody else in the world!"

He recalled that he had never met the evangelist alone; always Mother Kennedy was present during their discussions of his entirely fictitious researches. Each time he arrived, Sister would guide him to a settee and would sit beside him. Now and then during the conversation she would nudge him with her knee, as if cautioning him, and his acute hearing caught the subtle tone of antagonism in the voices of the two women. He felt that, in front of her mother, Aimee would back up any claim he might make. Aimee Semple McPherson, he was convinced, lived in fear of her mother!

Shortly after this, McKinley laughingly told a friend that Joe Watts had called Aimee on the telephone and identified himself as Steve, whereupon she had gasped, "My God, is it really you?"

The next morning McKinley's body was found in an automobile overturned in a roadside ditch. In his pocket were letters from Judge Hardy linking the judge with the lawyer's pretended searches.

After they had been held for trial, real friction did develop between Aimee and her mother. To Minnie's alarm and indignation, her daughter suddenly placed herself under the guidance of some of the newspapermen who had been much around the temple during the commotion, and whom Minnie mistrusted and disliked.

The man seeming to have the most influence with Sister was Ralph Jordan, a husky reporter with tight reddish curls employed by the *Los Angeles Examiner,* a Hearst newspaper. James Kendrick, a reporter for the *Los Angeles Times,* seemed to be working closely with Jordan. And there was also Reginald Taviner, who had political connections and whom Aimee had hired as a press agent during the hearing, saying that he could get her a "good press." To Mother Kennedy and many temple members, it seemed that Taviner was getting Sister the worst possible press, but Aimee trusted him implicitly.

Minnie detested these interlopers—worldly men who swore, drank whiskey, smoked cigars in the temple corridors, and swaggered around—and she quarreled with them hotly when they presumed to interfere with her own and Aimee's legal defense. Again and again the temple attorneys were brushed aside, Jordan and his associates dictating strategy, until W. K. Gilbert, Aimee's chief of counsel during the hearing, confessed that he did not know where he stood from day to day. Another leading attorney, Roland Rich Woolley, withdrew entirely from the case. Since Mother had to pay these attorneys their fees—ten thousand dollars in each case—she despaired of a favorable outcome. But Aimee persisted in adopting every suggestion her new advisers made, calling them her "deliverers."

Meanwhile the temple and the city seethed with rumors. After the close of the preliminary hearing, Kenneth Ormiston had returned to Los Angeles, offering no explanation of where he had been. He ridiculed all attempts to associate Mrs. McPherson with him in the cottage at Carmel, and although he was held for trial together with Aimee and her mother, he displayed little anxiety.

District Attorney Keyes was badgered from all sides. Pressing for a final, stern determination was the church federation of the city, whose executive committee stood on its call for a cleanup of the mystery, let whom might suffer. Said the committee:

"Either a crime of the most terrible nature has been committed against Mrs. Aimee Semple McPherson, or else a fraud and hoax that is a shame to Christianity has been attempted, and the Christian religion itself is being criticized and even condemned as a result."

Los Angeles, always a focal point for cults and faddists, was agitated and the chamber of commerce expressed alarm that the sensational publicity should tarnish the city's good name.

Keyes insisted that he would press the case vigorously, yet seemed to be in no hurry. He went traveling in the East.

Another puzzling development, which Minnie Kennedy could only watch and deplore since Aimee was telling her hardly anything any more, was her daughter's sudden need for money in large sums. Again and again Aimee demanded that her mother withdraw thousands of dollars from their several accounts, and when Minnie handed over the money gave not the slightest explanation of its intended disposal. One night, just before Christmas, Sister hurried out of the temple after the evening service, accompanied by her three "deliverers." She did not say where they were going. On her return Aimee seemed greatly excited, and told her mother that she had just talked with "certain officials" and was sure the charges against them would be dismissed without a trial.

January 10 was the last date on which Keyes could start the trial, or he would have to drop the case. Shortly before that date the *Examiner* reported that he had decided to waive prosecution. Keyes was a good-natured man who wished harm to no one, above all to the leaders of Angelus Temple, but he was holding a political hot potato. He promptly repudiated the *Examiner*'s statement and said he would carry out his duty vigorously.

After this announcement, it seemed to Minnie that for the first time her daughter showed fear. This was something new, for no matter what the emergency, Aimee had never in her life showed fear before; throughout the preliminary hearing her courage and confidence in ultimate vindication had been commented upon again and again. Aimee was by nature dauntless; but now she seemed harried by inner qualms. That their plight was serious Minnie was well aware, for if the charges against them were proved before a jury, the consequence would be not only the probable downfall of Angelus Temple and their own financial ruin, but quite likely a term in prison. Nevertheless, Minnie wanted no quasi-clearance, no equivocal finish; she wanted the charges to be disproved in court, beyond question.

With rumors thickening, a report circulated through the inner circle at Angelus Temple that tended to explain the influence which Ralph Jordan had gained over Sister. This report said that Jordan had gone to William Randolph Hearst, the publisher, and had argued that continuation of the "Aimee case" would be bad for the city and on the grounds of the public good should be halted. Hearst, it was said, had been inclined to agree. His influence in Los Angeles was potent, and a few days after the reported talk with Jordan, Hearst's *Examiner* did quote Keyes as saying he intended to shelve the case. The disclaimer from Keyes had followed, after which it was understood that extreme pressure had been put on the district attorney to yield.

Still the issue remained in doubt, so far as the public was concerned; and it was still indeterminate on January 10 when Keyes entered court. There he stated that the evidence had become so vitiated by contradictions and rebuttals on the part of witnesses that the case could no longer be prosecuted "with honor or with any reasonable hope of success." Thereupon he requested that the charges be quashed, though he was not sparing of Mrs. McPherson personally:

"The fact that this defendant fabricated a kidnaping story, or that she spent a time at Carmel, are not, in themselves, offenses of which this court can entertain jurisdiction. Reputable witnesses have testified sufficiently concerning both the Carmel incident and the return of Mrs. McPherson from her so-called kidnaping adventure to enable her to be judged in the only court of her jurisdiction—the court of public opinion."

The judge granted the request and the defendants were discharged.

Aimee received the news at the temple. As the word came over the telephone, she gave a long gasp of relief and fainted. Quickly revived, she faced reporters lying on a couch, and apologizing for making a scene, said, "I couldn't help it; I'm sorry." Then, between sobs of joy:

"It has been so hard, all these months, for two defenseless women to fight against this tower of lies. But all through the trouble the Lord prepared a table before me in the presence of mine enemies. His work will now go on bigger than ever."

Mother Kennedy was asked for a statement. With tears streaming from her eyes and her sturdy frame shaken by convulsive sobbing, she replied, "Sister has said it all."

Later, alone with her mother, Aimee was jubilant. Waving a newspaper "extra" announcing the dismissal, she cried triumphantly:

"Mother, I'm sitting on top of the world!"

Minnie didn't think so. To her mind, nothing had been cleared

Certain of "vindication," Aimee helps Santa Claus with the presents around the Temple Christmas tree in December, 1926.

up, and she told her daughter that far from getting a vindication, she had been "left in a dirty hole." Suspicion would never die down now, she muttered, and for herself, she was bitterly disappointed.

Aimee tossed her head and marched out of the room.

Minnie had become inured to her child's secretiveness by now. What had been going on during the last few days she realized she did not know and might never know. But she trembled, both for her daughter and for herself and for Angelus Temple. What, for instance, had prompted Sister, the very day before the sorry windup of their legal trouble, to announce, from the temple platform and over the temple radio, that she was about to embark on a "vindication tour" of the United States—and couple that announcement with the prediction that the charges against her would be dropped?

What had Aimee known then that she had not seen fit to share with her mother? What folly was she bent on committing now?

Prayers and Pleading Versus
Watermelons and Lemonade

Her mother remonstrated with her, and attempted to forbid her to go, but Aimee had the bit in her teeth. In vain Minnie pointed to their narrow escape and urged the necessity of regaining the esteem of Los Angeles by renewing their earnest, sincere work at the temple. Get off the front pages, Minnie preached; the members of the church were indignant at the way the headlines screamed *Aimee* this and *Aimee* that; they had always addressed her with honor and respect as *Sister* or *Mrs. McPherson*. There was much dissatisfaction among the membership, Minnie went on, and there was all the cost of the legal battle to make up—more than a hundred thousand dollars. There was mighty little money in the till, she warned; even "The House That God Built" had been sold to satisfy the lawyers.

Aimee ignored the remonstrances, and all but ignored her mother. Now that the danger seemed past, every line in her mother's face became a reproach; Aimee felt she had to get away. So off she started, to meet people elsewhere, who had been reading "lies" about her, she said, and show them that she was not the monster of iniquity the newspapers had painted. In charge of the tour as managers and personal escort were Ralph Jordan and James Kendrick, and Minnie predicted that no good would come of that.

With Sister gone, Mother turned her attention to salvaging what was left of Angelus Temple, spiritual and temporal. Even without Sister, the church, she was determined, should not falter.

The Los Angeles press, after reaping the benefit of months of circulation-building sensations provided by Mrs. McPherson, treated her Eastern tour slightingly and haphazardly. They printed little about her reception in other cities, and most of that was unfavorable. The reports published elsewhere sometimes told a different story: in some cities Sister McPherson was an unqualified success, though in others she encountered hostility and criticism. When Mother Kennedy, in a radio broadcast, finally accused the Los Angeles newspapers of "printing a lot of funny stuff" about the tour, they mended their ways somewhat.

Among the temple membership there was uneasiness over the worldly publicity that Sister was getting. Mother began to drop hints that Aimee might not return to her pulpit for a long while.

The temple's board of elders—reputable, substantial men and women who were privileged to advise on spiritual matters but had no authority otherwise—grew distressed as stories of Sister's indiscretions came in. She allowed herself to be quoted on subjects she should never comment upon publicly—divorce, for example, and "green bathing suits." It was unedifying, it was derogatory to her dignity and the dignity of the church whose pastor she was, some of the elders felt. Responding to this uneasiness, Minnie sent a peremptory telegram saying:

"Come home. The temple needs you."

No reply was forthcoming directly, although in Chicago, Sister told the reporters that her board's affection had prompted the message; they were concerned for her health.

"They are afraid I may take on too much work," she explained brightly. "But my health is excellent."

When she said this she had just returned from a horseback gallop along the lake front, and she certainly looked the image of blooming health.

But the uneasiness at home increased, and it was decided to send two high-ranking temple officials east to join Sister's party and try to correct the situation. Gladwyn Nichols, who in addition to being the head of the temple's music department was an assistant pastor, was chosen for this mission, and Miss Churchilla Bartling, a nurse

Aimee with her entourage arriving in Washington on her "Vindication Tour," February 15, 1927. From left: Mrs. Bertha Daughter, Churchilla Bartling, Aimee, Emma Schaffer, Mae Waldron.

and a member of the temple advisory board. They caught up with Sister at Lancaster, Pennsylvania, and went on with her to Baltimore, Washington, and New York.

They were shocked by the change they saw in Aimee. She seemed to be completely under the dominance of her newspaper friends and cut off from any religious associations. Clergymen who called at Sister's hotel to pay their respects were turned away roughly by Sister's entourage. Some of these well-wishers were friends of Mrs. McPherson since her early barnstorming days, and they felt the rebuff keenly. Sister seemed to them to be given up wholly to worldly ambitions.

Gladwyn Nichols remonstrated, but Sister brushed his protests aside. She admitted that Jordan and Kendrick were worldly, without a spark of religious sincerity in them; she admitted that they smoked and drank whiskey and played cards in her anteroom and did other things foreign to a Christian atmosphere; but she added that they had helped her at a time "when you people at the temple couldn't." Being newspapermen, they knew how to handle the press, she insisted, although to Nichols it seemed that the press was using them. He warned that disaffection was growing at the temple, and there might be a walkout of some members. Her reply was flippant:

"Let them walk out of the temple. I'll fill it up again."

She wanted no advice from Mother or anybody else, she made clear; she was perfectly confident of her ability to "go it alone," with the help of her newspaper friends.

The climax of the tour—and the climax of the revulsion of Mother Kennedy at home—came in New York, where Aimee scored a decided success with her preaching, but received even more publicity for her visit to the notorious speakeasy of Texas Guinan, "queen of the night clubs." In the company of reporters, Aimee boldly penetrated this haunt of wickedness, unafraid to meet his Satanic majesty in his own domain (she explained). She was tastefully gowned, demure, and self-contained as she entered the club, which was crowded with revelers. At her hostess's invitation—elicited by a whispered suggestion from a reporter—Sister made a short speech, standing in the center of the dance floor, gently reminding the crowd at the tables that "behind all these beautiful clothes, behind these good times, in the midst of your lovely buildings and shops and pleasures, there is another life. There is something on the other side. 'What shall it profit a man if he gain the whole world and lose his own soul?' With all your getting and playing and good times, do not forget you have a Lord. Take Him into your hearts."

Texas called on the crowd to "give this courageous woman a big hand," and Aimee was cheered for five minutes. She extended an invitation to all, chorus girls included, to come hear her at the Glad Tidings Tabernacle on West 34th Street, and left amid more cheers.

This scene left a bitter taste in Gladwyn Nichols's mouth, and upon being sent ahead to Syracuse as advance man, he left the caravan and returned to Los Angeles, to make a sorrowful report. And again Mother Kennedy scattered hints that Sister might not return to her pulpit at all.

"We have heard that she is finding work enough to do to keep her busy indefinitely," Minnie said with a look full of innuendo.

And weeks did slip by while Aimee swung down to Florida and then moved leisurely westward, speaking as she went. From Dallas at length came a letter reporting tremendous revival success there and saying that she would arrive home on April 1. Immediately

In New York on her "Vindication Tour," Sister Aimee was photographed in her Hotel McAlpin suite in a favorite pose—looking at herself (and some prizefighters) on the front page.

preparations for a gala reception were got under way, and the temple buzzed with happy expectancy.

All this went for nothing when a day ahead of time, Aimee slipped into the city unannounced.

That evening, at the Friday night prayer meeting in the Five Hundred Room (the upstairs room at the temple reputedly set aside for what theologians call *glossolalia*, or "shouting sessions"), Minnie broke the news that Sister had returned. Even while she was making the announcement, a limousine purred up to the entrance and Sister herself came running up the stairs to a storm of hand-clapping, drum-banging, and hallelujahs. Breathlessly she embraced everyone with her smile, then gave a brief account of her travels, telling about going down into the Grand Canyon in Arizona, and wound up with:

"Then I just got homesick to see you all and came right on home!"

After which the evangelist retired with her children and her mother to the family residence, or parsonage, next door.

On Saturday evening Sister received the delayed welcome-home of her followers, and not even the outburst of joy at her "resurrection from the dead" ten months previously had been more dramatic or warmhearted. Angelus Temple had been transformed into a floral bower. Above the heads of the congregation fluttered streamers of red ribbon, and the platform was smothered in baskets of flowers presented by the twenty-eight branches of the church, while the altar rail and walls were draped with floral hearts and ribbons.

The newspapers published columns of description of this home-coming, for the city was curious to see how Aimee would look and act after her Eastern foray. The *Los Angeles Times*, a newspaper not conspicuous for overpraising the manifestations at Echo Park, assigned a woman feature writer, who found the temple already filled at 6 P.M., two hours before the service was to commence. Right on cue, Sister appeared, looking "the very epitome of success." A spotlight was turned on her as she "sailed down the runway with arms full of roses, her hair, with that famous glint of gold-red, perfectly marcelled."

The reporter thought she discerned one of the keys to Aimee's perennial appeal, and wrote:

"She observes and showers appreciation for every tiny service rendered. She knows the drama, the human reaction, the glow of reward that a few well-chosen words with personal application can achieve.

"Every tiny item on the program of her service is palpitating with drama. Dramatically, picturesquely, she became entangled in the festooning ribbons as she proceeded down the runway, as the spotlight followed her, and other lights illuminated the stained-glass windows depicting the life of Christ. She waved like a happy, joyous girl as the crowd applauded and cheered and seemed about to dance for sheer joy. And right away, Mother Kennedy, speaking carefully into the microphone, thanked God for Sister's safe return. Tumultuous amens! Fervid praise-the-Lords!"

The program was long and incessant.

"First some very small boys piped their little pieces. Sister smiled at each of them and patted their heads. Then came the tiny girls, much more self-possessed, singing, 'Praise the Lord, Sister is home.' Sister's smile of ecstasy seemed personal, and each and every parent's bosom swelled with pride.

" 'First attendants' at the Temple were asked to rise. Obediently scores rose. They were given an inclusive, yet somehow individual, welcome in that smile which passed swiftly from face to face. All ministers of the Gospel were then asked to rise. Perhaps one hundred responded, and received a blessing. Then she flattered and joshed the choir—the best ever—and told them how she wanted to take them and the band to a great revival meeting scheduled for the Coliseum in Chicago in June. Who wanted to go? It seemed that hundreds answered that call.

"Dozens of organizations in the church wanted to sing for her. Cleverly she kept this rather overwhelming musical program within bounds, yet distributing gay compliments the while. And in the midst of it all, she would be answering a little telephone, making notes, yet right on hand to start the applause always.

"About fifty girls and a few men had a surprise whistling chorus for Sister, and she promptly thanked the Lord for 'these sweet bird notes which added glory to His greatness.'

"At exactly the right psychological point Mrs. McPherson lowered her voice and told us we must sing 'I Ain't Goin' to Grieve No More, Precious Lord.' She led this number herself, with strong chest notes, singing many times in solo with ecstatic gravity, and concluded on a high tremolo top note.

"There followed another prayer in which she thanked the Lord that this great church was not founded upon a personality—and complimented the Deity upon the fact that the Temple had thriven mightily while she was away harvesting souls for the Lord."

At ten o'clock, just as the reporter was leaving to catch the morning edition, Sister was telling her followers about her trip—"every hall filled in every city, sometimes to the extent of twelve thousand souls, and all the country ripe for 'a good, old-fashioned Holy Ghost revival.' From coast to coast they are 'waiting for Angelus Temple,' which she declared stood for a Gospel that would solve all human problems. The entire country, she said, knew of Angelus Temple and yearned for it—for 'its marvelous unity, its oneness, its loyalty, its love.' Not a word about recent distressful experiences; nothing but one long, inclusive, all-pervading hallelujah. She didn't look tired. She merely radiated triumph, triumph, triumph."

Four days after this convincing demonstration of "oneness," Mrs. McPherson moved out of the parsonage and into a rented furnished house at the beach—at Ocean Park, almost overlooking the spot where she had disappeared in the sea. With her she took her children, three secretaries, and a couple of Filipino servants, and the city buzzed with the rumor that the Titian-haired evangelist was about to shake the dust of Angelus Temple from her feet forever.

II

Denials came, but in a noticeably cool manner.

"Absurd!" said Minnie Kennedy at the temple, speaking between compressed lips. "Mrs. McPherson has a lot of writing and planning to do; she needs rest and quiet. Sister is still the head of the temple and always will be, but, as in all great works, there are those who misconstrue things."

This merely stoked the fires of speculation, and reporters posted out to Ocean Park to question Aimee herself. They found her looking very fit in tennis costume, just back from an early round of golf. Her tennis rackets stood beside a phonograph that was grinding out the popular fox-trot, "Blue Skies."

"Mother and I are on the best of terms," said Sister calmly, "always have been and always will be—as far as I can foresee."

It was not surprising that there was some talk, she went on; there always had been.

"After all, I have twelve thousand followers, and there undoubtedly are some in our organization, as in others, who misinterpret things. I am merely resting here as the guest of Mr. and Mrs. Emmil, members of my congregation, who have taken this house."

Mrs. H. Emmil was the married name of Mae Waldron, the temple stenographer who had brought first word of an impending scandal linking Sister and Kenneth Ormiston in Europe. Now Miss Waldron was one of the secretaries with Mrs. McPherson.

Looking as if she could say more if she chose, Mother Kennedy explained that her daughter intended to leave Los Angeles in June for an evangelistic tour of the East and Canada. Mother seemed resigned.

"While we should love to have Sister here," she said, "she has made a great sacrifice for her people. It has been a wonder to me that she has been able to remain four years at the temple. While we should hate to lose her, we must bear our loss."

Would Sister continue to preach at the temple until her departure? Minnie sighed.

"You will have to get the answer to that from Sister," she said enigmatically, and closed the door on her questioners.

The sequence of events that had precipitated this apparent estrangement of mother and daughter was learned only gradually by the press. When pieced together, it ran about like this:

Directly upon her return from the "vindication tour," Aimee informed her mother that henceforth she intended to be the head of Angelus Temple in every respect, and demanded that Minnie turn over all funds and records and resign as business manager. And she seemed again to be in desperate need of money. Mother prided herself on her business efficiency, and had a poor opinion of Aimee's ability to manage the enterprise alone. When Minnie objected to her daughter's peremptory demands, Aimee accused her of always standing in her way, of treating her like a child, and reproached her for many omissions and slights that seemed to have assumed disproportionate significance in her mind. The money contributed to the temple was given to *her*, Aimee insisted, and she was entitled to have it.

One concrete demand was that Minnie immediately draw out the fourteen thousand dollars in their joint personal "sinking fund," their savings over the years. Minnie prayed over this and, concluding that Aimee was entitled to have her share if she wished it, drew out the money and handed over her daughter's seven-thousand-dollar half. The next day Aimee, in great agitation, Minnie thought, said she must have more, and when her mother asked what had happened to the seven thousand dollars she had received the day before, replied nonchalantly, "Oh, that's all gone." This puzzled and alarmed Minnie, but after consulting the department heads and securing their consent, she turned over the temple funds entirely.

Meanwhile, the women quarreled over Aimee's evangelizing tour plans. Minnie reminded Aimee that she had "much ground to make up" right in Los Angeles, and said her place was in the temple, to heal the wounds and get things on an even keel again. Aimee retorted that she was sick of bickering, and would rather resign. During one dispute on this score she sat down and wrote out her resignation as pastor of Angelus Temple. Minnie brushed this aside; she knew her daughter's inveterate propensity to "act out" her impulses. Ralph Jordan, Minnie believed, was at the bottom of this new foolishness, and she said so; wasn't Aimee planning to take him along as manager of this new trip? The thing was a scandal, Minnie went on; that worldly, grasping man would get everybody into trouble. Finally, to escape her mother's reproaches, Aimee had fled to the rented house at the beach.

Her course was not clear to herself. The one thing that she did see plainly was her need to get out from under her mother's dictation. To Minnie Kennedy, Aimee had never ceased to be her "child," who direly needed correction at times as well as affection. Aimee, on her side, ever since the kidnaping episode, had found her mother insufferable; Minnie's every look and word was an accusation. For her self-respect, she felt that she had to throw off her mother's discipline. At heart Aimee realized that without her mother's assistance there would never have been an Angelus Temple, but she pushed that thought out of mind. She wished her mother well, but she could no longer stand her presence. She had indeed changed as a result of her Eastern junket. That tour, under worldly direction, had opened to her a world that she had not penetrated before—a world wider, more varied, and more interesting than either her followers' or her mother's cramped mind could take in. She had discovered that she could move worldly audiences, as well as those religiously inclined, and the demonstration that this power could be immensely profitable as well as a source of self-fulfillment was exhilarating. But first she must be freed from her mother's tutelage, and confusedly she was fighting to gain that release.

As she would do again and again in other crises, she turned to her board of spiritual advisers for support. These advisers were not consulted on financial matters and had no control over the church property or revenues; appointed by Sister, they could be, and sometimes were, arbitrarily dismissed upon suspicion of disloyalty or opposition to her wishes. They were not strong-willed individuals, and they were eager to bask in the reflection of Sister's approval. Now Aimee called the board into session, and Minnie, aware that a showdown was impending, kept a record of what was said and done at the meeting.

The session was opened with prayer, in the midst of which Sister entered. In her hand she clutched a paper that Minnie recognized as the previously written resignation. In her most imperious manner, Aimee began, saying:

"I find that someone has sown tares, and there is a ripple of criticism. The church has been sown with poison."

Then she reviewed the events of 1926 and her recent tour. Stating her intention to leave shortly on another tour, she delivered an ultimatum: either they, the board, representing the members of the temple, must approve her conduct, past, present, and future, or she would retire as Angelus Temple's pastor. She demanded that a written vote be taken, and ballots were passed around. These had been prepared previously, and bore three typed questions:

"1—Did I do right in obtaining dismissal of my case?

"2—Did I do right in making this tour and taking Ralph Jordan as manager?

"3—Will it be right to go on tour again and take him along?"

The marked ballots were handed to Sister, who counted them and announced the result: all except two, she said, gave her a clear vote of confidence. One of the two dissenters had written, "I don't know," and the other, "Yes, if others go along."

Gladwyn Nichols then expressed his "disillusionment" with the whole trend of affairs. Whereupon Sister curtly told him, "You take a vacation."

Anybody else who objected to her actions could also "take a vacation," she added, looking directly at her mother.

Minnie sprang up angrily.

"Stop right where you are!" she cried. "We have never discussed these things before this board. This board is a spiritual board, and this meeting and the spirit of it are a disgrace! Furthermore, this board did not elect me to office and it has nothing to say about my vacation! But I am free to say that I am ready to take it!"

Without replying, Aimee stepped to the door, opened it, and beckoned. Ralph Jordan entered.

"Here he is," said Sister. "I want you all to meet him."

Shouted Mother Kennedy, "If Ralph Jordan goes in, I go out!" and she stalked out of the room.

Sister went back to her beach house with her board's complete endorsement.

But the next evening Gladwyn Nichols publicly severed his connection with Angelus Temple and led the choir, the band, and about three hundred members in a secession of the first magnitude. Setting up his own Church of Philadelphia, convening in a tent, he issued a series of announcements baring the basic cause of the walkout. This was Sister McPherson's surrender to worldliness, as exemplified in "fancy gowns and personal adornment," and culminating in the bobbing of her hair.

Throughout all Los Angeles, and indeed throughout the nation as a result of the 1926 furor, Aimee Semple McPherson's luxuriant hair had been her trademark. It was long, auburn-brown in tint, and she wore it piled high on her head. That long hair had figured in court testimony as an anomaly in the age of bobbed hair; it had stood out as a symbol of her womanly conservatism.

She had returned from New York with an unmistakable "shingle." From their position rather behind the preacher's lectern, the temple choir could observe the back of Sister's head, and they had been both saddened and indignant at the transformation. Yes, Sister had succumbed to worldliness, they grieved. Her modish clothing, too, they considered unbecoming a preacher of the Gospel. Stated Nichols:

"The God of the Gospels is being replaced at Angelus Temple by the god of materialism. When Mrs. McPherson bobbed her hair, she hurt her followers terribly. Bobbing of the hair is not according to the Scriptures."

Nor, he intimated, were elegant evening gowns and expensive motorcars.

Aimee met the attack ingenuously.

"Mr. Nichols is a dear, sweet man," she cooed, "and I can say nothing about him except that he was very loyal and very fine to all of us. Of course, you know, as everyone does, that musicians are very temperamental. Why should I get into controversy with a bandmaster? Mr. Nichols couldn't have meant me, with his talk of short skirts and bobbed hair. You don't really think my skirt is too short, do you?" She appealed to the reporters.

As for her hair, after the worry and strain of her "troubles" it had started to fall out, and she had been warned that unless she had it cut, she would lose it all. So it had been just "trigly trimmed," and "of course I'll let it grow back in again." And far from having expensive automobiles, she had no car of her own at present, and was using "a nine-hunded-dollar car that belongs to a friend." What had happened to the expensive Kissel she had been driving she did not explain.

"I have nothing but the kindest of feelings for Mr. Nichols and those who followed him," she concluded. "I will do everything in the world for them." But she would "rather not make a statement as to whether Mr. Nichols would be welcome if he wanted to return."

It developed that the schism had come into the open on the preceding Friday evening, when the choir failed to show up for regular practice. Minnie hastily swung into action to prevent any spreading of the disaffection, although she intimated that she rather sided with Nichols on the prime question. She told the press:

"Mr. Nichols has never been disloyal to the church. It has been said that the music department of a church is its war department. Mr. Nichols brought the band and choir into existence, and I am certain that everything will be settled."

But nothing was settled, and she was forced to telephone for help to her daughter at the beach. The welfare of the temple taking precedence over personal feelings, Aimee hurried into town and assumed charge of the church's defenses.

At the Saturday services music was provided by volunteers. By Sunday an auxiliary choir that had been partially disbanded—the Foursquare Choir—had been reactivated, and over the radio Sister announced intrepidly that plans were under way to form a new choir, a new band, and a symphony orchestra. Mother Kennedy retreated from her initial sympathy for Nichols, and while deploring the breach, which according to her "never should have occurred," announced that in the crisis she stood with Sister "foursquare." Addressing four hundred Bible students, Aimee asked them whether they wanted her to resign, and back came the cry: "Never! Never! We are with you foursquare!"

Monday and Tuesday Aimee spent interviewing the heads of the departments and the pastors of the branch churches. She also spoke with many of the seceders by telephone, assuring them that they could always count on her affection. And gradually, thanks to the concerted efforts of mother and daughter, the revolt was stemmed and the tide turned; so that within a week Mrs. McPherson was able to dismiss the secession as the act of "a few disgruntled, self-seeking members," while Gladwyn Nichols countered with fuliginous statements that somehow sounded slightly windblown, such as:

"I wouldn't go back if they gave me a deed to the temple!"

On May 18, less than four weeks after the walkout, temple members by the hundreds foregathered on the beach at Ocean Park for a double victory celebration. It was the first anniversary of Sister McPherson's descent into the sea off that spot, preparatory to resurfacing in the desert in Mexico. And the celebration marked the return to the fold of most of the Angelus Temple choir and the restoration of hymnal harmony at Echo Park.

The gladsome festivities took the form of a marshmallow roast and taffy pull.

Sister herself was not on hand. Minnie or no Minnie, objections or no objections, she had taken her departure for the Midwest, far from the temple's turmoil. And from that distant vantage point, she proceeded very effectively to roil the waters more.

III

There was no doubt that tares had been sown, and they had been sprouting vigorously for months past.

Reports from "the front" indicated that Sister was having her usual success in Chicago, the first point of attack in her fresh assault on the strongholds of Satan. She was quoted liberally as denouncing a particularly rowdy night club known as The Stables, calling it "the trapdoor to hell." The owner of the club claimed defamation and a lawsuit resulted, remunerative to the lawyers conducting it but to nobody else. The publicity was tremendous, and Mother Kennedy anguished over her daughter's having even been seen in such a place.

The Chicago revival, according to meager press reports reaching Los Angeles, was in every way, except perhaps the spiritual, a rousing success—police reserves were required to restrain the crowds battling to see Sister. Then Aimee moved along to Alton, Illinois, to hold forth in a circus tent during the month of July.

Traveling with Sister on this safari of righteousness were faithful Emma Schaffer; pretty Mae Waldron; Thompson B. Eade, the scenic artist who prepared the settings for Sister's illustrated sermons; and a temple quartet. The Alton revival was just gathering momentum when it was abruptly terminated by news of a fresh uproar at Angelus Temple. This time the cause was admittedly money, and the target of the revolt was Mother Kennedy.

As with most happenings in that cockpit of turbulence at Echo Park, the facts of the commotion were heavily obscured by a smudge cloud of words.

The first hint of trouble had come on the evening of Sunday, July 17, when a group headed by the Reverend C. E. Jaynes, pastor of the Riverside Foursquare Gospel branch church, forcibly took possession of the collection receipts, acting, they said, on the authority of Sister. Minnie Kennedy vigorously protested, but the Tuesday night collection was similarly seized, and a report reached the newspapers about "burglaries" at the temple and a new flareup of dissension. Mrs. McPherson was said to be hastening home from Illinois.

In dispatches from Alton, she was quoted as saying that "business reasons" were the only cause of her suspending the meetings—the first instance in eighteen years of her breaking off a revival campaign when it was only one-third completed, she added regretfully. But "matters at Angelus Temple" demanded her immediate return.

At the temple, Minnie was evasive.

"Sister is a darling and I love her and we all want her to return home," she said. "Everybody feels that this is her place. For the past two Sundays I have taken a vote among the congregation to learn their viewpoint as to her absence, and they are almost 100 percent for her to return and remain in the pulpit here."

Minnie also hinted at her own imminent resignation from the Temple's business management, saying:

"It has been a great strain on me and I feel that I should retire, and will do so and turn the reins over to Sister when she gets back. I haven't had a real rest since Sister returned from the Holy Land two years ago, and I think a trip would do me good, too."

But the next day Minnie confessed that a new insurrection was the cause of Aimee's hurrying home.

"I am not worried about the situation in the least," she assured the press, "but I, as well as members of the church board, felt it was a matter for Mrs. McPherson to take charge of."

The self-designated "committee" that had taken charge of the collections had no right to do so, Mother continued. Mr. Jaynes?

Yes, she had heard of that gentleman, but was "not well acquainted with him."

"This group still has charge of the money," she explained, "and no one is worried about it. I feel that this group, knowing I was about to resign from the business management of the temple, seized this opportunity to try to assume command, but they never will succeed."

She exhibited telegrams exchanged with her daughter. One from Minnie read:

"REJOICING IN YOUR RETURN. THE ENTIRE CHURCH IS SOLID. AM PERSONALLY UNDISTURBED IN SPIRIT AND MIND."

Aimee's answer:

"STAND FIRM. DON'T WAVER. REACH LOS ANGELES 9:30 TOMORROW MORNING. LOVE."

Preparations were begun by Minnie for the customary gala reception of the evangelist at the railroad station. But then came a telegram from Sister—addressed not to Mother but to Jaynes—ordering:

"NO RECEPTION AT DEPOT BUT MASS MEETING WILL BE HELD ANGELUS TEMPLE SATURDAY EVENING. ALL BRANCHES TO BE REPRESENTED."

At the same time, the Reverend Mr. Jaynes stated formally that he had been designated by Sister to take charge of the temple until her return "to protect her interest." He also, more sensationally, released to the press a letter written to him by Mrs. McPherson, which was an amazing confession of strife rending the temple and of her own unwillingness to continue under the "present regime"—meaning her mother.

When she left Los Angeles the last time, she wrote, she had thought she was leaving Angelus Temple forever:

"It having been impossible to remain longer as pastor of my people under the present regime, I chose, rather than to strive, to step quietly out, penniless, in the field, leaving behind me that which tangibly represents eighteen years of most exacting labor."

Unless there should occur some "action by the church," she concluded, it would be impossible for her to return, for she would rather work in the field than fight with her mother, and she was heart-

Mother Kennedy and Aimee on latter's arrival in Los Angeles after summons home from Illinois revival to quell an insurrection at Angelus Temple. Requested by reporters to kiss her mother, Aimee said it was "not necessary."

broken. She did suggest one way out of the dilemma, and that would be to "build an entirely new church to absorb the old." If this should be undertaken, she pledged, she would stand "shoulder to shoulder."

The letter contained authorization for Jaynes to occupy the temple pulpit, and he was releasing it to the public, he said, because when he tried to exercise his right, Minnie had refused to let him on the platform to address the congregation.

Minnie retorted that she had barred him from the pulpit because she didn't want to disrupt the religious service. As for that letter, she, too, was heartbroken if Aimee really had written it, but this she would not believe unless her daughter herself told her so.

"I told Sister before she left for Chicago that I would hold on here until her return," Mother said. "She knows I am to retire from the business end of the church. And I will retire just the minute she arrives. If she wants me to quit, I'll do it, but it will break her poor mother's heart. After all these years of work and strife to make this church a success!"

That Friday Mother got her hands on the collection money first and refused to surrender it to the self-styled committee. And the situation became further confused when Mrs. McPherson, interviewed in Utah on her way home, said emphatically:

"I have no intention of deserting my congregation in Los Angeles. I am not returning for the purpose of investigating any asserted financial shortages. I am merely going home."

Saturday's sensations started on Aimee's arrival at 9:10 A.M. Minnie had boarded the train at a way station up the line and had been closeted with her daughter. The Reverend Mr. Jaynes had done the same, and he, too, had a consultation with Sister in her stateroom. At the station only a small group, including members of Jaynes's committee, was on hand; there were more reporters than temple adherents. Aimee and her mother posed for the cameramen, but when one photographer suggested that they kiss, Sister replied coolly that it was "not necessary." The tension between the two women was evident, but Aimee warded off questions about a supposed breach skillfully.

"She is my mother and I love her," was the evangelist's comment. "I have the greatest respect and admiration for her and for all her invaluable services to me during the last eighteen long years. Even if these things were all true, I could not make a statement about them. There is no trouble between us. My mother signified her intention of retiring long ago. She deserves a good rest, and she shall have one."

But the reporters were intrigued by the fact that after spending most of the day in conference with her mother at the parsonage, that evening the evangelist moved into a rented house at 333 South Manhattan Place, taking along her retinue of secretaries, servants, and sympathizers. Minnie Kennedy was left in the parsonage alone.

And there the reporters found her, tearfully packing to leave also. And at last it came out: Aimee had delivered an ultimatum. Either her mother accept one of three alternatives that she offered, or Aimee would go back to Alton and wash her hands of temple affairs for good; she had already telegraphed orders not to start dismantling her tent there. She made clear that she intended to run the temple without assistance or opposition. She would enter into no explanation of why she wanted her mother out of the organization but merely repeated that she wished to be in full charge, to operate every branch and department as she saw fit, and to have the finances under her sole control.

The three alternatives she offered Minnie were:

1—To take over Angelus Temple entirely, and Aimee would found a separate church with which Mother would have no connection;

2—To remain at the temple and cooperate with Aimee in matters of policy and spiritual work;

3—To retire from temple work and receive an income for life.

Minnie's tears flowed as she stood beside an open suitcase on the dining room table and told this story. She was torn between two impulses and had actually started to leave and go to a friend's home, but had changed her mind and would try to have one more talk with her daughter. Probably it would be better to do what Aimee wanted, Minnie sobbed, "but I love her, and I don't know what to do."

The mass meeting called by Sister for that evening brought a capacity throng, and she was loyally greeted. (It seemed to the press, however, that Brother Smith Wigglesworth, athletic English evangelist who had been substituting for Sister, got a bigger ovation when he manipulated several ailing members heroically in a healing demonstration.) Sister spoke briefly, but made no mention of the current difficulties; instead, she talked enthusiastically about her plan to reorganize the church and extend branches all over the nation, calling them "lighthouses."

Mother Kennedy did not appear, and the next day she journeyed to Taft, California, to speak in the branch church there, confiding to a friend that her daughter had ordered her to go. This allegation Aimee disposed of effectively by the undeniable observation:

"Those who know my mother know that she cannot be ordered anywhere."

The only difference between them, the evangelist said, concerned business matters and had nothing to do with their relationship as mother and daughter. But that relationship seemed dangerously menaced again when, at the Sunday services, Sister announced from the pulpit that the weekly pay checks for the temple staff were being held up because Mother had left without countersigning them. She was sure it was an oversight, and that Mother would return and straighten out the tangle, but meanwhile a collection would have to be taken to enable the staff to get their pay. The collection was taken, and Sister said it would do nicely, thank you.

When word of this performance reached Minnie on Monday, she blew up. Although she had just previously declared staunchly, "I won't say anything against my beautiful daughter; I love, I am loyal to her," this latest "outrage" aroused her fighting spirit, and she denounced it as "the most insulting and unjust insinuation of the many that have been made by Mrs. McPherson.

"My daughter, before the world, told her congregation that I had not signed pay checks for temple employees and that they could not get their money. The insinuation cast was that it was spite work on my part. The unjustness of such a statement is shown by the fact that the account on which the checks were drawn is in both our names. Her name on the check is as good as mine."

Minnie's wrath reached the boiling point shortly thereafter, when, in a flurry of statements from the temple, she was presented with four more "insulting" propositions by the so-called committee, claiming to speak for their pastor.

It began when Mother called Aimee on the telephone, only to have her daughter (according to Minnie) hang up.

Nothing of the sort, said Aimee:

"Mother used language that I couldn't bear others to hear if they were listening in on our party line. I tried to tell her that it would be ruination for us if her language to her daughter were heard by others. I hung up, waited five minutes until she cooled off, and then called again."

Retorted Mrs. Kennedy:

"That statement is untrue. I did not use any but the best language at my command, and my daughter did not call again."

Instead, Aimee secluded herself in her rented home, and the church committee handed out a statement filled with verbal dynamite. This manifesto read:

"The committee which called Mrs. McPherson home is composed of the heads of all departments at Angelus Temple and pastors of more than forty branch churches, in other words, the entire church.

"We are shocked and grieved that Mrs. Kennedy should attack her evangelist daughter, as she has been quoted as doing. Mrs. Kennedy has no quarrel with Mrs. McPherson. We are the ones, the church, who want a change of business management at the temple.

"Mrs. McPherson has made no move, we are sure, which would embarrass her mother in any way. But the committee does think that for the good of the work Mrs. Kennedy should let someone else take her place.

"The board of the church and the committee desire that Mrs. Kennedy be cared for in splendid style and would be delighted to assist her in working out any one of the several courses open to her:

"1—Mrs. Kennedy might remain with honor and respect as the evangelist's mother.

"2—Mrs. Kennedy might tour the world or take a trip to the Holy Land at the expense of the church, who would, we believe, contribute to the fund for a vacation so well deserved.

"3—Mrs. Kennedy might permanently entertain work of her own in other fields as she has suggested.

"4—Mrs. Kennedy might return to her wealthy husband, Mr. W. Whittebeck, who is a well-to-do engineer on a big Hudson River liner. He lives in New York where Mrs. Kennedy resided until eight years ago."

This lit the fuse for a detonation. Aimee remained incommunicado, but Minnie erupted.

"When my daughter gets ready to come to me and talk these things over, some thought will be given to them," she said with finality. "But this so-called committee, who never has had nor ever will have a legal position of authority in this temple, is not going to dictate my course."

The options offered Minnie rejected as "ultimatums of the most unjust nature." And she denied categorically that she had ever said that the trouble with her daughter started in her disbelief of the kidnaping story.

"My only statement made in answer to an inquiry as to whether I was satisfied with the ending of the kidnaping case was that I always felt that Kenneth Ormiston could have cleared Mrs. McPherson by revealing who was with him at Carmel," was her carefully worded, defensive explanation. "I have never intimated that I didn't believe her story. Every effort has been made by newspaper reporters and others to revive the kidnaping case and get me to commit myself. But this I have refused to do. This trouble has nothing to do with the disappearance of Mrs. McPherson, and I don't propose to have it brought into our present difficulties.

"The situation has become nearly intolerable when it has reached the point where I can talk with my daughter only through an attorney," she added, and burst into tears.

"She ordered me to get an attorney and said she would do the same, and hereafter all our conferences would be through attorneys alone. That certainly is unchristianlike! Mrs. McPherson has continued to tell the press that everything has been satisfactorily settled at conferences, when she has not given me one conference since her return from Alton!"

As for that startling suggestion that she return to her "husband" in New York, to that steamboat engineer, Minnie refused all comments—or nearly all.

"I will not make any statements regarding *that* until the proper time, which is not now," she said firmly. "I do not know by whom, or why, that statement was issued, but it will be heard from later on. Just let them go on and have all the rope they want," she muttered. "They'll soon enough hang themselves—and *then* they will hear from me!"

The "Mr. Whittebeck" mystery was compounded when a man of that name was located in New York, but he denied that he had ever set eyes on Minnie Kennedy.

"I never saw the woman and know nothing more about her than what I have read in the papers," he said. "I am married to Mrs. Mabel Archer Whittebeck, we have a home in Catskill, New York, and I am a grandfather. I can't understand how such reports can start."

This Whittebeck had been engineer on the Hudson River Dayliner *Clermont* for sixteen years.

Reporters managed to question Roberta Semple about the matter and quoted her as saying:

"Grandmother married William Whittebeck, an engineer on a Hudson River boat, but I do not know just when."

Roberta was sixteen. At the time mentioned in the committee statement, when Minnie Kennedy was living in New York, Roberta would have been eight. She could not recall the name of the boat in which Whittebeck was supposed to have worked, but she thought it was the *Clermont*. At least, so the press quoted her.

As had always been the case when her mother went on the warpath, Aimee kept out of sight; but on the evening of the same day on which the famous propositions were presented, another statement emanated from Angelus Temple (where no statement was ever issued over Sister's veto), quoting three temple aides as accusing Minnie Kennedy directly of malfeasance and subversion in her conduct of temple affairs.

Mrs. Letha Mae Brooks, registrar and secretary of the Temple Bible School, was represented as saying:

"Mrs. Kennedy told me that she would break Sister, crush her, and bar her from every pulpit in America. She said she would draw everything out of the temple accounts and when Sister returned would fool her with bills. She would have no cash and the place would go into the hands of receivers. She said she would drive Sister to her knees."

Roderick H. Morrison, Gladwyn Nichols's successor as head of the temple music department, was quoted:

"Mother told me she would give a story to the world that would wreck Sister if she didn't do as she wished."

And Brother Jaynes:

"Mrs. Kennedy told me she would take McPhersonism out of the temple; if it was the last thing in the world, she would break Mrs. McPherson."

After that, the only converse between mother and daughter was in the presence of their attorneys. Aimee played her trump card in the temple, however, by telling a special meeting of the members that she was preparing to resign as their pastor and give her entire time to evangelistic work in big cities of the East, Midwest, and Canada. In a half-hour talk she never mentioned her mother's name, but after praying that she might be guided aright, launched into a résumé of the events since the dismissal of the perjury charge against her. She repeated that her story of being kidnaped was true and said she thought her members believed her.

Applause seemed to confirm this impression.

After her preliminary hearing, she said, she had still felt like facing the world and telling of her innocence, and that had been the reason for making the "vindication tour." She told of people coming to her and asking questions until she had doubted her own physical health and sanity, and how she had gone to reputable physicians, who told her she was in perfect health, and an alienist whom she had consulted had said she was one of the sanest women he had ever encountered.

As for her new venture and her resignation, it would not mean that she was abandoning the temple, for she would still preach there from time to time. But she had simply received "more calls to bring our work into various parts of the country than I could answer in ten lifetimes," and she must start to serve others. She confessed that she had family troubles, but said they were probably no worse than those of anybody else—"only mine get into the newspapers." But she believed that she could handle them and asked for a chance to do so without interference. Still without mentioning her mother, she spoke of the desirability of a long trip for someone— stipulating that a return ticket should be provided.

When this sweet reasonableness was relayed to Minnie, she scoffed. No need to become alarmed about that resignation threat, she advised, because this was "at least the sixth time she has said she would resign."

Proceeding then to "unload the burden of her heart," Minnie said that doubt of Mrs. McPherson's kidnaping story by a portion of the temple membership was really "what is driving us both out of the temple." She referred to a "diabolical plot hatched during the kidnaping episode to rout both me and my daughter from the temple." Then, after making clear that she was insisting upon a business settlement with her daughter before she would yield the reins, and that neither Angelus Temple nor the Bible School would be affected or injured in any way, she went for an automobile ride with a covey of Bible students who were loyal to her cause.

Reaching a settlement proved difficult. Minnie would take nothing less than a fifty-fifty split of their personal property. The temple and Bible School were separate; but jointly the two women owned some sixty-five thousand dollars' worth of real estate that they had purchased during the last year, and there was more. Nor would Minnie budge from the fifty-fifty split. She likened her contribution to their mutual success to grubstaking a prospector or gold miner.

"Mrs. McPherson didn't have anything when I joined her," she explained severely. "It was my money that financed our work through all these years, and that ultimately brought Sister to the greatest church in America. When we started we agreed to go fifty-fifty on everything we made during the ensuing years, and it is upon that agreement that I want her to settle."

Then Minnie's mood changed, and she asked how any agreement could be reached when "watermelons and lemonade have broken up every conference we have ever had to settle this matter." As soon as they met with their lawyers, she complained, Aimee would insist on eating watermelon and drinking lemonade.

Responded Aimee:

"I like to eat watermelon and enjoy drinking lemonade, but if Mother objects to them, I will promise not to eat or drink while talking business. We have attempted several meetings, but it must not be overlooked that I have a pulpit to fill and cannot sit all day talking.

"When this began," she went on with candor, "I did not realize how degrading a misunderstanding or disagreement, which certainly is not uncommon among business partners or even in families, could look in print. I am just as sorry as I can be that I ever answered a word, no matter who spoke unkindly about me or what was said.

"I am sure the public must be, to put it kindly, fed up on all this nonsense that has been published the last few days, and I will promise, and do my level best to keep that promise, that I will not inflict any more such stuff on newspaper readers."

Which pledge, it happened, coincided with a bulletin from the lawyers that a settlement had been reached. The terms were not disclosed, by mutual agreement, but it was ascertained that Minnie Kennedy received approximately one hundred thousand dollars in cash and property, and Aimee was handed, as her share of the fifty-fifty division, roughly the same amount in canceled checks representing the money paid out for her defense in the kidnaping case.

Mother stepped out of the temple management, turning over full control to her daughter. The attorney's statement said that the settlement would allow "the work of the church and the Foursquare Gospel to go on, the accomplishment of which aim has been uppermost in the minds of both principals at all times."

The gag rule applying to differences with her mother apparently did not bind Aimee in regard to others. Gladwyn Nichols, who had been taking potshots at the evangelist, saying that both she and her mother had a confession to make to the world, took the occasion to demand that Mrs. McPherson "stand trial before a church board" on the truth of her kidnaping story. Aimee shrugged.

"Mr. Nichols needs the publicity," she said, "so let him go to it."

A Judge Is Judged

"The judgments of the Lord are true
and righteous altogether."
—*Psalms 19:9*

So here was a mother distraught and a daughter equally distraught, who, in addition, in Minnie Kennedy's belief, was heading toward ruin. The quarrel *had* been sordid, and neither woman had risen to the crisis gracefully. Minnie had been too long accustomed to domineer, and Aimee, naturally compliant and avoiding disputes wherever possible as long as her will was not thwarted, had conducted herself with what suggested the petulant perversity of an insecure, spoiled child. The break had been long coming. It reached back into basic antagonisms in the two women's characters; but since it finally had come, and their interests had finally been sundered on businesslike lines, both were prepared to drop the argument for the sake of Angelus Temple.

Each, in her way, was solicitous for the temple's welfare. Its well-being had been their well-being. As the symbol and tangible proof of God's blessing on their labors, it had crowned their lives with justification and meaning. And it had made them important in the world. The concerns of the temple therefore were their concern—although not their only concern, to be sure. The crux of their 1926 dilemma had been their mutual realization that if Aimee fell, the temple would fall; and in the ultimate reckoning of the motives and means by which they had slid out of that dilemma they themselves had little doubt that they would be absolved of all but righteous intent.

Although shut out now from the engrossing activity at Echo Park, Minnie could not help fretting as news of developments there was relayed by faithful adherents, of whom she retained not a few. It seemed to her that Sister had embarked on a course of recklessness that could serve no purpose except to demonstrate, if it succeeded, that her mother was not indispensable to the temple or Aimee herself, but that she, Sister McPherson, had a head for business, too. Minnie foresaw a grievous outcome.

Aimee's first step was to reorganize the church with herself as the supreme authority. She formed an eight-member "board of control," comprising herself and the heads of the temple's seven departments. This board, she said, would decide on church policy "by majority vote." She would remain business head. Thus in effect she insured that the board would be a shadow group, possessing no authority in vital matters. All they could control would be their opinions; the reins were held tightly in her strong hands.

Next she announced that within a short while she would take the field to recruit branch churches under the new name of lighthouses. These would function as "soul-saving stations," occupying buildings constructed to look like lighthouses—round towers with beacons atop, flashing hope to perishing sinners and guiding the storm-tossed to snug harbors. The first lighthouses, she said, would be established in Chicago, Des Moines, Canton, Ohio, Wichita, Kansas, St. Louis, Philadelphia, Rochester, Dallas, New Orleans, New York, San Francisco, and San Diego—all cities in which she had preached and was known. Later she would extend the movement to the British Isles, Australia, and Shanghai.

"I have visualized a great movement of the Foursquare Gospel into all parts of the world," her announcement read, "and feel that now is the opportune time to begin."

The Reverend John D. Goben, an evangelist who had been enjoying success in Des Moines, was named chief field agent to start organizing the lighthouses at once. An architect's sketch of the international headquarters was placed on display; it graphically depicted a lofty tower one hundred and fifty feet high with a revolving beacon at the top, rising from a base of artificial rocks, on the site of the parsonage, which would be torn down. The rubric said the building would provide office space and one hundred guest rooms for visiting delegations.

The nautical theme had captured Aimee's fancy, and she foresaw the transformation of her entire church into a "Salvation Navy."

Here comes the navy! Sister Aimee starts reorganizing her church as a "Salvation Navy," complete with rank and uniforms. Aimee salutes the camera in her rear admiral's cap.

As a starter, she put the temple staff into uniforms, with designations of rank right up to herself as "admiral." She posed for publicity pictures in her admiral's cap, standing in a lifeboat mounted on a Ford truck, the first of the "fleet" that she envisioned carrying the Foursquare message worldwide.

This innovation soured, however, when her crew quarreled over questions of rank and precedence, some members protested that the uniforms were gaudy, and the United States naval authorities called the attention of the district attorney to an apparent misuse of the navy's uniform. A prosecution was hinted; but Sister ridiculed the whole matter as a tempest in a teapot and mustered her tars back into civilian togs again.

Lined up for inspection—Admiral Aimee, left, down to the littlest middie. But the workers squabbled over rank, the United States Navy objected, and the uniforms were scrapped.

When Minnie had vacated the parsonage, she had moved into a flat on Lemoyne Street, next door to the Bible School building, but she had not remained there long. Very quickly she left the city, saying only that she was going to take a long vacation; and when her mother was well on her way, Aimee announced the dawn of an era of good feeling, telling her flock:

"The day of discord is past. Mother and I are closer than ever before. We have reached an absolute understanding. I am offering her an opportunity of taking an active part in her lifework, the missionary field."

Skeptical onlookers noted that activity "in the field" would keep Minnie Kennedy out of Los Angeles; and whether the "day of discord" had entirely passed was thrown into question when Mother showed up in Portland, Oregon, traveling in her big blue limousine, with Kharvina Burbeck, her secretary.

"I am still Mrs. Aimee Semple McPherson's mother, and she is still my baby," Minnie told the newspapers. "But there are times when every baby would be better off for a good spanking."

She declined to discuss the break with her daughter, saying:

Admiral Aimee launches the first "lifeboat" of her "Salvation Navy," pointing the way to the nearest "soul saving station," or Foursquare Gospel mission, to be renamed "lighthouse."

"There were other people involved. They had an influence over her. But I don't want to go into that."

Neither would she discuss Aimee's still celebrated disappearance of 1926; this subject neither woman seemed able to get clear of.

"I don't want to go into that either," Minnie said firmly. "It wouldn't do. I want to help Mrs. McPherson, not harm her. Some day I may put it all into a book, and then a great many things will be explained. But there is nothing I can say now."

She fixed the reporter with a meditative stare.

If this alarmed Aimee she did not show it. When asked to comment, as of course she was, on her mother's enigmatic "threat," the evangelist said smoothly:

"I'm sure that if my mother were to write a book about me, it would be inspired only by mother love and would be much the same type of book any mother would write about her daughter. As to the spanking which the dispatches say my mother intimated might be good for any mother's baby, no matter how grown up it might be—

well, I think it is awfully foolish for us to give out statements about each other regarding any misunderstanding which may have existed between us. It has all been a very unfortunate affair. Too much has been said over something that really had no significance. I still love my mother very dearly. I don't believe that she would purposely say anything to harm me."

By that time Mother Kennedy had left Portland for Seattle, which she would make her headquarters for some time to come.

Aimee, meanwhile, was busy with extraneous enterprises. One was the promotion of a Foursquare summer resort called Tahoe Cedars, on Lake Tahoe, in the high Sierra in Northern California. Another was the promotion of a Foursquare cemetery named Blessed Hope, in the nearby community of Burbank. Temple members were being solicited assiduously on behalf of both projects—to buy cottage sites in the one and grave sites in the other.

Ralph Jordan, whom Sister was introducing everywhere as her business manager, was active particularly in the Tahoe Cedars promotion. To launch the expected boom in building lots, Sister announced that she would lead a motorcade of prospective buyers on the four-hundred-mile journey north to dedicate the ground. But when the pilgrimage was made, with Sister bravely leading, only a trickle of followers came behind her.

The project was miscalculated from the start. Aimee's followers were, in the main, not well-to-do; they were working people, regularly employed, or pensioners living on small means, and extended vacations and summer cottages were beyond their reach. And Lake Tahoe was far from Los Angeles. The enterprise floundered along until a few temple members who had bought cabin sites complained to the authorities, and Mrs. McPherson, Ralph Jordan, and the real estate developers were involved in very unpleasant investigations. It was brought out that Sister had been working for a commission of 10 percent on all sales, plus a free gift of from four to sixty-one lots (the stories differed), in return for which she was to build a tabernacle on the grounds and conduct services there. The Angelus Temple magazine, *The Crusader*, had carried promotional articles vaunting the project, and temple members had been worked upon. In the end the complainants were refunded their money, and Sister was the loser.

T HE site which has been selected for the Blessed Hope Memorial Park is to be laid out, beautified, and landscaped to become one of the scenic spots of Southern California. Centrally in this Park will be placed the beautiful "Chapel of the Angels," in which Sister McPherson's own family crypt is to be built and where, amid the accompaniment of singing birds and pipe-organ music, she will, d. v., personally conduct the services for those of her members who desire their awaiting-place to be near that which she has chosen for herself.

Sister's own desire for herself and
her family in our own charming
"Chapel of the Angels"

A scheme that went awry. Page from brochure promoting the sale of grave plots in her Blessed Hope Cemetery, where she promised to be laid to rest herself. The sales slogan was "Go up with Aimee!"

The cemetery scheme turned out badly, too. In the announcements of the purchase of a tract for a Foursquare Gospel "tarrying ground," no allusion was made to the rough, weed-infested condition of the land; it lay adjacent to a landscaped and immaculately maintained cemetery in full occupancy. In the promotional brochure Sister was quoted as saying:

"When my time comes to fall asleep, I do not want to be taken to some dark, solemn, gloomy cemetery where the atmosphere is a pall on life."

And this somewhat confusing note was the theme of Sister's dedicatory pilgrimage to the new "rest home," when she led a band of the faithful out on the greensward and knelt in a ceremony of solemn consecration. Only later was it realized that she had been kneeling not on her own repellent acres but amid the lush greenery of the cemetery next door.

Ignoring this lack of directional sense, Sister did her best to further the efforts of salesmen who clogged the corridors of Angelus Temple peddling chances to "go up with Aimee." In the beautiful Chapel of the Angels to be erected would be Sister's own family crypt, and the price of the lots rose according to their proximity to her tomb. There, in that chapel, the official brochure said, "amid the accompaniment of singing birds and pipe-organ music, [Sister] will, d.v., personally conduct the services for those of her members who desire their waiting place to be next to that which she has chosen for herself."

The conditional "d.v." proved to be well chosen, for no Chapel of the Angels was constructed, the promised "perpetual care" proved to be anything but everlasting, and eventually, to the tune of lawsuits, the venture was liquidated. It was said that the promoters had reaped a profit, while Sister was left to shoulder the debts and the criticism.

Mother Kennedy was scornful of Aimee's "boneyard." Her daughter's generous nature was being imposed upon by conscienceless schemers, she asserted. In the Pacific Northwest, Minnie had developed new interests. She had hit the trail as a revivalist on her own account, and according to reports reaching Angelus Temple was meeting with success. Her services were said to be bringing the liveliness, the foot-tapping music and the platform innovations of Angelus Temple into local tabernacles; Mother's methods were, in fact, a road-show version of her daughter's spectacles. Preaching before a responsive crowd in Seattle, Minnie exclaimed:

"There are many of these modern churches trying to bring the world into the church. They advertise Wednesday night chicken dinners to get folks out to Wednesday night prayer meetings. But what we need is less fire in the church kitchens and more fire in the pulpits!"

With fur-trimmed white satin cape flying, she moved agilely about the platform, preaching the "open Bible" and indulging in vivid pantomime. For her baptisms she had a huge tank placed on the stage, stated to contain four and one-half tons of water. On two evenings Minnie told "the story of my life" (a sure-fire topic with Aimee), reserving for the second evening the part "pertaining to Angelus Temple." This lecture was particularly heavily attended but was devoid of revelations.

Plainly Minnie was enjoying her release from the responsibilities of the temple management. She was seen dashing about in her car with her secretary, and she took up horseback riding; her favorite mount she named Billy Sunday. And when Aimee announced a forthcoming preaching tour of the Northwest, Mother was amused.

"I guess I'm still the trailblazer," she chuckled. "She is advertising her appearance in the very cities where I have successfully conducted campaigns."

Aimee did tour the Northwest, and her failure to look up her mother in Seattle upset Minnie, especially since Minnie's hotel was only a few blocks from the railroad station.

But this grief was nothing compared to the anguish Minnie's sentimental soul suffered on Christmas Day of 1927, when she was back in Los Angeles for a brief stay, in her flat beside the Bible School. She could hear the joyful bustle going on next door in preparation for the holiday, though shut out from it all. Calling over the janitor of the building, she gave him a message for her daughter, begging her to come and greet her "dear old mother on that day of days." But, as she recounted:

"The janitor came back in a few minutes. He looked very sad. He said Mrs. McPherson told him to say to me that if I wanted to see her, to write a letter asking for an appointment."

Tears welled in Minnie's eyes as she told of this cruel rebuff.

Like daughter like mother. Minnie Kennedy, ousted from the Temple management, embarks upon a tour of the Pacific Northwest as a barnstorming evangelist on her own. Here she carries out the total-immersion baptism of a convert in a park lake.

The truth was that Aimee was afraid of her mother still, and she always would be.

Minnie went back to her work in the Northwest, but Mother's Day brought fresh tribulation. Friends in Los Angeles began telephoning her congratulations. For what? she asked, and they said because of her reconciliation with her daughter. This was news to Minnie, but gradually she learned what had happened. Standing in the pulpit, Aimee had said that she had sent her mother flowers on Mother's Day, "as tall as herself," and a collection had been taken to defray the cost.

Minnie was outraged.

"My daughter never sent me flowers of any size, color, or description!" she fumed.

Her wrath turned to fury when she read in the newspapers that her daughter had informed the temple congregation that notes had been found, totaling twenty-five thousand dollars, which were due and must be paid, although there was no money in the temple treasury to pay them. In Minnie's opinion, the plain intimation was that these notes had been signed while she was still in charge of the temple's finances and had been carelessly or spitefully left behind. Any reflection on her business competence aroused Minnie Kennedy's ire, and she made abundantly clear that she knew nothing whatever about the asserted notes, had never seen them, and positively had never signed them.

The misleading statements being put out at Angelus Temple were trying Minnie's patience, and she also feared that Aimee and the temple itself were in jeopardy because of mismanagement there. To a confidential friend, Mrs. W. J. Crawford, a temple member living in Los Angeles, Minnie unburdened her anxieties in a series of long, intimate letters. The first one, written from Longview, Washington, where Mother was conducting a revival, read, in part:

"Precious Soul:—Thanks for your very interesting letter. I sincerely appreciate every true friend and also all the news of how the old ship is 'a-moovering' along. My very life blood is intermingled with the warp and woof of it all, and although I am out of it in person, yet I am interested in watching developments under the newspaper regime. Then, too, it is a great spiritual study, for as far as I can see, it is being run on totally unscriptural lines and for purely mercenary and publicity purposes. If God continues to bless His word and save souls under those conditions, it is very wonderful.

"Wasn't that a terrible statement that A[imee] gave out on her return? Seems it would turn anyone's soul sick that had any sort of right mentality. . . .

"What I would like to know is, have the people no spunk to clear up the situation? Surely they must see through it all. . . . But God bless them all. They are standing for things that cost John the Baptist his head. And it might cost anyone's head that dared speak as John spoke! I'd give my life to see A. clear of the Egyptians, but as long as she seems to like them and put them ahead of the people that have pledged to stand by her and the work, there is nothing that I can do. When she is so insincere as to put across the Mother's Day flower farce and get away with it! . . . The board there are nothing but a cover, and so flattered at having a position that they will swallow everything, although they must know the facts."

This letter was signed: "The Least of His, Mother Kennedy."

It had two scribbled postscripts: "Love to my little tea party girl & your own dear self," and "Some wonderful meetings here."

It was followed by even more pointed commentary in a letter urging "all good true members" of Angelus Temple to "do the Lord's service . . . and also be a better friend to Aimee by sitting tight in the place you now hold, and instead of leaving right now, try to get it cleaned up once and for all. I am fully satisfied it could be easily done, and that until it is the spiritual unrest and undertow will continue.

"Why on earth don't a few of you members who have stood so loyal through it all, and who really love little Sister and would share the last dollar with her, get together and write a request for a complete change of all boards and also an internal investigation that would set everything at rest? I have thought much over the matter, from the knowledge that I have on various lines, and I believe it could be done very readily. Then I know a big blond man with curly hair, who travels with Sister and seems in charge generally behind the scenes, who would not stand very popular. . . . I am sure it would be the best thing that could happen, and in the finals, if properly handled, Sister would be freed of those blackmailers and parasites that are bleeding her and the Temple to death.

"It is pitiful that Sister has got the press started again. . . . Several weeks ago I wrote to Brother Arthur concerning the faked financial statement and letter they had issued to work the poor long-suffering members for money, and trying to make it appear that I had left the notes and that they had just found that they were coming due, etc. I requested an explanation be issued explaining that these had been all after I left. But I have not even had an answer. . . . Of course he [Brother Arthur] is helpless, only to give it to the board or to Sister. . . . So much has been put out over the pulpit, radio, and press, which I have borne in silence, but I feel the time has come when the actual facts should be known. She is in need of real help, although maybe she won't admit it or even realize it. . . . I am sending a long telegram today. Her heart seems like flint."

The culminating indignity, for Minnie, occurred later that spring of 1928, when Aimee at last sought an interview with her mother. As Minnie recounted the incident, Aimee had deemed it "wise and diplomatic to get in touch with me," on account of seething unrest at the temple, and "the danger of an upheaval which would expose the rottenness underneath the tinsel."

"I have a very well developed sense of truth," ran Mother's account, "and in my heart was no witness whatever as to her sincerity, and I told her so. First she called me on the phone. I said I did not want any further publicity connected with her, and she said she did not either. . . . Then she called twice from P[ortland], saying she wanted to see me. [Minnie was in Longview.] So I could do no other than to say: 'If you are even a little bit sincere, you can come.' All that was talked about was business and a lot of money matters."

What Aimee wanted, Minnie quickly grasped, was help in locating the first minutes of the Echo Park Evangelistic Association, the corporation that held title to Angelus Temple. Aimee needed the minutes to negotiate a mortgage on the temple. The amount of the mortgage was to be a quarter of a million dollars, and the money was to be for her benefit. This Minnie stated positively, and to her the proposal seemed like sacrilege. "Her trying to mortgage the temple after my giving my very life to get it out of debt!" she exclaimed indignantly to friends. Impetuously she rushed to protect her life's work by alerting "loyal" members and the press of the danger. Thereafter the statements flew.

Mrs. McPherson denied categorically that she had ever contemplated mortgaging Angelus Temple. That could never be mortgaged, she insisted; the only building that would be mortgaged was the Bible School, and that solely for the purpose of erecting a much needed residence hall for students across the street.

By telegram Minnie Kennedy retorted:

"You told me about arranging to mortgage the Temple for yourself personally. Am horrified at your attempt to sidestep the truth by stating that the mortgage would be for dormitories and school only. You know and God knows what you told me here, that it was for yourself and to be a blanket mortgage over entire properties and that members are willing. Why didn't you state the facts and keep in the clear? Nobody would begrudge you all that is rightfully yours but action should be open and aboveboard.

"Your flat denial today and your attempt to make your mother a falsifier convince me that your whole mortgage proposition was a scheme which you were attempting to put over in a manner which, for some reason, cannot face the light."

Praying that her daughter's "heart would be softened," Minnie then struck home:

"I fear that your present headlong course will prove your complete spiritual downfall and possible loss of Temple. Conditions have at last come to a pass that I am coming to the conclusion that the proper steps for me to take will be for me to return and with information and evidence now in my possession endeavor to completely cleanse and clear up the whole matter, past and present."

Past and present. . . . The public mind harked back to those unexplained, mystical events of 1926. If anyone could, Minnie Kennedy should be able to "cleanse and clear up" that tantalizing riddle.

II

The dovecote at Echo Park fluttered, and Sister attempted to blunt her mother's wrath by a display of winsomeness and sweet reason. In a carefully composed statement, the evangelist replied:

"When Mother left the Temple she took at least nine-tenths of our personal property, leaving me the Temple to carry on God's work. It is not mine and never can be mine. Mother promised that in view of my willingness to give her whatever she wanted, she would leave me alone to preach the Gospel. All I ask of her is to do that. Surely, that is not too much for a daughter to ask of her mother? Why she wants to send telegrams to the newspapers and to my people I cannot understand.

"First, several days ago she sent a long telegram to all the newspapers attacking me. Then followed another long, bitter telegram addressed to me and signed 'Mother.' I never received it, but copies of it were sent to all of my people and my branch church pastors. I have said before, and I repeat, I have no intention of turning the Temple to my private use. To say anything further I feel is beneath my dignity. I do not intend to be drawn into any more disgusting controversies with Mother, or to enter into any public controversies of any kind. I am going to stick to my business of preaching the Gospel and staying out of newspaper headlines if possible.

"Almost a week ago I sent Mother a telegram which read in part as follows, and which reflects my attitude entirely: 'Dear Mother: I am sorry you feel as you do, for you are mistaken. But I will not enter into any more distressing incidents with you. Please let us both conduct ourselves only as true Christians should, and be the Christian examples our positions call for. I will always love you as a mother.' "

Undaunted, Mother released her reply:

"I expected to have some trouble about that telegram, so I saw to it that I got a signed receipt from Aimee when the telegram was delivered."

This did nothing to cool the hot winds blowing across Echo Park; but still in the role of a misunderstood, long-suffering daughter, Sister McPherson frankly told the press all about her visit to her mother, and called it "lovely."

"Mother was highly pleased that I called and complimented me on my appearance and dress," the evangelist said. "During the course of the conversation I told her I was considering building the hotel for Bible students across the street from the temple, which she had planned when she was here, and she said that she would have had it built by now. . . .

"I asked her how one would go about raising the money, and she said by a mortgage and bond issue on the school building. We parted very friendly. I can't understand the attack. Our church books are open to everyone here and they know all the business of the institution."

On her side, in another long letter to her confidential friend, Mrs. Crawford, Minnie poured out woe and indignation:

"I have done everything in my power to keep from talking, although I have had telegrams asking me for statements and information. . . . Now, she stated here that it would be a blanket mortgage covering everything, and was for herself, as she felt she should have it. I am sure that nobody would begrudge her everything, for it is hers and she worked for it and so did I. But the trouble is that everyone fears, if she gets it, it will go to that same bunch that has been causing all the scandal, and that she will lose the Temple and all. . . . The idea of saying that we talked of cabbages and kings! . . . Why couldn't she let me alone, after the terrible way she has treated me and done her best to ruin me? . . . Her calling me a liar does not make it so, thank God. Does she dare to deny her negotiations to secure the mortgage? The press clippings have just arrived, 'hurling the lie.' Awful!"

After which outpouring, the dam broke.

In an interview with a newspaper reporter lasting five hours, Mother Kennedy "told all"—or nearly all, it turned out—and shed some light on questions that had baffled folks for years.

The interview took place in the lobby and dining room of the hotel in Seattle where Minnie was living. The interviewer had made the trip especially from Los Angeles, on an intimation, or feeling, he said, that Mrs. Kennedy, who had hardly been seen in Los Angeles since leaving Angelus Temple, was ready to talk.

Rumors at Echo Park had suggested that Minnie was failing in mind and body, broke, and looking for any kind of a paying job at all.

The interviewer found her healthy, in fine spirits, and giving no indication of having any money worries. She was dressed in a smart white serge ensemble, with a large corsage of brightly colored imitation flowers on the left shoulder. In a jolly voice she explained that she had spent the afternoon in a Turkish bath trying to steam off some of the ten pounds she wanted to lose; she was dieting, she said. But at ten o'clock in the evening, when the interview began, she was full of vivacity, sprightly in her speech, and at all times keenly aware of what she was saying. Her penetrating gray eyes filled with tears when she touched on painful portions of her narrative, but she brushed them back with her hand and never lost her self-command. The reporter was impressed by the acuteness of her "bright business mind," and he also commented on her skill in parrying questions that she did not wish to answer. She admitted that in regard to exact dates and places her memory sometimes was at fault, but so much had happened it was impossible to keep all the details straight.

"Sister used to leave everything in the way of business in my hands," she began, "and thus we worked lovingly, hand-in-hand, to spread the Gospel. It has all changed now. I may have theories and opinions about many things in connection with the trouble that has come to Angelus Temple, but I want to tell only what I know, or is a matter of record."

She seemed reluctant at first to enter into any discussion of the kidnaping episode, explaining that there were "so many blind alleys and mystifying angles that it leaves me baffled when I think back over it. I have lain awake many nights trying to solve some particular circumstance, only to find myself utterly baffled. Sister did not confide in me, and many people think I know a lot more than I really do."

She accompanied this confession by a look full of meaning.

When her daughter disappeared at Ocean Park, Minnie went on, she honestly believed Aimee had been drowned.

"This is the Gospel truth," she said earnestly. "Those days of agony I have lived over countless times. We at the temple were being deluged with anonymous letters, threats, appeals, offers of assistance, and I don't know what. It seemed that everybody had seen Sister, but no definite clues were furnished. I say solemnly in truth that I believed Sister was drowned. Someday the whole truth of this matter will come out."

The interviewer asked whether Mrs. McPherson's appearance, when Mother first saw her in the hospital in Douglas, seemed to indicate that she had been kidnaped and suffered privation or that she had just passed through an ordeal of desert heat.

"I won't answer that question," was Minnie's response, and her lips tightened.

Asked point-blank whether she believed the kidnaping story, she repeated firmly:

"I won't answer that question."

But about the subsequent entanglements—the grand jury, the false leads, the shoal of witnesses, and the dubious characters on the side-lines—about these she was voluble. Up to that time, she said, her dealings with lawyers had been few: "about the only time we saw a lawyer was when there was a matter of building contracts or something of that sort." But after that it had been lawyers, lawyers, lawyers.

She then went on to her daughter's sudden demands for money.

"One night we were undressing in adjoining rooms when the telephone rang. Mrs. McPherson hurried to the phone and answered it. I didn't hear the conversation, but to my surprise she came into my room after hanging up the phone, and said:

" 'Mother, I want you to turn over to me the bankbooks and other books of the association.'

"I didn't know what to say, and I didn't reply. I haven't the slightest idea who phoned. I felt then, as I have felt recently, that an effort was made to entangle me in the finances. Odd things have happened at the temple and I am at a loss to understand them."

Minnie traced in detail the hunt for Ormiston, while Sister was in

Europe, and the baffling clues that developed during the preliminary hearing; but she added little new except to emphasize her dislike of Mae Waldron. The report Miss Waldron had brought to the temple, about the intended scandal article linking Sister and Ormiston abroad, seemed to Minnie to have been the starting point of the whole long sequence of troubles.

"Strangely enough," she added darkly, "this stenographer who brought the story to the temple was elevated by Sister to an important position in the church, and now is an officer."

Coming down to recent events, Mrs. Kennedy said that it was her background of knowledge of temple finances that had prompted her to inform the members of the mortgage proposal.

"When I handled the finances there were seventeen different funds, all monies received being kept in separate accounts, but I understand now that all monies go into one fund. Why Sister wants to mortgage the temple I can't understand. She has plenty of money for her own needs, and new money is constantly coming in. I can't understand where all the money is going.

"If the time comes for me to take up the battle for the church, I shall return to Los Angeles. I have only the greatest of love for Sister, and the interests of the temple at heart. The church is suffering from all this talk. Sister wants to travel. She once said to me, 'I'd like to turn my face toward every port.' My great concern is that if Sister should leave the temple, it will not stand up under another leader. I think the temple needs her. She handles crowds in a masterful way. There is no one in the world who can equal her. She is a changed woman when on the platform."

It was 3:30 in the morning when Minnie ceased talking, after the interviewer had tried one more searching question. Referring to the "little blue trunk" that had been produced by the district attorney, containing clothing alleged to be Aimee's, the reporter asked:

"Did you recognize the clothing in the 'little blue trunk' as that of Mrs. McPherson?"

"I never saw the contents of the trunk," Mother replied. "I only saw the photographs in the newspapers."

"Did you, from the newspaper pictures, recognize any specific garment as that of Mrs. McPherson?" the reporter pressed.

Mrs. Kennedy laughed.

"Well, they certainly weren't garments an evangelist should wear," she exclaimed, and broke off the interview.

In Los Angeles the reported conversation filled columns of newsprint, and reporters tried to get Kenneth Ormiston's comment on Mrs. Kennedy's extensive mentioning of himself. He was living quietly in Los Angeles, engaged in radio work; his wife, after the kidnaping prosecution had been dropped, had returned briefly to California and obtained a divorce on grounds of desertion.

"I can't be annoyed," was his indifferent reaction. "It doesn't concern me in the slightest what Mrs. Kennedy says. I haven't even read the interview."

Mrs. McPherson's reaction was not so casual. At first sight of the published interview she exclaimed:

"This is unbelievable—just too vicious and unkind to be imaginable, as well as being very largely untrue!"

But after careful study of the article, she handed out a less affirmative statement:

"It is difficult indeed to ascribe the motive which inspired these attacks to a mother's love. As for the attacks themselves, it is unbecoming a daughter, even when she is attacked by her own mother, to attack her mother in turn. At such a time, because of the sacredness which must always belong to motherhood, one necessarily suffers in silence."

Orally she added:

"There must be something wrong with Mother."

Right or wrong, now that Minnie had started to talk, she kept on, in interview after interview, and in articles of her own composing, signed in her capacity as "Evangel of the Everlasting Gospel." Her revelations were sometimes piquant. In one chapter she recounted an asserted meeting between her daughter and Ormiston just before their trial was about to start. It took place on New Year's Eve, Mother said, and it fitted in with the melodramatic air of the whole bizarrerie.

At the conclusion of the regular evening service on New Year's Eve, Minnie said, there was an interval before the start of the "watch night" service.

"Sister slipped quickly from the pulpit, hurried past me, and rushed up the ramp, threw a cloak about her shoulders, and ran across the street," Minnie recalled. "She sprang into an automobile and was driven away."

When she returned, just in time to conduct the midnight service, she appeared very nervous and excited, Minnie said, and continued:

"I was very much alarmed and asked my daughter where she had been. At first she wouldn't tell me. Finally she told me of the pre-arranged meeting with Ormiston and details of what happened there."

She said Aimee had told of being taken to an isolated part of the city. Shortly another car had driven up, with Ormiston in it. Several men armed with pistols had got out of the second car and patrolled the street during the brief interview. Aimee and Ormiston had had only a few minutes to agree on the story they would tell to the court and the public. Such was Minnie's story. She resumed:

"Previously my daughter had told me she was working on a plan toward dismissal of the case. When I pleaded with her that I feared she was following a dangerous course, she replied, 'I have placed myself in their hands and they have got to stand by me now.' "

Mother's answer to repeated questions as to whether she believed the kidnaping story remained cryptic:

"I'm not saying it's not true; I'm saying it's strange."

She did hint at the payment of large sums of money to unidentified persons just before the case was dropped, and alluded to a six-thousand-dollar contract that had been given to "a certain person of influence" prior to dismissal of the case.

"My daughter should make public the names of all persons who were not part of the Angelus Temple membership who received money as gifts from Mrs. McPherson or Angelus Temple, through the payroll or otherwise, before the kidnaping case was dismissed," Mother mused. "Everybody should know the truth."

She provided a glimpse of the way Aimee managed to get her board ("a set of tin soldiers," Mother called them) to approve measures against their better judgment.

"My daughter," said Mrs. Kennedy, "has a magnetic personality and an ability to win people to her. When she wants to accomplish an important purpose, she tells with feeling of the tragic death of Robert Semple, her evangelist husband, who died in China. She moves everybody to tears, and then they hold up their hands in approval."

One canard that Minnie disposed of was that she was suffering from poverty. Breaking the secrecy that had surrounded the terms of her settlement with her daughter (Minnie called it an "adjustment"), she said that she had got one hundred and six thousand dollars in cash and "certain outlying properties which we had secured for development work," and that Mrs. McPherson received "Angelus Temple and the entire association property, valued at a million and a half dollars, achieved through ten years of united effort. These were turned over to her with a considerable amount of money, both association and personal funds."

In working out the "adjustment," the hundred thousand dollars spent on their legal defense during the kidnaping troubles was "taken into consideration," of course, Minnie confirmed. And finally, "a record was made of all bank accounts and all properties, including our many branch churches, and signed over to her." So her daughter could not justly be said to be impoverished either.

The reaction to these disclosures in circles loyal to Sister was not restrained. So unrestrained was it, a group of snoopers set out for Canada, determined to prove from the records there that Aimee Semple McPherson was not the daughter of Minnie Kennedy, but must be James Kennedy's daughter by a previous marriage.

Both women were amused by this development.

"Why, we even look alike!" Minnie exclaimed, and Aimee joined in with, "Of course I am Mrs. Kennedy's daughter. Any other idea is ridiculous." Discreetly she put the quietus on the researches of her overzealous zealots.

But Mrs. Kennedy's talking did revive the gossip that had been heard all over Los Angeles to the effect that the dismissal of the case against the Echo Park evangelist had been effected by the payment of large sums of money to somebody. Already one attempt had been made in the state legislature to investigate the expenditure of public funds in pushing the famous case. The resolution, however, had been pigeonholed, after one baffled assemblyman moved that it be laid away in the "little blue trunk" with other futilities and unsolvable questions. District Attorney Keyes did state at that time, however, that the cost of the prosecution to the state had been negligible—something like four thousand dollars—because the major expense of unearthing evidence and locating witnesses had been borne by the daily press.

Meanwhile, however, Keyes's office had come under suspicion in

When irate Temple adherents claimed that Aimee McPherson could not possibly be the daughter of Minnie Kennedy, both women laughed and said, "Why, we even look alike." This photo was taken May 30, 1929, upon announcement of their reconcilation and Minnie's temporary return to the Temple.

connection with other matters, and an investigation by the grand jury uncovered an Angelus Temple check for twenty-five hundred dollars made out to Superior Court Judge Carlos S. Hardy and cashed by him. The check had lain for months in Keyes's private files.

Judge Hardy readily admitted receiving and cashing the check, which he said was a "love offering" from the temple leaders, in recognition of their long friendship and gratitude for the assistance he had rendered them over the years. The payment was not for legal services, he insisted, but was a voluntary gift.

Strange stories had been circulated about Judge Hardy's behind-the-scenes activities during the early stages of the McPherson case, and the California Bar Association moved to look into the matter of the check. Although at first Hardy volunteered to appear for questioning, he changed his mind and denied the right of the association to meddle with the judiciary. But the American Bar Association considered the facts and dropped him from membership for violation of its professional and judicial canons, and the legislature moved to impeach him. The counts against him were practicing law while a judge, in violation of the state constitution; obstructing justice;

intimidating a witness; and conduct unbecoming a judge. The ghosts of 1926 were astir again.

Mrs. McPherson professed to be unconcerned by this development. Mrs. Kennedy confirmed that the check given to Hardy had been a love offering, and in no sense a fee for legal services. The judge had already explained that, as a friend, he had helped both the temple leaders and various members of the church in regard to plans for branch churches, setting up the Crusaders, and so forth, but had never given legal advice. He estimated that between 1923 and 1926 he had spoken over the temple radio perhaps seventy-five times, for which there had been no question of receiving any remuneration.

It was just at this juncture that Aimee took the step of incorporating Angelus Temple as a church, in legal form—the Church of the Four-square Gospel. Up to this time, although the name was used loosely, it had been only a nondenominational religious association, without corporate identity.

At the same time, Sister announced her imminent departure for Europe, where she would undertake a speaking tour through the British Isles.

III

Last-minute legal complications threatened to prevent her sailing. She was defendant in several lawsuits, precursors of dozens that would dot her tempestuous career. The most troublesome action was the one being pressed by Mrs. Virla Kimball, twin sister of the "hoax woman," Mrs. Wiseman-Sielaff. Mrs. Kimball, who was married, had five children, and lived in Oakland, was claiming a million dollars' damages for defamation, charging that Mrs. McPherson had named her over the radio as the woman who stayed with Kenneth Ormiston at Carmel. Aimee's lawyers had been trying unsuccessfully to compromise the case, and it was only after Mrs. McPherson agreed to pay an undisclosed sum of money that it at last was dropped. That cleared one hurdle out of the way of Sister's departure.

Then there was the suit brought by a temple organist, who wanted two thousand dollars for breach of contract. The Tahoe Cedars settlements were hanging fire, and the architect who had drawn the plans for the master lighthouse was suing over his unpaid bill. Up to the last minute Aimee was busy, in and out of courtrooms and law offices,

The 1926 kidnaping episode continued to haunt Aimee. Here, two years later, she prepares to sign a settlement of a slander suit brought against her in that connection. At left, S. S. Hahn, the plaintiff's attorney; at right, Jerry Geisler, representing Aimee.

and when everything was finally disposed of, she had to sprint to catch the train.

"I'm glad it's all over with!" she exclaimed. "I hope now they will leave me alone for a while; I'm tired of the hullaballoo."

But the temple band and two hundred members were waiting to provide a singing send-off, and the train pulled out with Sister blowing kisses from the rear platform and promising to be "home by Thanksgiving." Rolf McPherson, her fifteen-year-old son, and Mr. and Mrs. Eade were traveling with her.

At New York the party boarded the *Aquitania* (they had missed the *Ile de France*) and Sister was corralled by reporters for the customary ship-news interview. They asked her about her stand in the coming presidential election, and she said that she would not be in the country on election day, but if she were, she would vote for Herbert Hoover. She thought Hoover might count on two hundred thousand votes among her following. She was not against Al Smith, she explained; she simply didn't know him. No, she said, she received no salary from her church, but did get the collection on the first Sunday of each month; she estimated that this averaged about ten thousand dollars a month. Asked to explain the secret of her ability to draw crowds into Angelus Temple year after year, she said with a self-assured smile:

"The people can't get anything at the theater that we haven't got."

And when asked what sort of people responded to her appeal, she defined her area of influence with discerning accuracy, saying:

"I bring religious consolation to the great middle class, leaving those below to the Salvation Army, and those above to themselves."

Debarking at Cherbourg, Sister and her party went on to Paris, where it was surmised that Parisian dressmakers were the attraction. Meanwhile, across the Channel in England, protests were being made against allowing her to land in the country, and the Home Secretary was besieged by demands to exclude her as an undesirable alien. The Reverend W. E. Pietsch, former Foursquare Gospel evangelist who had renounced McPhersonism as a result of the kidnaping episode, told a congregation in Hounslow that Aimee McPherson was a "twentieth-century Jezebel, as dangerous as a person who goes to a schoolhouse to sell poisoned candy. If she is coming to London to chase out the devil, let her pack her bag and go first!"

The Reverend R. J. Hall, a pastor in Swansea, Wales, feared audibly that "Mrs. McPherson's meetings might generate an orgy of religious emotionalism comparable to that of the devil dancers in pagan ritual; her credentials appear to be those of a type of booster who has turned religion into a business."

It all formed wonderful advance publicity, and while the Home Secretary was trying to make up his mind, Aimee slipped quietly into England. In her suite in the Hotel Cecil in London she was given a severe grilling by reporters, and impressed them by her poise, charm, and candor. She denied that she was a sensationalist, although she did use spectacular effects to fill Angelus Temple. With newsmen she toured London's night life and voted it less wild than that of Paris and other cities she had seen. In the theatrical district she tried the doors of locked churches and said they ought to be kept open; Angelus Temple was never closed.

The publicity she generated made her the most advertised woman in London when she first appeared in Albert Hall. Billed as "Everybody's Sister," she packed the huge auditorium, and many were turned away. The police were on hand in case of disorder, but they had noth-

Tourist Aimee. In London in 1928, she had her photograph taken at the Tower of London with a Yeoman of the Guard.

ing to do. Aimee was heckled during the service by "Bishop" Alma White, hard-featured founder of the Pillar of Fire Church, who shouted from a box, "Couldn't Mrs. McPherson explain her kidnaping incident on the Pacific Coast?" But the interruption was sung down by the crowd, while Aimee beamed goodwill at her persecutor.

On tour she had a mixed reception. Crowds turned out to see and hear her, though religious feeling sometimes seemed lacking. At Glasgow she was ragged by university students, who greeted her with deafening shouts in a hall decorated with beer bottles and signs reading, "Ladies May Smoke," and "Whiskey Is Good for the Complexion." In the front row co-eds smoked cigarettes ostentatiously. Aimee stood up to the rudeness gamely and, managing at length to make herself heard, asked the students to join in prayer. This calmed them, and she followed with a ten-minute talk, at the close of which she was cheered for her pluck. As her car rolled away, long streamers of toilet paper fluttered out from rolls fastened there by ribald students.

All the while, the news from home was not reassuring. The move to impeach Judge Hardy was going forward, and Asa Keyes was indicted for accepting bribes in connection with an oil-company scandal. The Los Angeles grand jury was said to be hunting a strongbox belonging to Mrs. McPherson, believed to contain documentary evidence of the payment of large sums of money—as much as eight hundred thousand dollars, one report had it—to secure the dismissal of the felony charges against her.

Aimee showed no alarm. The accusations against Keyes she belittled as "some political dodge, the sort of thing we get around election time. One party wants to get Keyes out and another wants to keep him in, and anybody in the middle is a football between them. Personally I believe the charges against him will go up in smoke. I have not been asked to testify in the case, and there is no reason why I should."

As for any payoff to quash her case:

"No payment was made at all. I was vindicated when the lying accusations against me were dropped, and I have no further concern in the matter."

She radiated the same jaunty confidence when she reached New York on the North German Lloyd liner *Columbus,* quipping:

"If I had had eight hundred thousand dollars, I would have kept it myself and not given it to anybody!"

She called her tour the most enthusiastic and satisfying of her life and thought English people much more emotional than Americans. The opposition she had encountered she dismissed as not amounting to much ("it only made people more anxious to hear me"), claimed thousands of converts, and reported a hundred Foursquare Gospel churches already established in England, with the number growing. At home, she said, "we have opened three hundred and forty churches in eleven months, which is nearly one church a day."

Before such sunny optimism the cloud in the West seemed paltry, and when Sister was greeted in Los Angeles by three thousand supporters waving blue-and-gold pompons, she told them she had never been so happy. She spoke for the newsreel cameras (the "talkies" had just come in), and then, true to her promise, preached a Thanksgiving Day service before a joyful throng at the temple.

But events were moving rapidly. Brother Arthur, the temple's bookkeeper, had already been called to testify before the legislative impeachment committee, and had identified the temple ledger in which the check to Judge Hardy was entered. The entry was made in a column headed "Legal and Defense," and the check itself had typed on it "Legal." Every other item in that column was a payment to a lawyer, a detective, a witness, or other person concerned in Sister's defense. Arthur was unable to account for the Hardy check being entered there also.

"Do you know the meaning of legal services?" asked one legislator.

"Yes," said Brother Arthur; "what you are doing now."

He remembered Mother Kennedy telling him:

" 'I want to give Judge Hardy a check. How much shall it be?' I ran over in my mind and recalled he had been with us four years. I decided about six hundred dollars a year was about right and told her twenty-four hundred dollars. She said, 'Make it two thousand five hundred.' "

Brother Arthur learned fast. The next day he asked to correct his testimony. He had inquired what "legal services" meant, he said, and had found out it meant "hiring a lawyer."

Amid laughter he admitted that the numerous temple funds (though he knew nothing about a "Fight the Devil" fund) sometimes got intermixed, because he was not a regular bookkeeper; he was a preacher really, though he had studied bookkeeping for three months.

"Did anyone instruct you to mix up the accounts so they can't be figured out?" an exasperated member of the committee asked him.

His reply was meek:

"No, sir."

"Then it was just natural?"

"Yes, sir."

When Mrs. McPherson was called to testify she arrived with Mae Waldron Emmil, her secretary, and the crowd in the hearing room craned to admire the evangelist's modish attire. She gave her version of the love offering to Hardy. She had wished to give him something, she said, because he had done so much for them—had spoken

over the temple radio and at youth meetings on Friday nights, had
given spiritual advice to members of the temple, had turned the first
spadeful of earth for the Bible School building, and in many ways
had used his time, automobile, and gasoline for the benefit of the
temple. There had been no thought of remunerating him for legal
services, she was quite sure; however, her mother had dealt more
often with the judge, and she had the records, so she was the one who
could better explain what services in a business and legal way, if any,
Judge Hardy had performed.

"When the matter of the check came up," Aimee was asked, "did
Mrs. Kennedy say he wasn't worth that much, that he had used the
radio for political purposes, but you insisted on paying him the
amount?"

"No," was the scandalized response. "That's absurd! She couldn't
have said that, because it isn't true!"

It was a mistake, she said, for Brother Arthur to enter the check

As an uncooperative witness in the Judge Hardy impeachment hearings,
Aimee's strong profile expresses her total impenetrability in January, 1929.

under "Legal and Defense," but that was a detail of no importance. Some members of the committee thought it was highly important.

Judge Hardy's testimony was to the effect that he had remarked casually that he was planning a vacation trip, and Mrs. Kennedy had urged him to visit Alaska. He quoted Mother as saying:

" 'Take this check and go.'

" 'I make no charge for what I have done for the temple,' " he said he had replied, and Mother had answered:

" 'Well, you have earned it. Our members want you to have it and so do we. It hasn't been convenient to give you anything before, but we are in funds now.' "

The judge denied that he had done anything unethical or improper in connection with the kidnaping investigation, and contended that his motive throughout had been one of simple friendship mixed with a certain amount of self-interest. When scandal and innuendo began to swirl around the temple, he explained, he feared that if it went down, he would go down with it, because he had become so closely identified with it.

A resonant "Amen!" from the spectators greeted this admission.

The hearing dragged on, the temple witnesses providing little pertinent information, and Aimee headed north to Vancouver to conduct services there. While passing through Seattle (where she did *not* call on her mother) she told reporters that she realized she was only a pawn in a political feud.

"It's all politics," she said with a gesture of resignation. "They want to get Judge Hardy out, and so they are using the check to try to oust him and I'm the political pawn. But I'm used to it. That seems to be one of my chief roles, being a pawn."

Would she return to California to testify again if called, she was asked. Her manner changed, and she replied with a rush of feeling:

"I'd go to India if it would help Judge Hardy clear his name. He is a dear, fine, sincere man, and I'd be as much surprised and disillusioned if Judge Hardy went wrong as if God went wrong. You know, I realize what it is to be falsely accused, because I have gone through all of that. If we had had a real auditor at the time the check was written, this would not have happened. But we had a Methodist minister doing some of our bookkeeping. I asked him why he wrote 'Legal' on the check, and he said, 'Oh, I saw it was to a judge and thought of course it would be classified as legal.' "

Mrs. McPherson with Brother Arthur, Temple bookkeeper, explaining his weird system of ledger-keeping by the fact that he was "only a preacher," and ignorant of business.

This indirect slur on her business methods brought Minnie Kennedy into the fray belligerently. She had been refusing to answer the door or the telephone, although denying that she was hiding.

"I hope to die before I run away!" she had shouted from inside her hotel room.

Her daughter's innuendo, however, brought forth a bristling statement, addressed to the world in general.

"I ran all the business of the temple in good shape and in an unquestionable manner," she said defiantly. "Dear little Aimee would do better if she did not talk so much, or if she would first consult her mother. My memory seems to retain the details of all our affairs. The facts are—and nobody knows it better than Aimee herself—that she and Ralph Jordan demanded that I deliver the check to District Attorney Keyes shortly before the charges against her were dismissed. I felt that her action was a definite betrayal of the confidential nature of the check, and I protested against its being given, but was overruled by my daughter and Jordan."

A newspaper reporter already had testified that Mrs. Kennedy had told him that when Ralph Jordan came into her room and demanded the check, she had defied him with, "Look here, big boy, who do you think you are talking to?" But Jordan had "stormed around," and said he had to have the check, although she and Aimee had agreed that its existence should be kept a "sacred secret" between them, until finally she handed it over, but only after making a photographic copy.

Her daughter's idea that she was a "football between two political factions" aroused Minnie's scorn.

"They don't know she exists until something of this kind brings her to their attention," she scoffed. "When the check to Judge Hardy was made out under the heading of 'Legal Expenditure' it was not accidental. The check was made out under the correct heading, just as I ordered it. I do not do business in such a slipshod manner that I could make a mistake in this matter. We were two little strange women when we opened the fine, big Angelus Temple, now owned by Aimee alone. Judge Hardy came to us and we became very close friends. It's sometimes hard to tell where friendship and private counsel leave off and legal advice begins."

The assembly voted impeachment of the "gray-haired patriarch of the bench," as the press was styling Hardy, and the state senate summoned him to trial. It was the first judicial impeachment in California since 1862, when another judge, also named Hardy, was impeached for proposing a toast to Jeff Davis.

Aimee received word of the legislature's action on her return from Vancouver. She expressed shock that "any body of men could make such a decision."

"The whole business is much ado about nothing," she said with a trace of acerbity. "Judge Hardy never gave me any legal advice. He is my dear friend and admired counselor. It would seem that both of us are the objects of considerable criticism."

Mother Kennedy had more to say and said it, in a flowery telegram to the judge reading in slight part:

"Esteemed Friend:—On the eve of impeachment proceedings instituted against you because of Aimee's betraying love offering to Asa Keyes, I cannot let the occasion pass without sending a personal message of assurance, sympathy, and prayer. With your experience I know it is unnecessary to warn you against the pretended friendship which poses in Parisian gowns and tells the press 'the judge is such a lovable soul.' . . .

"Had I known that morning when I phoned you information that Aimee and Jordan had ordered the check given to the district attorney, what it would mean, I would have made a bonfire with it rather than cause sorrow and shadow to those who stood by me when my daughter left me without explanation. But as you seemed willing then, I thought it proper. . . .

"Am waiting and praying and will shout 'great jubilee' when the good word goes forth, 'Judge exonerated,' as you surely will be. Meanwhile tell Aimee to keep quiet or back her talk by paying all your legal bills. Your loyal friend, MOTHER KENNEDY."

The whole 1926 entanglement seemed to have been revived. Just before Hardy's impeachment, Asa Keyes had been tried and convicted of bribery in an oil-swindle case, and had been sentenced to a long term in prison: and there was much comment on the irony of events that were bringing him down to disgrace.

It had been the inextinguishable public suspicion of justice having been corrupted in the McPherson case that had caused the grand jury to look into Keyes's conduct in office. And though the grand jury subsequently absolved him of the least taint of misconduct in the temple leader's prosecution, its investigation of the matter had brought to light corruption elsewhere.

Also, in the legislative debate on the impeachment, hot words had been spoken against Judge Hardy, but hotter words against "the woman at the bottom of this mess. Her filthy money got him into this trouble." One assemblyman called on the legislature to show "no sympathy with money-grafting hypocrites who operate in the name of religion," and another stated bluntly that the trial of Judge Hardy would be, in effect, the trial of Aimee Semple McPherson.

"Ninety-five percent of the people of Los Angeles believed this woman perpetrated a gigantic hoax," exclaimed this legislator, "and yet we find a judge of the Superior Court acting as her chief counsel, assisting her in her trouble with the law. . . . There is testimony to show that no step was taken by Mrs. McPherson's lawyers without consulting Judge Hardy, that detectives were [sent to] Carmel to suppress evidence, and that Judge Hardy [sought] to intimidate a witness."

Letters favoring the impeachment flooded into Sacramento, with a few that charged the Angelus Temple leader was being traduced and persecuted.

Two assemblymen, acting under a special authorization, went to Oregon to obtain Mrs. Kennedy's deposition, and spent two days questioning her without eliciting any useful information. Minnie admitted that the Hardy check was not entirely a love offering, and was paid out of the legal fund that was set up after Sister's reappearance. She said that Judge Hardy "was the only person we could go to for advice, particularly after trouble arose with the grand jury and the prosecuting attorney." Her lawyers, she recalled, had simply gone into court and got her into more trouble as fast as they could, so she had to turn to Hardy for advice. But she was evasive about just what that "advice" consisted of.

At one point she broke down and sobbed hysterically when asked whether she could remember the date of her daughter's vanishing.

"Just like asking you if you remembered the day your mother died!" she wept.

She never used the word "kidnaping"; it was always her daughter's "disappearance" or "absence." And at the close she knelt with the two examiners and prayed that truth might prevail.

The impeachment trial did unroll as a virtual rerun of the McPherson hearing. The same witnesses were examined again, and some were more forthright than they had been before. Wallace Moore, the young Santa Barbara newspaperman who believed he had identified Aimee and Ormiston in Ormiston's car on the day after the mysterious couple vacated the Carmel bungalow, at the preliminary hearing had declined to make the identification positive, giving every appearance of a terrified witness; now he told of Judge Hardy's frightening him with a lecture on the peril he would expose himself to if his identification should prove false. Then he was asked, while the senators hung on his words:

"Can you identify the woman in the car as Mrs. McPherson?"

"Yes, sir, I think she was," boomed the answer through the loudspeaker.

A deep hush fell over the chamber. The crucial identification had come three years too late.

Aimee was in a nearby hotel, waiting to testify, although the impeachment managers expressed doubt that she would assist the prosecution. Terming her an "unwilling and evasive witness," they said she would "only state facts already proved, and then only after an examination in the nature of a cross-examination."

The gravity of her own situation was indirectly confessed by Aimee herself, by the act of voluntarily reopening the kidnaping episode before her people. During the course of a sermon in the Pasadena branch church, she told of the welter of false clues that poured into the temple during that episode, and of the distraction there:

"It was hard to tell which way we should turn so that I could get the vindication I know I am due. I had one report that [the woman at Carmel] was a Denver girl, and then again I heard she was a Pasadena woman. Someone said the woman was forty years of age. Others said she was twenty-five. It was no wonder that the investigation failed to clear up the situation. My story is as true today as the day I told it," she wound up ringingly. "I was kidnaped as I stated, and these futile attempts to prove otherwise are nothing short of malicious persecution."

When finally, after Judge Hardy had testified in his defense for several hours, most of the time with eyes closed wearily, and after he had been asked bluntly, "Did you believe Mrs. McPherson had been kidnaped?" and had replied, "There was no evidence to the contrary"—though later he alluded to the "alleged kidnaping"; after the "hoax woman" had changed her story once more, and Ormiston had appeared and had said virtually nothing; and after newspapermen, and detectives, and lawyers, and temple officials had testified; and after Mother Kennedy's deposition had been droned through, all two hundred and sixty-eight pages of it, requiring seven hours to read and proving so rambling it put several senators to sleep—when, finally, after all the sensations had been exhausted, Aimee herself took the stand.

A ripple of laughter spread through the room at her response to the clerk's courteous inquiry as to whether she was accustomed to speaking through a microphone, and understood its use.

"Yes, a little," she murmured.

But that was her only admission. From then on her replies were along the lines of "I don't remember discussing that," or "I don't recall." She seemed at ease on the stand, and her attire had the women spectators envious.

The summations were made, and Judge Hardy, in an emotional appeal, pleaded frankly for a merciful judgment. He reviewed his forty-odd years as a lawyer, spoke of advancing age, and beseeched the senators to send him back to his wife, children, and grandchildren without the loss of office or good name. The plea had an effect, and when the vote was taken he was acquitted on all counts, although on some of them by a narrow margin. Off the record, several senators said they had voted to acquit because the impeachment process had been outmoded by passage of the law permitting the recall of judges by popular referendum.

Hardy returned to Los Angeles and issued a statement saying that he had aided Mrs. McPherson "and the church which I attended as any man would aid his church, his lodge, or his benevolent society, whether he be lawyer, judge, bricklayer, banker, editor, carpenter, or laborer. I feel that the hue and cry was all brought up as a gesture against the lady whose name was particularly mentioned at my trial."

Thus the impeachment settled nothing, and cost the taxpayers fifty thousand dollars. The bill for printing the 1,378-page transcript of the proceedings alone came to twenty-five thousand dollars.

The cost to Judge Hardy, however, was heavy. One year later, in an appeal to what Asa Keyes had called "the only court of Aimee Semple McPherson's jurisdiction, namely, the court of public opinion," Judge Carlos S. Hardy was decisively denied reelection by the voters of Los Angeles County. He retired to private law practice and remained active until his death at eighty-one, outliving both the women he had devotedly if indiscreetly served.

Aimee returned from Sacramento and called her stay there a vacation. To the applauding congregation at Angelus Temple she said briskly:

"I am back and ready to carry on my work. I have gone through fire ever since I started this work and I suppose there is much more in store for me."

The public, at long last, seemed to be tired of the "Aimee case." Keyes's successor as district attorney, Buron Fitts, pointed out that

Home from the Judge Hardy impeachment trial, Sister Aimee waves to followers and says that since the California Legislature had been unable to disprove her kidnaping story, so "they might as well have stopped bothering me long ago."

under the statute of limitations the charges against the evangelist would be outlawed in four months, and he had no intention of trying to reopen the prosecution. Aimee was satisfied. Said she:

"Three years in the limelight is enough for me. My story is as true today as it was on the day I told it, and since even the legislature couldn't shake it, they might as well have stopped bothering me long ago."

But stepping out of the limelight was less easy. Barely had the Hardy agitation subsided when the city was startled by Mrs. McPherson's announcement that she and her mother were reconciled, and that Minnie Kennedy was back at Angelus Temple. Radiating happiness, Aimee said:

"Mother and I are again in accord, and I am sure there will be no more so-called breaks between us."

Did this mean that Mother Kennedy would resume the management of the temple's business affairs? Mrs. McPherson preferred not to say.

"We want to be let alone and allowed to go ahead and enjoy each other," was her dulcet response. "Our troubles, both private and legal, now are at an end and we are happy."

But there were those at Angelus Temple who were not happy at all.

Rebellion, and a Broken Nose

꧁

"Why should calamity be full of words?"
—Richard III

The first intimation that harmony between mother and daughter had been restored had transpired during the Hardy impeachment turmoil. On the day Judge Hardy's trial opened, the Los Angeles newspapers had carried streamer headlines proclaiming the fresh difficulty besetting Minnie Kennedy in distant Seattle. There, on that day, the "Evangel of the Everlasting Gospel" was sued for breach of promise to marry, the plaintiff being an unattached, middle-aged, mild-mannered, melancholy, and, it turned out, impecunious preacher named the Reverend H. H. Clark. He wanted fifty thousand dollars to assuage the grief, shock, and disappointment produced by the asserted shattering of his asserted dream of love.

(The headlines proliferated "pastors" on that day—the pastor of Angelus Temple, the suing pastor in Seattle, and pastoral Minnie in Oregon.)

The Reverend Mr. Clark had no reluctance to tell his story to the press, averring and avouching, as the lawyers say, that Mrs. Kennedy had enticed him into moral lapses under a promise that they would be married. He said that Mrs. Kennedy, a spendthrift in promises, had undertaken to procure a tabernacle for him to preach in and also provide him with a "Gospel ship" to spread the Word along the coast to Alaska. None of these promises had been honored at the bank of performance, he sighed.

His complaint recounted alleged trysts at luncheon, tea, dinner, and the movies. It related that just before the previous Christmas, Mrs. Kennedy had rented a suite of rooms in a Seattle hotel and there had induced the plaintiff to visit her, not once but several times, and at her solicitation to make "violent and passionate love to the defendant," despite his remonstrances. To him the defendant had been known as "Mrs. Mary E. Clark," and he had learned her identity only when he saw her photograph in a newspaper. Subsequently, he charged, Mrs. Kennedy had told him that marriage was not in her plans, and consequently he was "brokenhearted, humiliated, disturbed in peace of mind, prevented from carrying on his religious work, shamed, dishonored, and broken in health."

This formidable bill of particulars was flashed upon the public while Aimee was in Sacramento, waiting to testify. Upon reading the headlines she was said to have laughed.

"Now who is calling the pot black?" she was reported to have crowed.

And immediately she telegraphed her mother assurances of sympathy and six dozen roses.

Mother, in Portland, was overjoyed by these tokens of restored confidence and affection, and the wires hummed with reciprocal messages of love and understanding between the two women.

Minnie was in no mood to put up with the nonsense coming from Seattle.

"Why, this man Clark must be crazy to do such a thing!" she fumed. "It's too funny—trying to make me out a love pirate! The last time I saw him in Seattle I gave him twenty dollars, just trying to help a down-and-out. He came to me and claimed to have attended our meetings in Denver and elsewhere, and wanted me to set him up as a psychologist. I offered to introduce my friends, to give him a trial, but he always refused. I've known this court action was coming. Why, he has written to me, to Aimee, and my friends, and his lawyer phoned to my lawyer as late as yesterday demanding a compromise."

Far from compromising, Minnie intended to fight the suit to a finish; this wouldn't be like former times at Angelus Temple, she said:

"Then we often paid petty tribute. But I have decided the right thing is to face the suit and show how ridiculous the charges are."

Fishing under the bed, she dragged out a cardboard box from which she extracted letters said to have been written by her accuser.

(In every hotel room Minnie was ever interviewed in, she seemed to have a similar box under the bed, stuffed with her "records.") One of the letters read:

"If you or your daughter are willing to loan me a few hundred dollars I am willing to fade out of the picture. I am willing to sign any kind of paper or agreement that you may have drawn up. . . . If I don't hear from you in the next few days, there remains but two courses, both drastic, and one of them means my death."

Aimee and Minnie's own secretary had received similar letters, Minnie stated. Then with a spunky, "This is a case of biting the hand that feeds it," she telephoned her lawyer and went for a horseback canter.

If the jilted Clark really had entertained suicidal notions, he had resisted them successfully, for reporters found him in health, but definitely downcast. Punctuating his revelations with doleful sighs, he told them his story. He had first encountered the mother of Aimee Semple McPherson, he said, in a second-run, downtown movie-house in Seattle.

"I was sitting there alone when Mrs. Kennedy came in." He sighed. "After looking around, she sat down right beside me. She began to lean over against me almost immediately, and kept on doing it even after I moved away as far as I could without actually leaving my seat. Soon she spoke to me. I thought I'd set her right, so I told her I was a minister and a public speaker. She told me, 'I knew you were. I'm a minister, too.' I didn't suspect anything wrong, and we chatted."

Later, he said, Minnie had asked him to dinner, and during the next several weeks they had taken in numerous movie shows together.

Reporters established that a "Mrs. Mary E. Klark" had been registered at hotels mentioned by the complainant in the case, on some of the days when he contended that he had been romantically led astray.

On her side, Minnie let her lawyer do the further talking, promising through him there would be no settlement, that the charges were "so scurrilous there must be a complete showdown." It was admitted that she had used the name "Mrs. Mary E. Klark" (Clark was the maiden name of Minnie's mother), but only because she had been "long prominent in the public eye, so much so that she is at all times importuned by all sorts of cranks, beggars, and others seeking her acquaintance." The suit was denounced as "a preconceived plan of blackmail and extortion."

When the action came to trial in Seattle on the last day of September, 1929, the courtroom was jam-packed. Clark was his own witness. He had been born on a farm in Michigan in 1875, he began, and wept as he pointed out that he was younger than the defendant. His tears continued to flow for the better part of a week. During the noon recesses, reporters would come upon him standing in the corridor, weeping like a male Niobe.

He testified that after the occurrences described in his complaint, he had felt "as if a moral hit-run driver had struck me down and sped away in the darkness. I called and called, but there was no answer."

Cross-examination brought on more sighs and fidgeting. He confessed that he had once been arrested as a Peeping Tom. He admitted writing the "fade out of the picture" letter. He admitted that Minnie had threatened to have him arrested for blackmail, and said he had to look the word up in the dictionary to find out what it meant. His hotel-room enticement he recounted step by panting step, insisting that Mrs. Kennedy had made all the advances, against resistance on his part.

"Did you make any outcry?" asked counsel.

"No. My resistance was so broken down I couldn't."

"What? You made no outcry?"

"No, sir."

The witness sighed lugubriously.

"And you went through this performance three or four times?"

"Four times all together. I consented after her promise that we would be married in the very near future."

Repeatedly the judge gaveled warnings that the spectators must restrain their laughter. Sitting a few feet from her dismal accuser, Minnie regarded him with an icy eye. In the rear of the courtroom reporters spotted Mae Waldron, Aimee's personal secretary, taking notes assiduously.

Clark was asked whether he had ever told Mrs. Kennedy that he loved her.

"Many and many a time."

He sighed.

"When did you first tell her?"

The witness gave the question doleful consideration.

"Well, it was a gradual affair. It is difficult to say just when one crosses the line." He sighed. "But I recall that my emotions were less easily aroused than hers, and she chided me about it."

"What!" exclaimed counsel. "You traveled from being utter strangers to the intimate relationship to which you have testified in seven days, and she said you were slow!"

"She did," was the sorrowful response, and again the judge warned against disruptive laughter.

Against the grain, Clark was forced to confess that since his so-called jilting he had become friendly with two Seattle women, from one of whom he had borrowed two hundred dollars and to the other of whom he had intimated that financial assistance would be appreciated.

During this questioning, a woman entered the courtroom and took a seat beside Mrs. Kennedy, whereupon the witness appealed in great agitation to the judge:

"Your honor, I want to call your attention to that woman sitting there!"

"Who is she?" asked the bench.

"She is the woman mentioned in testimony."

"The one you borrowed two hundred dollars from?"

"Yes, sir. She's"—his voice broke—"she's smiling at me!"

"Well, there isn't to be any smiling," the judge ruled fiercely, stroking his white goatee. "I'm not finding that she did smile—I'm just telling her not to. Every witness in this courtroom is going to be protected."

After hearing arguments on points of law, the judge took the case out of the hands of the jury and declared a nonsuit, finding that Clark (whom the bench described as "a creature of emotion and impulses and very poor judgment"), when he volunteered to "fade out of the picture," had indicated his acquiescence in Mrs. Kennedy's refusal to bestow a wedding ring.

"At least," the judge concluded significantly, "that is the court's interpretation. Otherwise it would be evidence of blackmail."

Minnie accepted her vindication grandly, bowing like a prima donna to admirers who crowded to congratulate her and even to kiss her hand.

The long strain had told on her, however, and she went to bed for a few days. Then she reappeared, fully restored, and declaring that her victory was a victory for women everywhere.

The rueful Clark unwisely appealed, and two years later the state supreme court rendered final judgment, rejecting the appeal. The learned judges advised the appellant that he should count himself lucky—that, in fact, he had reason to rejoice rather than despond in the failure of Mrs. Kennedy to ally herself matrimonially with him.

"It would seem," read the curtain speech of the farce, "that so happy an escape should not be converted into a cause of action."

II

During an interval in Minnie's legal troubles, a reporter had accidentally encountered her and her daughter emerging from a bank in downtown Los Angeles arm in arm. At sight of the newsman, Mrs. McPherson had jumped into her waiting automobile and sped away, but Mrs. Kennedy was cornered. After some initial coyness, she consented to be interviewed.

The reporter had not seen her for nearly two years, and he was struck by the change in her appearance. She looked years younger, was dressed smartly, and was cheerful and apparently at peace with the world.

The business that had brought her to Los Angeles, she said, wouldn't interest the public.

"There were some legal papers to be signed before my connection with Angelus Temple was completely severed, and that was what we did today."

She denied that she was returning to Los Angeles to live; but the next day workers at Angelus Temple whispered that Sister and her mother were fixing up the five-room flat on Lemoyne Street that Minnie had taken upon moving out of the parsonage but had seldom occupied since. In spite of expectations, however, Mrs. Kennedy soon returned to the Northwest and her evangelistic work there.

What she had glimpsed of the temple's disarray during her short visit did not reassure her. Aimee, she was convinced, was in deep trouble; and shortly after that the trouble came to a head in the most serious rebellion that had yet shaken Angelus Temple.

The leader of this revolt was the man whom Sister, in August, 1927, had appointed general field secretary of the lighthouse movement, the Reverend John D. Goben. Devoted to the glamorous evangelist, whom he believed to have been the target of malicious persecution in 1926, Goben had gradually become disillusioned. He was a member of the temple's "control board," and carried the additional title of assistant pastor of Angelus Temple.

From this vantage point, he saw much about the inner workings of the temple administration that was not visible from the outside, and he became convinced that Mrs. McPherson was as much the victim as she was the exploiter of her sharply divided nature. As preacher and evangelist, Goben found her without a peer and giving every appearance of sincerity; but as a woman, and in her private life, he judged her deceitful and greedy for money and worldly pleasure.

An instance that had brought him to this conclusion had been Sister's plea to her followers to make up the twenty-five-thousand-dollar deficit in the church's finances, supposedly incurred and left behind by Mrs. Kennedy when she quit the management. Goben was present when Sister made her appeal from the temple platform and over the radio for funds to pay these notes; and he was shocked by the explanation that Sister gave her followers.

Just previously, Aimee had called her church board together and told them about the notes, saying they had been given to secure a loan from Ralph Jordan that had been needed to tide things over after her mother had left. She said the notes were due. Jordan and his wife had appeared and confirmed the loan, stating that they had mortgaged their home to raise the cash. On the basis of these representations, the board had sanctioned an appeal to the membership for a special contribution.

Armed with that sanction, Sister had gone before her congregation and without making mention of Ralph Jordan or any loan implied that the notes had been left by her mother and had just been found.

This had seemed odd, but about that time Goben's faith in Mrs. McPherson had received a worse jolt by his discovery that at the time the appeal for an extra twenty-five thousand dollars was made to the church membership, Sister and Jordan were maintaining a secret account in a bank far from Angelus Temple, in which large deposits had been made and from which large sums had been with-drawn without the knowledge of the church board. This joint account had been at the 39th Street and Western Avenue branch of the Security-First National Bank in the names "Elizabeth and Edith Johnson." Subsequent investigation would indicate that deposits of roughly one hundred thousand dollars had been made, against which checks for sixteen thousand, fourteen thousand, eight thousand, and similar sums had been cashed. The account, opened in August, 1927, had been closed out in April, 1928.

These were about the dates between which Ralph Jordan had been acting as business manager of Angelus Temple.

Many other things occurred that disturbed Goben. For instance, the way Sister McPherson exaggerated over the radio. He had been present more than once when she told the radio audience that in response to her altar call, penitents were streaming down the aisles from the lower floor, from the balcony, when in fact none whatever were coming from the balcony, and only a handful from the floor. Sister would count the number responding—twenty, twenty-five, thirty—when there were only five or six. A visiting evangelist who was seated beside a temple Bible School student, known to be such by the visitor, was startled when, at Sister's invitation for all who wanted to "give their hearts to Jesus" to raise their hands, the student raised his and immediately was shepherded to the altar by an officious usher, where he knelt and was prayed over fervently by Aimee. The student later explained that his action was taught in the Bible School by Sister, that she called it good psychology, because it encouraged the timid.

But the way the money was mishandled troubled Goben most of all as he came to understand how the system worked. Outwardly everything was open and aboveboard. During Sister's "vindication tour," Goben had heard her tell audiences that she was raising three hundred thousand dollars to pay off the debt on the Bible School building, and collections had been taken for that purpose. Later he learned that there was not a penny of debt on the building when she made her appeal.

The bouquet of American Beauty roses that she customarily carried into the pulpit she would describe as provided by "kind friends," she did not know their names; yet Goben himself had once been sent out to buy flowers costing ten dollars, which Sister had carried onto the platform and there expressed gratitude to the "unknown dear friend" who had sent them.

After the uproar caused by Aimee's bobbed hair, Goben found out, the evangelist had worn a wig in the pulpit to fool her followers.

These were petty deceits and might be overlooked, but Goben found deception practiced in large matters, too. He recalled statements that Minnie Kennedy had made to the effect that even as a little girl, Aimee had been unable to tell a thing the way it happened; she must dress it up to accord with her imagination. She would not deliberately falsify, Minnie explained, but would stretch and alter the truth to what it pleased her to believe and to have believed by others. This weakness Goben began to see manifested in almost everything Sister said or did, with "seeming sincerity of purpose"; without her gift of convincing sincerity, he believed, Aimee would "never have risen above an actress." What profoundly disturbed him was that her cumulative deceptions, large and small, all seemed prompted by a single motive—greed for money.

Nor was he the only one who was upset. Complaints came to him from the pastors of churches in the field. The International Four-square Gospel Lighthouses had been incorporated as a religious association separate from Angelus Temple on December 30, 1927. There were seven incorporators, Sister McPherson, Goben, Mae Waldron, Harriet Jordan (dean of the Bible School), and three branch pastors.

The articles of incorporation and bylaws provided that the property of each participating church should be vested in a board of trustees to be chosen by the congregation and that through delegates sent to a general convention all the churches should participate in the affairs of the association. Any change in the form of incorporation or bylaws, it was provided, must be submitted to the individual churches in time for discussion and instruction of delegates to the next convention, which would pass on the proposals. If these were approved, they would still require the signatures of the original incorporators before they could become effective.

Sister McPherson had been named perpetual president of the lighthouses; the other officers were elected. Goben, chosen treasurer, had charge of the association's funds, and he banked them in a separate account against which only he was entitled to draw checks.

Goben felt that he had been mainly responsible for the dramatically rapid spread of the lighthouse movement. As the "salesman" in the field, he not only organized new congregations but induced many unaffiliated groups to come into the association. At the end of eighteen months he had recruited some three hundred units all over the country. The tithing (one-tenth of income) contributions from these independent churches made a sizable income. The churches all had enlisted under the McPherson banner on Goben's assurance that each would retain right and title to its own property and have a voice in the overall lighthouse management.

In July of 1928, Ralph Jordan, acting as temple business manager, informed Goben that a change would have to be made in the lighthouse setup, giving Sister firmer control. Goben had demurred, and shortly after this Jordan had left the temple. Sister then retained Cromwell Ormsby as her legal counsel, and he installed a friend, Frank J. Timpson, as temple auditor.

Ormsby drew up amended articles of incorporation for the lighthouse movement, giving Sister title to all properties of the separate churches as well as absolute control of appointments and funds. When the revision was read to the original incorporators, they failed to approve it. Despite this, Ormsby announced that the revision had been filed with the secretary of state at Sacramento and had been accepted, making it legally binding. Goben knew that this was impossible without the signatures of the first incorporators, which had not been given; the original rules of the association therefore continued in force. He determined to protect the interests of those whom he had brought into the movement.

Meanwhile, Timpson, by his arbitrary methods, was arousing resentment among the members and offending the temple staff. He issued such orders as forbidding the workers to close their letters with "God bless you," or some similar phrase, as they had always done and as they thought befit a religious organization.

Alarm also was aroused by the way in which Ormsby seemed to dominate Sister, leading her not only into risky business ventures but into risky personal associations. One venture that Ormsby "sold" to Aimee was a pilgrimage to the Holy Land at the head of her followers. The project was launched on a grand scale, Aimee charter-

Go with me to The Holy Land

AIMEE SEMPLE McPHERSON
MEDITERRANEAN CRUISE
·· AND PILGRIMAGE ··
EASTER in the HOLY LAND
S.S. Republic · March 20th to May 11th 1930
TRANSPORTATION AGENTS
UNITED STATES LINES and THOS. COOK & SON

Another promotion scheme—a personally led hegira of hundreds of her followers to the Holy Land. It flopped.

ing a whole Atlantic liner, the *Republic*, for the pilgrims' exclusive use. A talking-picture record of the trip was to be made and exploited later. Sister was to rebaptize the pilgrims in the River Jordan, and hold services at the tomb of Christ and other sacred shrines. Keen for the project herself, she aroused Goben's enthusiasm for it so successfully that he undertook to sell tickets among the lighthouse membership at six hundred to one thousand dollars apiece.

In July, 1929, Aimee conducted a revival in Detroit and caused dissatisfaction when a deficit of nine hundred dollars was left for the local church to pay. She also left behind a thirty-five-dollar beauty-shop bill, and an unpaid hotel tab for pitchers of orange juice sent to her room at a dollar and eighty cents apiece.

Goben saw no reason for a deficit. He had counted the last evening's love offering, and knew it came to about thirty-five hundred dollars. Yet Sister had told the crowd that it amounted to between a thousand and twelve hundred dollars and had thanked them graciously for it. The story got into the newspapers, with unfavorable comment, and Sister wired from her train to the Detroit pastor:

"PLEASE CORRECT IMMEDIATELY FALSE BEAUTY SHOP AND HOTEL STORY RUNNING IN HEADLINES. WIRED $500 TO COVER SAME. RIDICULOUS FOR THE CHURCH TO SAY THEY PAID THE BILL. SUCH NONSENSE. GOD BLESS YOU ALL."

But by then seven lighthouses in the Detroit area were announcing their withdrawal from the movement, and others were said to be tottering.

On his own return to Los Angeles, Goben found that Timpson had appropriated the lighthouse books, installed a new bookkeeping system, and had had the bank account shifted to his own name on the authority, the bank was told, of Mrs. McPherson. All this without consultation. Goben, outraged, consulted with other dissatisfied churchmen.

One of Ormsby's moves had been to get rid of Mae Waldron, and both she and Goben made a desperate attempt to alert Sister to dismiss Ormsby and avoid an impending storm. They said that Aimee rebuffed them haughtily. A delegation of ministers then met in Goben's office and declared that they would not stand for Ormsby's running the temple and the branches any longer; and soon a dozen churches were out, or on their way out, of the organization. In order to obtain irrefutable evidence, detectives were hired who shadowed Sister and Ormsby for several days. Affidavits of their findings, describing clandestine midnight visits paid by Mrs. McPherson to Ormsby's darkened bungalow, were sworn to, and with this and other evidence in hand Goben prepared for a showdown.

But one of the ministers had privately warned Aimee of the trouble brewing, and at 6 A.M. on October 2, 1929, the telephone rang in Goben's room. Sister was losing no time. Peremptorily she commanded Goben to come to her home "right away."

He arrived at half-past eight, and, according to his later account, he no sooner appeared than Sister "lit into" him in a fiery manner.

"Dr. Goben," he represented the evangelist as saying, "I understand that there is going to be a private meeting of the ministers today to question my character."

Goben replied that no meeting had yet been called; whereupon she herself called a meeting at ten o'clock that morning, in the lecture room of the Pasadena Foursquare Gospel Lighthouse. The ministers obeyed her summons.

Imperiously taking charge, Sister ordered all the people who were faithful to her to come down together in one corner; let the others stay where they were. Then she demanded that anybody who had said anything against her stand up and repeat what they had said. Nobody moved. The pastors who had come to Goben with their complaints about Sister's "double life" were silent, even when challenged by the wife of Goben's secretary to repeat what they had told her. When none replied, this woman then told Mrs. McPherson herself what she had been told, about Sister's "dual life," about how Cromwell Ormsby's chauffeur had come into her bedroom drunk and had pulled her out of bed and danced around the room with her, and similar things.

The hubbub that arose at this became so great that Aimee hurriedly adjourned the meeting until that night, after the evening service. They would assemble again in the roof garden of the Bible School building.

When this meeting came together, Sister had around her four stalwart supporters, although at the morning meeting she had been alone. The four defenders were Emma Schaffer, Brother Arthur, Harriet Jordan, and a Mrs. Oliver, a member of the *Bridal Call* staff.

After prayer, Aimee called the meeting to order and demanded that anyone who had made derogatory statements about her at the morning session prove them. One of the dissenters asked Emma Schaffer about certain damaging remarks that she had made, and then Mrs. Oliver was challenged to repeat what she had told some of those present. Neither responded. Sister then turned to Goben and asked him whether he had anything to offer. Goben started to read the incriminating reports of the detectives, describing Sister's apparent intimacy with Ormsby, but he had not gone far when Sister fainted.

Up sprang Harriet Jordan, wringing her hands and crying, "You are killing Sister!" There was a rush to Aimee's side, and the meeting was thrown into disorder. Goben felt a reaction of hostility toward him and sensed that it would be useless to continue. As soon as Mrs. McPherson recovered sufficiently, he announced his resignation. But the group for whom he had been spokesman protested against his leaving them and he agreed to meet with everybody in the morning and try to straighten out the affairs of the lighthouse organization in a way satisfactory to both sides. Aimee indicated that she would go along with this.

What happened at the "settlement meeting" on Thursday, October 3, soon became temple gossip and was vividly related by Goben. The participating ministers and church officials met at the temple as agreed. Aimee came in during the obligatory opening prayer, but before the discussion could really get going the telephone rang and she stepped outside to answer it. When she came back, she was all smiles.

"I am very, very happy to announce that Mr. Ormsby has received information from the secretary of state at Sacramento that the revised articles of incorporation of the Foursquare Gospel Lighthouses, over which there has been so much unsatisfactory argument and discussion, have finally been accepted," she beamed. "Now all we have to do is to make a few changes in the bylaws."

Goben knew that this statement could not be true; by law, the revised papers must be signed by all the original incorporaters to be acceptable, and they had not been so signed. He protested but was overruled, and discussion turned to technical changes in the bylaws.

At the luncheon recess, Goben telephoned to the office of the secretary of state and was informed that the articles had *not* been accepted and would not be accepted until signed. At Goben's request, the secretary of state confirmed this by telegraph, and when the meeting reconvened Goben announced that he had a telegram that he wished to read to everybody.

Couldn't he discuss it with her in private first, asked Aimee. Goben replied that it concerned everybody and then read the telegram from the secretary of state aloud.

Sister dashed to the telephone and called Ormsby. Goben, listening close by, overheard her say that "this man Goben has got in touch with the secretary of state and has a telegram from him, and that the scheme hadn't worked, it had been knocked into a cocked hat."

The discussion after she returned grew heated, and she was faced with the promises that had been made at the organization of the lighthouses, especially the pledge that each church should retain its own property. Aimee turned on Goben and for fifteen minutes blistered him with a scorching denunciation, until he broke in to remind her that although he had come there to help, his resignation still stood. With that he started to leave.

Just then Cromwell Ormsby entered the room, and Aimee drew him into a corner and told him what had happened. She was furiously angry, and several ministers heard Ormsby mutter, "I'll get Goben!" Since, around the temple, Ormsby was credited with having underworld connections, that "get" sounded sinister.

Leaving the meeting to settle its business as it might, Goben walked out and just outside the door encountered two eavesdropping newspaper reporters. They begged him to tell them what was going on, for they could hear through the door that a row was in progress. He declined to be quoted.

Later he found out that the two reporters had gone to Aimee and had told her that they had talked with Goben (without mentioning that he had said nothing quotable), and the dread of seeing the rebellion erupt in the headlines had cooled her down. She dispatched two messengers to find Goben and bring him back.

The messengers did not locate him until the next morning, and at their insistence he went with them to Sister's residence.

Aimee gave them a smiling welcome.

"Mr. Goben," he quoted her as saying, "you are a gentleman, and the only man I have ever had in my employment whom I could trust and know was filling the place you have been called to. Why didn't you set me down when I was so mean to you yesterday?"

"When you get something in your head, nothing can stop you, not even a buzz saw," Goben replied.

Thereupon Aimee gave him her word that if he would come back and resume his place, she would let Ormsby, Timpson, and that whole crowd go just as soon as she could.

"I promise you I won't ever see them again except in the presence of members of my church," she said earnestly.

Goben was willing to be conciliated.

"That is all anyone can ask," he answered. "If you get those ungodly leeches out of official positions and replace them with godly men and women, that the work of the Gospel may prosper, there isn't anything in the world that I wouldn't do for you."

Aimee insisted he stay for dinner and during the meal she was charming. Then she suggested that he join her in the evening service. But first, to quiet the newspapers, they dictated a joint public statement—an innocuous communiqué, saying that certain questions of procedure, respecting appointive and elective powers, were being referred to a general convention, and that Sister McPherson was still the head of the lighthouse association. Both signed this sop to the press; then they stepped across to the temple, where Goben sat on the platform with Sister and led in prayer. At the close of his invocation, he was puzzled by a spattering of applause. It gathered volume and lasted an appreciably long time, while he wondered what it could mean.

"Then," to use his own words, "it dawned on me what this clever woman had done."

The report of a serious disagreement was abroad. The church members had heard it, and they interpreted Goben's friendly appearance on the temple platform with Sister as signifying that harmony had been restored. And the joint statement to the newspapers, which the members would read in the morning, would clinch that impression. The ground had been cut from under Goben's feet; he realized that from then on any opposition he might raise against Sister would be looked upon as inspired by spite and selfish motives. He had been boobytrapped.

Later that evening Aimee requested Goben to come to her home in the morning. When he arrived, the two previous intermediaries also were there, and Sister led them all out on the patio. From her appearance she had passed a restless night. Goben thought she seemed uneasy and nervous. After a few generalities, she suddenly said:

"Brother Goben, I wanted you to come here this morning to talk things over about those affidavits you have. I feel that you should destroy them or prove them."

Then quickly she turned to inconsequential topics—her pet turtle named Noah, a painting of herself—and rambled on for about ten minutes. At length Goben reverted to the affidavits and said he would not destroy them but stood ready to prove them at any time.

Aimee appeared to be taken aback.

"Now, Brother Goben," he quoted her as saying, "that was not my suggestion at all, to destroy those affidavits. I want you to come back with us. I have arranged to increase the salary of your office to a thousand dollars a month and will give you the love offerings of four church conventions a year. You can put off the destruction of those documents one month, two months, six months, a year, five years, or ten; I don't care if you never destroy your evidence."

Goben sensed that she was obeying instructions given to her by Ormsby. Concluding that she was trapped and led by that baleful influence, he picked up his hat and went straight to the district attorney's office, determined to force a grand jury examination of the temple finances.

Aimee countered by formally dismissing Goben for being "unfaithful to his trust, disloyal to the supreme authorities of the lighthouse corporation, and causing dissension among the membership."

Cromwell Ormsby issued a stinging retort to Goben's "ridiculous charges," called the revolt a "minor windstorm," and expressed confidence that a thorough investigation would absolve Mrs. McPherson of all suspicion in connection with the church's funds.

District Attorney Buron Fitts, after hearing Goben's story and looking over the documentary evidence submitted, announced that the matter would be placed before the grand jury.

Then, so swiftly the eye could scarcely follow the changes, Mae Waldron was back at the temple, Cromwell Ormsby was out as temple counsel, Timpson was out, and the public became aware that Minnie Kennedy's steadying hand was again on the helm of the storm-tossed church.

III

There was need of Minnie's help.

Far and wide, Foursquare Gospel congregations were either renouncing their temple ties, or were being racked by internal dissension. Goben and his sympathizers rallied support at crowded meetings and set up committees to formulate their own plan of action. Sister outwardly denied that there was any serious disaffection and claimed many of the seceded churches were coming back; but Goben listed many lighthouses as definitely out, among them the Pasadena, Whittier, Lomita, Santa Ana, Oakland, Hyde Park, Bell, Corona, Stockton, Long Beach, and Huntington Hills branches, all in California; plus the branch in Bremerton, Washington. Many of these churches had women pastors, all in active revolt.

Minnie had arrived from Seattle during the height of the fracas. She was looking a little peaked from the strain of her heart-balm victory, but was still gamely smiling. She declined to take any part publicly in the furor, although expressing willingness to help her daughter and the church "the little that I can." She would not return to the temple in any official capacity, she made plain, adding:

"Once I make a decision I stick to it."

However, her hand in developments became evident when Ormsby publicly laid his ouster to Minnie's influence and sued Mrs. McPherson for breach of contracts, seeking three hundred and twenty-four thousand dollars. He accused a "mendacious triumvirate" (all feminine) at the temple of distorting the facts in statements to the press, thinking that "the world will believe anything they say."

A formal announcement soon came from Echo Park, issued by Sister herself:

"Mother will be back in the work with us from now on. She took up her duties last week at the Temple. We are in full accord despite the rumors circulated that there has been a difference between us. Any difference that we once might have had has been settled."

The two left for the Northwest immediately after this announcement was released, and it was reported that Minnie had consented to invite the following she had built up in Oregon and Washington to come under the lighthouse beacon.

In Portland, Aimee rode on a fire engine, and at Eugene she spoke in three fraternity houses on the University of Oregon campus. Then she hastened back to lead the orchestra in a production of her latest oratorio, "Christ the King," staged with a chorus of five hundred at Angelus Temple; to push the preparations for her Holy Land pilgrimage; to fire rebellious pastors; to rally the heads of her departments to renewed loyalty; and to woo back seceders.

But the real threat lay in the interest the district attorney's office was showing in the temple finances and especially in that mysterious bank account held in the names of "Elizabeth and Edith Johnson."

Goben had given the district attorney two temple ledgers covering the two years prior to April 28, 1929. The sort of dynamite they contained was typified by the entries on a single page for the month of March, 1928—the month in which Aimee had made a desperate appeal to her congregation for $25,000 to pay the mysterious notes presumably signed and left by Mother Kennedy and in reality given to Ralph Jordan and signed by Aimee.

According to the ledger, that month Sister had received in her regular love offering collection on the first Sunday the sum of approximately $1,200. This collection, she had repeatedly stated, was the only remuneration she received, but the entries showed that she had also received a salary as editor of the *Bridal Call,* another salary for teaching in the Bible School, and the regular contribution of $500 from the missionary fund of the branch churches. On top of these direct payments, $8,603.29 was taken in special collections for the commissary—all of which had been banked in the account of "Elizabeth and Edith Johnson." Thus the traceable "take" of the temple's pastor in March, 1928, the month when she was representing the church as flat broke and threatened with ruin unless $25,000 was forthcoming quickly, was $12,000, if the ledger was to be believed. Add the $25,000 that was subscribed in answer to her appeal and that passed from Aimee's hands to Ralph Jordan's—from "Elizabeth" to "Edith Johnson" (Elizabeth was Aimee's middle name)—and in March, 1928, the temple pastor had received about $37,000, almost none of which was devoted to temple uses, the operating overhead of Angelus Temple being covered by the regular tithes of the members, which were separate from the proceeds of special collections.

After a hasty preliminary study, Chief Trial Deputy District Attorney Daniel Beecher announced that the accounts would be sifted to the bottom, and such action would be taken as the law warranted. He subpoenaed all the temple's books and a parade of witnesses including Aimee, her mother, Mae Waldron, Harriet Jordan, Brother Arthur, Ralph Jordan, and others.

Aimee produced the books with a flourish, taking the huge, "elephant-folio" ledgers personally to the district attorney's office and posing with Harriet Jordan in front of the grand jury's door as if in the act of carrying them into the room.

John Goben, who was on hand, smiled. He recognized the books Aimee was surrendering so nonchalantly: they were the ledgers show-

When the Los Angeles grand jury indicated a desire to examine the financial records of Angelus Temple, Mrs. McPherson brought them personally, posing with Harriet Jordan, dean of the Temple's Bible School, outside the grand jury room. A former Temple aide said they were only one of three sets of books; he produced pages from a different set.

ing the tithe payments of the membership, which were placed on display in the lobby of Angelus Temple every month—a sort of honor roll—where anybody might inspect them and incidentally check on who was falling behind on his or her pledges. These books, Goben said, were only one of the *three* sets of accounts kept at the temple.

With Goben at this confrontation, waiting to be called to testify, were two former employees of the temple, the former financial secretary and her assistant. They were there to certify—and they did certify—the ledgers submitted by Goben as authentic; they had made the entries themselves.

On her birthday in 1929, Aimee preached in a sunbonnet and afterward cut her birthday cake in the shape of Angelus Temple. She said she was thirty-seven. *Who's Who in America* said she was thirty-nine.

When Aimee saw the three, she walked up to Goben and said audibly, "God bless you, my avowed enemy." Goben replied nothing; he just looked at her. Aimee turned to the two women and said something in an undertone, causing one to reply hotly that she "had better prove it." The second woman, cuttingly reminding the temple pastor of "what happened the last time we met," coldly removed Aimee's hand from her shoulder.

In due course the procession of witnesses passed through the grand jury door. Minnie Kennedy, looking entirely competent, smart in a dress of brilliant red velvet, was before the grand jurors only about five minutes, and Aimee told the jury all about that so-called "mystery fund." No mystery about it, she contended; it had been opened as a device to elude the people who had shadowed her everywhere after her return from abduction, and the balance had never exceeded $25,000.

Back at the temple that evening, the scene was reminiscent of the tense days of 1926. Before a packed audience, Sister told all about her questioning by the grand jury and called it no more than "a formal tea party." She alluded scathingly to her opposition, but named no names, making her point by remarking that the Archangel Michael had fallen from Heaven through pride, and had taken a third of the angels with him. But "this work is going on and no one can stop it. . . . If certain persons had received Bible training, this trouble would not have been stirred up for us at the district attorney's office." And as in 1926, she demanded that she either "be indicted immediately, or be given a chance in court to prove the falsity of the charges." And as in 1926, she was to achieve neither alternative.

A complete audit of the temple financial records was ordered, but after one week of work the accountant took to his bed with a fever. More records were called for and produced, and another auditor took up the task, while detectives scoured the town for information.

In the midst of this, Aimee exuberantly celebrated what she said was her thirty-seventh birthday by preaching in a gingham dress of pink and gray, wearing a pink sunbonnet—just the way she used to dress as a girl on the farm. An enormous birthday cake was cut and passed around among the congregation, and a message from Mother Kennedy, sent from Seattle, was read over the radio. It was in Mother's best style:

"Tenderest greetings with heart's deepest wishes for many happy returns of your birthday which seems but a day of sunlight and a night of shadow since God gave you to Mother for the world's greatest service since William Booth.* Born through prayer, raised, trained with healthy mind and body, sustained by every available means for many years, now assured God's guardian angels will protect and guide, which Mother no longer can do. Heaven's richest blessing shall ever follow thy ministry of His preached word and generations to come shall call thee blessed."

The newspapers unfeelingly remarked that the latest edition of *Who's Who in America* gave the date of Mrs. McPherson's birth as 1890, which would make her age thirty-nine.

John Goben smiled his understanding smile.

And lawsuits rained on Aimee. Timpson, ousted temple auditor, demanded $7,600 back salary. A building contractor sued over an unpaid bill of $199.77 for tile and other building materials. She was involved in a scheme to sell building lots in a San Fernando Valley

* Founder of the Salvation Army.

subdivision over the temple radio; in this promotion, which went sour, she was said to have received $20,000 plus free lots valued at $5,000. A contractor sued for $216,418 in damages over her failure to construct a thirteen-story hotel for her Bible students. A promoter brought an action for $143,380 against Mrs. McPherson and Ralph Jordan over their failure to go through with a contract to establish a Foursquare Gospel camp in the San Bernardino Mountains.

Meanwhile, the district attorney's office wrestled with the tangle of temple accounts, and Beecher said it might be necessary to audit the church's records clear back to 1923 to trace the interlocking transactions. Handwriting experts had been called in, and the complete job, Beecher estimated gloomily, might cost the taxpayers thousands of dollars. Beecher began to look dejected. Not so Aimee.

She answered the legal actions with one of her own, regretfully however, by procuring the arrest of a man who dropped obscene letters into her mailbox expressing a wish to marry her. The court ruled the fellow was obviously demented. And when the Pasadena lighthouse congregation remained obdurate in its rebellion and refused to let Brother Arthur, although personally beloved by all factions, speak on behalf of his pastor (drowning him out by singing the Doxology), Aimee obtained, at Minnie's instance, a court order, and backing a truck up to the church building, carted off the entire furnishings, including twelve collection plates, a communion service, four pianos, a saxophone, bankbooks, and twelve white "angels' robes."

In addition, when the newspapers felt parched by a dearth of temple doings, Aimee obligingly visited Luna Park Zoo and demonstrated before the cameras how divine healing worked on an elephant and a mangy lion, that obediently flopped down, and then struggled up at her command, "cured" of a distemper. To wind up the day, she rode the zoo's trick mule in a circus routine, impressing reporters that she really could ride. She stabled her own riding horses at the zoo.

Of greater moment was her incorporation of her own moving-picture company, Angelus Productions, Incorporated, to produce a film based on her life and adventures. The title was to be *Clay in the Potter's Hands,* and Sister would star. The temple's acoustics were tested and were found to be nearly perfect, and Harvey Gates, the scenarist who had turned out the script for *The Jazz Singer*, was engaged to write the scenario. Filming would start on her return from the Holy Land, Aimee announced, and Steve and Rose of kidnap fame would be portrayed in all their devilish wickedness.

In the midst of these buoyant activities, the district attorney was unexpectedly handed those letters that Minnie Kennedy had written to her friend eighteen months before, denouncing her daughter's growing worldliness and accusing her of "the most vicious scheme, trying to ruin me, body and soul, rather than I should have a friend or a penny." The woman to whom Mother had written these bitter words had confided the letters to Gladwyn Nichols, the onetime bandmaster of Angelus Temple, still heading his rival Church of Philadelphia. Nichols had confided them to other hands, and finally they reached the grand jury room and the newspapers.

This disclosure failed to ruffle the serenity at Echo Park. Reporters found Mother Kennedy presiding over a missionary conference, which she suspended long enough to answer questions.

"What of it?" she asked placidly. "Merely old enmities aroused again."

And back she went to her missionary meeting.

In an adjoining room Sister was working on a sermon. She, too, took the development lightly.

"If Mother did write those letters," she said, "I'm sure she doesn't feel that way now. Anyhow, let 'em whoop it up; it's good publicity for us and the temple—every shot worth a million dollars—and I hope they keep shooting!"

But events in the world beyond Echo Park were already vitally affecting Mrs. McPherson's activities, as they would affect the fortunes of millions of Americans. October, 1929, was the month of the stock market crash, and the start of the Great Depression of the thirties. One immediate effect was to scale down Sister's Holy Land pilgrimage sharply. Reservations already received were canceled by the dozens, and instead of leading a thousand or more of her devotees aboard their own chartered liner in the spring of 1930, Sister was forced to depart with a meager handful of followers.

The departure was staged with full fanfare at the railroad station, Aimee conducting an hour-long service from a flatcar before the train pulled out. Roberta Semple accompanied her mother. The party sailed from New York on the liner *George Washington*, a few among the

When no other publicity idea occurred, Aimee would oblige photographers by such stunts as riding a trick mule, as in these poses taken in 1926. She was a daring horsewoman.

many tourists who were bound for a land no more holy than Montmartre.

The temple's affairs had been left in the capable hands of Mother Kennedy, and gradually the tumult there subsided. Some of the seceding churches stayed out, and others felt the loneliness of their Sister-less independence and crept back into the fold. They were made welcome. Goben's support frittered away, he hit the evangelistic trail, and the schism petered out. The intricacies of the temple bank accounts continued to baffle the experts of the district attorney's office, and that investigation languished and died. Nothing was resolved and Aimee was neither indicted nor exonerated, but again she was able to "shout victory."

The reports coming from Sister's party were spotty and conflicting. Aimee did preach in hallowed surroundings and did carry out some baptizings in the River Jordan. On the other hand, the British authorities in Palestine were reported to have looked upon Sister as a disturbing element (especially after she claimed to be converting Arabs), and to have invited her to get hence, which she did. Altogether, the pilgrimage lacked luster, and letters from her latter-day palmers contained grumbling.

As the party approached Istanbul, Roberta became seriously ill, according to dispatches, and she and her mother remained in that city while the rest of the party moved along. Next, Sister was reported in Budapest; then in Northern Ireland, where she left Roberta for an extended stay with her grandparents, the James Semples, and proceeded home alone. She reached New York in June, 1930, and got into a tiff with customs inspectors who wanted to fine her for failing to declare "a few simple dresses picked up in Paris." Sweeping into the customs house, she protested the injustice and emerged saying she had found the officials to be "perfect gentlemen," who allowed her to pay only a fraction of what had been wrongfully assessed by the dockside inspectors.

To welcome Sister home, four thousand of her followers, or of the merely curious, gathered at the station. A representative of the mayor of Los Angeles extended the city's greeting, and Aimee sang a song which she said she had composed for the occasion: "This Is My Honey, This Is My Sunny California." She was escorted to Angelus Temple by a flower-decked motorcade. The temple, the parsonage, and the Bible School were bright with bunting, and several hundred children assembled on the front lawn sang for Sister. Mother Kennedy wept for joy and applauded with the others.

Six weeks later, the city was startled by reports that Mrs. McPherson was blind—was paralyzed—was dying—lying in a cottage at fashionable Malibu Beach, surrounded by armed guards—and that Minnie Kennedy was in a hospital, under bandages, and the Temple's harmony again had been blown to smithereens.

IV

Two questions convulsed Los Angeles. They were:

Where, when, how often, and how much, if at all, had Aimee had her face lifted?

Who broke Ma's nose?

In the mythology of the city, Minnie Kennedy had come to occupy a niche only a little less prominent than the one filled by her

On her trips abroad Aimee collected hundreds of costumes for use in her Temple pageants. Here she brightens a Palestinian costume with her warmest smile.

iridescent daughter. And as Aimee Semple McPherson, to the millions as to the few, had become ineffaceably "Aimee," so her mother, in affection or in repugnance, was everywhere referred to as "Ma." Her salty sufferings and doughty fighting spirit were about to add another sizzling chapter to the history of the temple pair.

When Minnie returned to Angelus Temple in 1929 to extricate her daughter from a managerial mess, she stipulated, among other things, that Mae Waldron was to be eased out of official connection with the church. To say that Minnie Kennedy and Miss Waldron hated each other might be an exaggeration, but certainly there was between them no spark of empathy. It was said around the temple that on one occasion Miss Waldron, driven to distraction by the clack of Minnie's tongue, had pushed her into a closet and locked her there; despite which, Ma kept right on talking through the door. Aimee's partiality for her secretary Minnie could not understand, and Mae Waldron's rise to eminence in the church's affairs precisely at the time of Mother's decline and banishment was a coincidence that rankled. In Minnie's opinion, Aimee was under the spell of three close associates—Emma Schaffer, Mae Waldron, and Harriet Jordan, dean of the Bible School. While they were in the ascendant, Minnie obviously could not be, and she had made her return to Echo Park conditional on at least Mae Waldron's leaving the inner circle.

What offended Mother above all was Aimee's retention of Miss Waldron as vice-president of the Echo Park Evangelistic Association, the key corporation at the apex of the temple setup, which exercised the real control. That had been Mother's proud position in the old days; and when Aimee failed to carry out her promise and supplant Mae with Minnie herself, the latter suspected that her daughter was not dealing frankly and truthfully. On Aimee's return from the Holy Land hegira, Ma resolved to have the matter out, for she saw plainly that she was on a day-to-day basis as temple manager, liable to dismissal at the whim of the "unholy three" (her words), Emma, Mae, and Harriet Jordan, who had Sister's ear. After what she had been in the temple, Minnie's spirit rebelled against filling a subordinate and dependent role.

Consequently, soon after Sister's welcome home, whisperings were heard at Echo Park that Aimee and her mother were at loggerheads again.

But this rumor paled before a more startling—and to many temple followers more shocking—rumor that Aimee Semple McPherson had had her face lifted. Plastic surgery and "rejuvenating operations" were much in the news just then (as heart transplants would be forty years later), and the permissibility, or the shamelessness, of having one's face remodeled for the gratification of vanity was hotly debated. Many religious fundamentalists had no doubt that face-lifting was another form of ungodliness, sinful and reprehensible to the last degree. If God had wished a woman of eighty to look like one of eighteen, He would not have created wrinkles, ran the hypothesis.

The newspapers took the scent and quickly established that Mrs. McPherson had recently been a patient in Brentwood Sanatorium, a hospital favored by the Hollywood set. They learned that she had checked out late one night, apparently in great urgency and agitation, and had taken refuge in a rented cottage at Malibu Beach.

Coincidentally, they learned that Mother Kennedy also had been a patient in Brentwood and after checking out had returned a few days later—this return being on the very evening when her daughter had departed in such apparent haste.

The curiosity of the city's newsrooms—which were conditioned to expect the unexpected where Aimee McPherson and her indomitable mother were concerned—was piqued. What connection, if any, might there be between these simultaneous arrivals and departures? Reporters were put on the trail.

A watcher for the *Los Angeles Times* established an observation post overlooking Mrs. McPherson's retreat at the beach. Spying through binoculars, he saw a doctor who was attached to the Brentwood staff drive up to the cottage, enter the house, and after a short while come out and drive away. This happened on two successive evenings.

The third evening the reporter cautiously followed the doctor's car. From a vantage point close to the house he saw, through an open window, the doctor remove bandages from the face of a woman who was undoubtedly Mrs. McPherson and swathe her features again in fresh gauze.

After the doctor had left, the intrepid reporter went to the door and rang the bell.

In an instant, all the lights in the house went out.

Aimee is welcomed home from Europe on June 20, 1930, by her mother and her son, Rolf McPherson. This was probably the last picture of Aimee and Minnie taken together. A short time later Ma Kennedy was in the hospital with a broken nose.

The reporter rang and knocked repeatedly.

At length the door was opened a crack, and a woman's voice came from the darkness, asking:

"What do you want?"

"I want to see Mrs. McPherson," answered the intruder. "We understand she is having her face lifted again."

A gasp was heard and some mumbling, and the door closed.

The listening reporter caught the sound of whispering and shuffling feet. Then the door was opened a crack, and somebody said:

"Mrs. McPherson cannot see anyone. She is having a breakdown. We're holding a meeting of the board of directors right away."

Since no lights appeared, this meeting seemed to have been held in the dark. However, in a few moments a typewritten statement was handed out at the door, which closed smartly again. This announcement read:

"After twenty-two years of unselfish, unremitting evangelistic work, it is no wonder that human strength cannot indefinitely endure the pressure of work. We are continually praying that God may soon restore Sister to her pulpit. The physician, a nerve specialist, will issue bulletins daily, which will be posted at Angelus Temple."

"Just a minute," said the reporter. "Anything to that story that there has been a row between Mrs. McPherson and her mother over a third party?"

"Nothing to it!" fairly gasped the voice, and the door was double-latched on the inside.

The reporter had his story and the *Times* made the most of it. The *Examiner* thereupon published a dispatch from Budapest saying that in May, Mrs. McPherson had been a patient in the Cottage Sanatorium there and that Dr. Alexander Spegler had performed a plastic surgery operation on her. Later, from May 10 to May 15, it was added, Mrs. McPherson had been in a well-known rest-cure sanatorium in Budapest, St. Margaret's.

If this report were accepted, might there possibly have been *two* face-lifting operations? The story became twice as titivating.

Hoping Mrs. Kennedy might shed light on this darkness, reporters converged on Brentwood Sanatorium, where they found Mother indeed a patient, lying in bed with her face heavily bandaged.

At first she declined to say anything; but after being coaxed and badgered for twenty-four hours, she—as usual—talked. Once started, she made no effort to control the freshet, the flood, the deluge of words that poured from her quivering lips.

Nine months ago, she began, sitting propped up in bed wearing a flowered negligee and a protective framework over her scarified nose, her daughter, beset by difficulties with the grand jury and "others," had begged her to "come home and clean house." Mother had consented to do so—on certain conditions—and had returned to Echo Park with "nothing but love in my heart" and "a burning desire to grasp the helm of the tottering church." But her stipulations had not been fulfilled, and "some weeks ago I felt I must drop out again. Evil influences were again at work which I was powerless to combat. So I began to lay my plans.

"About that time, however, Aimee approached me with a proposition that we submit to a rejuvenation process. I discouraged the idea, for you see, I am sixty years old and that sort of thing is behind me now—but she persisted, and finally we went downtown to the office of a surgeon [here Mother gave the name of a specialist in plastic surgery] and Aimee made all the financial arrangements. As we left, Aimee suggested that I go first—let the experiment be tried on me, as it were. I agreed.

"Well, anyway, I came in here and went through the ordeal on the table, then arose, although weak and still far from well, to visit Aimee and announce my resignation. I had promised to go to Olympia [Washington] to dedicate a new church. We chatted a while in the patio, then my daughter hinted that she wished to see me alone."

At this point Minnie bit her lip and struggled to keep her composure.

"How did you receive the broken nose?" asked an interviewer.

"It was because of something she said to me." There was a pause. "She said, 'Is it true you have said those things?' It was about this person who had come between us. And I told her it was true, that I had said them. . . . And then it happened."

Tears trickled down Mother Kennedy's cheeks until the reporter prompted:

"You mean—she struck you?"

Mother nodded and wept.

"Yes," she blubbered. "But a broken nose isn't half as bad as a broken heart! There I was, on the floor, trying to struggle to my feet and warding off, like this [she demonstrated] . . . warding off with my free hand . . . and then I got to my feet and went into the kitchen, and Emma Schaffer rushed out and brought back Miss Jordan and Brother Arthur . . . and they all watched me, the four of them, as I stooped over the sink and held my wrists under cold water . . . and the most appalling aspect of the whole terrible thing, as I look back now, is that there stood four of them, all God-fearing members of a great religious organization, watching me bathe my wounds—and not one of them to say, 'Let us pray!' "

Ma lay back wearily.

"Yes," she murmured, "I have told Brother Arthur since then about my thoughts in that connection, and he agreed I was right—someone should have prayed. Emma Schaffer, she said to me, 'You know, Ma, you laid down on that floor!' I kept bathing my wrists and finally I turned to Aimee and told her that she would have to make her choice between me and this other person . . . and my daughter told me, 'I'll make you eat your words!' "

"Did she strike you more than once?" asked the interviewer.

Mother waved the question aside:

"Let that be, let that be. I managed to totter home several hours later, and at 3 A.M. my little secretary brought me here and the doctor treated my nose and remained with me until train time . . . for in spite of my condition, I was bound to go to Olympia."

Mother said this encounter had happened on the night of July 29. But she had kept her engagement in Olympia and carried out her part in the dedication ceremonies. Afterward, among the congratulatory telegrams coming in, she had searched in vain, she said, for one that might read, "Mother dear, let us have peace." Only silence.

Taking the train south, she had gotten off at Santa Barbara so as not to attract attention and with her secretary had driven straight to Brentwood Sanatorium to be patched up.

"And whom should we meet in the driveway," she exclaimed, "but Emma Schaffer! She was carrying in an armful of bundles—and I knew at once that Aimee in the meantime had entered the sanatorium for her operation. Miss Schaffer denied that Sister was there, but I knew different."

Minnie had checked in, and thereupon (it was later pieced together) Aimee had moved out in extreme agitation and had bundled off to

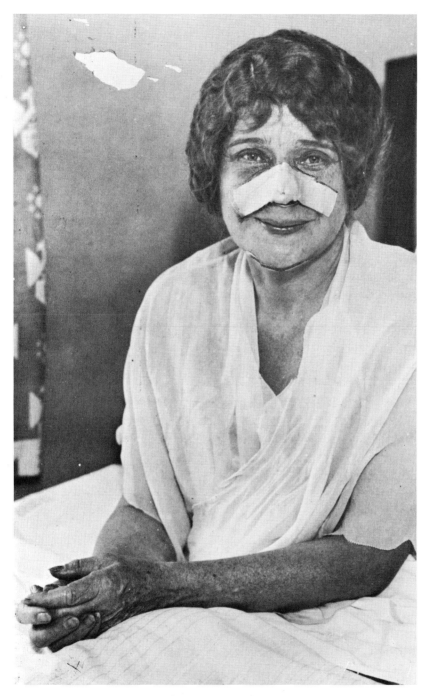

"You mean—she struck you?" Minnie was asked as she lay in a hospital bed with bandaged nose. Minnie wept and nodded.

Malibu with Emma, Mae Waldron, two other secretaries, three nurses, a houseman, and a chauffeur.

While Mother's account was unreeling, Emma Schaffer, at the Malibu cottage, was distractedly giving out bulletins saying Sister was paralyzed—was blind—was dying. At Angelus Temple, Harriet Jordan assumed command temporarily and posted Emma's bulletins and read them over the radio; they spread consternation among the faithful. Mother was racked by anxiety.

"They came today and said my daughter is threatened with blindness!" she protested. "Then the superintendent assured me that when Aimee left here she was all right. Then the doctor, too, told me there is nothing wrong with her. Then why, oh, why do these people around her have to give out such statements and frighten people to death? It is driving me frantic. . . . But I have telephoned down there and told Miss Jordan to shut Schaffer's mouth and issue an official statement, and if my daughter is all right, let her get up and go to the temple and show her flock that she is all right. When she was in trouble before, and all had deserted her, she yelled for Mother . . . and I came to her. . . . I hope she will do it again!"

For a week the turmoil raged, with Mother in the hospital and Aimee reported to be lying in a trance, poised over the abyss of immortality. Her followers gathered in clumps and clusters to pray and wail—in the hallways of the temple, on the sidewalks, across the street in Echo Park, on every floor of the Bible School, and around Sister's deserted home next door. When one group arose from their knees, others knelt in replacement. The praying and moaning at times was heard a block away.

No two temple spokesmen could agree on what was wrong with Sister. A doctor who had been called into the case told reporters as he emerged from the strongly guarded beachhouse that Mrs. McPherson was not seriously ill. The report of blindness he dismissed completely ("nothing to it"), stressing that he had examined the patient's eyes fifteen minutes previously and "her vision may be a little blurred because of nervousness, but there is nothing organic. She will be all right in a few days. The only trouble with her is that she can't get a rest."

But Harriet Jordan posted at the temple:

"Sister McPherson is still blind. No marked improvement. Suffering greatly. Please continue in earnest prayer."

"Jordie" said that additional telephone lines were being installed to cope with the flood of inquiries. And the board of elders added their report:

"Mrs. McPherson is suffering from a serious breakdown. We are having continual prayers and fasting for her recovery."

Cornered at the beach, Emma Schaffer blamed overwork for Sister's collapse: in addition to her normal schedule, she had been writing a book, composing two oratorios, and taking film tests, said the gaunt, hollow-eyed secretary, herself looking on the verge of collapse. Sister had been dieting drastically to slim down for her film role, Emma revealed. But Emma insisted:

"Her optic nerves are paralyzed and she has temporarily lost her sight. She has lost twenty-eight pounds."

Trying to ascertain the truth, the newspapers hunted up the plastic surgeon mentioned by Mother Kennedy, but though he admitted that Mrs. McPherson had been his patient recently, he said he had withdrawn from the case and could not comment. The doctor regularly visiting the Malibu cottage was a specialist in nervous disorders, and he continued to discount the gravity of the evangelist's illness, stressing again that in his opinion her marvelous recuperative powers would pull her through. But Harriet Jordan advised a sobbing congregation not to believe published reports; Sister was blind, and tests made by a church committee had convinced everybody of it.

The press was clamoring for an interview with the evangelist, and for four days was rebuffed. Then, consent at last being given, the reporters and photographers were briefed on the procedure they must follow: above all, they must maintain absolute quiet in the sickroom.

The door of the bedroom was opened slowly, and Aimee was seen in one of twin beds. The window shade was pulled down and the room was in gloom. Sister's eyes were closed. The coverlet was pulled up to her chin, and her hair was drawn down over the temples. On her forehead rested a gingham-plaid icebag. Her face was wan and thin; she appeared to have lost much weight. Through parted lips she breathed heavily, while a nurse held her hand reassuringly. The cameramen clicked away (no flashlights were allowed), Emma Schaffer glaring at them from the bedside. Then the photographers tiptoed out, and there was an uneasy pause. Aimee lay as though dead. A reporter's voice broke the stillness:

"Mrs. McPherson, are you able to make any statement on affairs between you and your mother, and are you planning to take any action against her for what she has said about you?"

Another silence, broken only by the grinding of heavy trucks passing on the highway a few yards away. Presently the patient's eyes fluttered, the leaden lips twitched, and she murmured:

"No one ever needed their mother worse than I."

"Well," said one insensitive representative of the press, "what did you smash her nose for?"

It was unnecessary to announce that the interview was terminated. Aimee began twisting and jerking, her lips moved in an incoherent mumble, and a nurse hustled everybody outside. As the reporters trooped into the brilliant sunshine, they collided with a newsreel camera crew arriving to make a film sequence. These were told to come back another time—Sister was too sick to pose for them now.

Later, through a secretary, word was conveyed that Mrs. McPherson did not intend to take legal action against her mother, nor would she offer any detailed reply.

Minnie was not impressed. Temple officials were spreading the report that Mother had broken her nose when she accidentally slipped and fell on the parsonage kitchen floor, but Minnie spurned such assertions.

"I don't care how many denials are issued that my nose was not broken in a fight with my daughter," she declared. "My nose was broken during a heated argument between Sister and myself, and that is all there is to the matter! The attendants at the sanatorium, the surgeon, and friends of us both know about the trouble, and that it was caused by my objection to Mae Waldron in the official family at the temple!"

At Echo Park, an officiating elder offered prayer for Mrs. Kennedy, saying:

"We love her. We think she is just a poor, misguided woman."

But a delegation of temple elders shortly appeared at Brentwood armed with a resolution stating:

"Whereas, Mrs. Kennedy has been making derogatory remarks detrimental to our pastor. . . . Therefore, after prayer and waiting upon God, be it resolved that a committee wait upon Mrs. Kennedy and demand that she cease her statements, which interfere with our religious work."

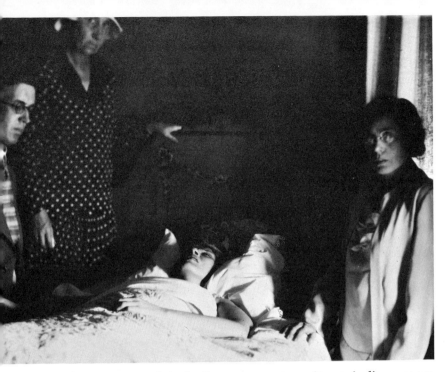

Aimee's attendants grudgingly allow reporters to see her as she lies prostrate in a Malibu Beach cottage. Photographs were taken in semidarkness; no flashlights were allowed. At left are a reporter and Emma Schaffer; at right, Harriet Jordan.

Minnie's secretary intercepted the group on the front porch, and by Mother's direction delivered to the elders *her* resolution, to wit:

"Mrs. Kennedy is not connected in any way with Angelus Temple, she is not a member of any board, she is not an official, she is not even a member of the congregation, and she will see no one on any matters except the head of the temple."

The crestfallen committeemen trooped away, and Minnie spent a congenial hour defying anybody to make her stop talking:

"I will not quit talking until they put me in my grave, and there is no group from Angelus Temple that has any right to tell me to! I am for my daughter first, last, and all the time, and if I could only be with her for five minutes, I know there would be some people on their way—up or down!"

The main worry on Ma's mind was lest Aimee's condition had been caused by an attempt to have her legs, as well as her face, reshaped. Rumor had it that the evangelist had had surplus flesh removed from her legs. Aimee had wanted to, Minnie said, and they had discussed the possibility with the surgeon, but had been told the operation was dangerous. Still Mother saw no reason why Aimee should not have her legs slimmed, if she felt like it, and could. In an age of short skirts, thick legs were a blemish, and Mother observed sensibly that "women have their hair bobbed, faces lifted, bodies massaged, and take reducing treatments, so why should it be out of order for my daughter to have her legs made more shapely?"

She gave this opinion while having the stitches taken out of her reconstructed nose. (Aimee, she said in an aside, would have to pay her hospital bills, or she would sue.)

Twenty-four hours later Minnie wept for joy when a basket of roses arrived with a card attached: "From Aimee with love." The bouquet had been delivered by Emma Schaffer, and Mother felt so happy she posed for photographs with the bandages off her nose. She was delighted with the improvement:

"My new nose—I love it! I think it looks a lot better than the old shape. You'd be surprised how many people are writing to me about face-lifting operations—not all of them women, either. I'm a bit shaky, but I think the doctors have done a splendid job. Modern surgery is just wonderful!"

Out of the basket holding Aimee's flowers she fished a second card that had tumbled to the bottom.

"Oh!" she groaned. On the card was written: "To Sister, with hopes for a speedy recovery." Aimee's love-bouquet was secondhand!

Tears dripped off the tip of Ma's new nose.

In the Shadow

~✺~

"Goldsmith tells us, that when lovely woman stoops
to folly, she has nothing to do but to die; and when
she stoops to be disagreeable, it is equally to be
recommended as a clearer of ill-fame."
—Jane Austen, *Emma*

While Mother Kennedy rantipoled in Brentwood Sanatorium, her
daughter, late one night, was spirited away from the Malibu cottage
in an ambulance, shielded by a train of nurses, secretaries, servants,
and armed guards. Minnie had been serving notice that Aimee must
be transferred to some place where she could have seclusion and
immunity from distractions. She had even threatened, if it became
necessary, to swoop down on the cottage, "wrap her in a blanket,
like I used to do when she was a baby, and carry her in my own
arms to a hospital." To the suggestion that she probably would never
get inside the house, she flung back: "If I went down there I'd
get in, or my dead body would be found on the doorstep!"

It seemed that Sister's hasty decampment had been inspired by
fear of just that: around the temple it was said that Mother had
actually planned to kidnap her daughter. Minnie scoffed and said
uncomplimentary things about "those people," but she was relieved
to hear that Sister was being well cared for in a rented house in
Santa Monica, set in tree-shaded, isolated grounds, and that Rolf
McPherson was with her. Roberta Semple was said to be hastening
home from Ireland.

Indications multiplied that Sister might not return to activity for
months. The temple's current business manager, A. C. Winters,
reported:

"Her brain is active, but her body is very weak. She is liable to be away for a long time."

Winters denied categorically that Sister had undergone facial surgery. He had been a member of the church committee that had made a thorough inspection of their pastor's face, looking behind the ears, lifting the ice pack from her forehead, and otherwise searching for telltale scars, and no scars were found, he said.

"I am ready to make an affidavit or swear on my death bed that there are no scars on Sister's face, and I am satisfied that there has been no such operation as has been reported," was his testimony.

Winters had come up through the ranks of temple workers, and was implicitly loyal to Sister. Although earnestly honest, he was not a forceful man.

Gradually the hubbub simmered down, but there was great despondency at Angelus Temple. Sister's fortieth birthday was observed there with a musical program, and shortly after that word was given out that she had departed on a Caribbean cruise in an effort to recuperate. Newsmen found her at Panama, traveling under the name "Miss Betty Adams, English governess," but when they accosted her while ashore in the Canal Zone she refused to be interviewed. Upon her arrival back at New York, she appeared very ill; her face was thin and her eyes were haggard. During a brief talk with the not-to-be-denied ship newsmen, a nurse and the ship's purser supported her, and she kept clasping and unclasping her hands nervously; when she reached out to take a newspaper clipping, her hand trembled.

A week later she was taken off the train at Pasadena, east of Los Angeles, and carried to the temple in an ambulance. The parsonage gate was padlocked, the runway between the house and the temple (so haunted by reporters it was called Newspaper Alley) was closed off, and a dozen watchmen patrolled the grounds. Sister could not be reached by telephone. Winters (who had met her in New York and had ridden back on the same train) said the strain on her heart coming across the Rockies had been severe, and though she had been intermittently unconscious since reaching home, "we hope that a few day's rest, at this lower altitude, will see an improvement."

Mother Kennedy had returned to her flat behind the Bible School. She was vexed by the contradictory rumors about her daughter's condition, but when she attempted to see for herself, a guard refused to let her through the parsonage gate. During the argument she saw a long, heavy box being carried into the temple and cried out that it was a coffin.

"What can I believe?" she wailed. "If Aimee is such a sick girl, what is she doing at the temple, and why isn't she in a hospital where she can receive proper care?"

Winters assured her that the sinister-looking box contained only furniture that Sister had bought in Palestine and that had finally been shipped after many delays, but Minnie remained skeptical. She prowled around the parsonage enclosure for an hour, berating the watchmen. Her grief and fretfulness were not caused by being shut out from the temple's anxieties (Minnie was finding that she could disregard temple affairs with more and more ease) so much as by her exclusion from the presence of her wonderful, wayward, totally exasperating daughter.

Shortly after this, announcement was made that Sister would preach her usual Thanksgiving Day sermon. Minnie offered to bet she wouldn't. And though a throng packed into the temple on that Thursday, the faithful were not rewarded by a glimpse of their pastor. Instead, they heard her voice over the loudspeakers as she spoke into a microphone placed beside her bed. It was the first time they had heard her voice in four months. It sounded listless. She told her flock that during the past summer she had expected to die and had felt happy at the prospect of reaching the end of her troubles, but apparently her work on earth had not been completed. With a faint "Good night—God bless you," she wished happiness to all, and the talk ended; she had made no mention of any return to her pulpit.

For several hours that evening a dense crowd stood in silence outside the parsonage, almost motionless in the garish glare of blue and red floodlights playing on the house—keeping vigil, awaiting a sign. But the only sign visible was the one on the front gate reading, "Keep out."

At Mother's flat a few doors away all was still. The shades were drawn down, the screen door was latched on the inside, and dangling from the doorknob was a penciled card saying, "I wish you all a happy Thanksgiving—now please leave." The doorbell button was taped over and marked, "Out of order." A further placard warned peddlers and salesmen to be gone.

Friday and Saturday automobiles moved in a steady procession past the house where Sister was said to be dying. The cars were counted in the hundreds, in the thousands, and expensively dressed women leaned out of the windows as they crept slowly past, to gaze up at the window of Sister's sickroom. Only once was the eerie tension disrupted, when police cars raced up with sirens wailing to arrest a drunken man who was trying to scale the fence.

Then on Sunday the true believers were rewarded with a glimpse of their beloved pastor.

The setting had been arranged for utmost dramatic effect. The standing-room-only throng at the morning service was worked up to shouting pitch by a succession of song leaders and preachers, each of whom promised that Sister would appear in a few minutes. At length the lectern was shoved aside, and the curtains of the proscenium arch at the back of the platform parted slowly. A spotlight was focused on the opening, and as the orchestra sounded a muted fanfare, the evangelist stepped into view, leaning on her son's arm. Her glimmering white satin gown reached to the shoetops, and on her bosom flashed a cross embroidered in brilliants. She was thin, pale, and looked extremely ill, but she was beautiful.

Her appearance was the cue for cheers that smote the sky-blue-painted dome. Six girls standing above the proscenium rained rose petals upon Sister's blond hair, while tears streamed down her face. In a faltering voice, she expressed her gratitude for such a welcome. A temple official handed her a huge bouquet of red roses in token of her people's affection; her words of acceptance were barely audible. She alluded to her illness, but mainly dwelt on her plans for the future, when she should have regained her health. Several times she was gently urged not to tax her strength, but she went on, stressing that her work was "only begun." With a final, smiling "God bless you all," she was led away, amid thunderous applause.

It was estimated that six thousand persons—all temple members holding special admission cards—witnessed this return to life, and reporters counted at least as many more who were turned away. Hundreds who were unable to get inside stood on the sidewalk, straining to catch Sister McPherson's voice over the loudspeakers rigged there.

Mother had not received a card of admission, and from the inner recesses of her flat she criticized the performance. Through her secretary she said:

"I am glad to hear that Sister was back on her platform, and very glad to hear that she was wearing a long dress. I told her to years ago. She has my blessing, and I wish her God speed. But I can't for the life of me understand why everything had to be built up so carefully and arranged so dramatically. Sister didn't need the aid of those temple hirelings; she could have walked out and given her talk. Why can't those payroll people tell the truth? Whose business is it if Sister had her face lifted? I think most of her illness is due to her efforts to reduce. However, these things are all past. They need have no fear of me trying to force my way into Sister's presence. I wish my daughter all the success in the world, and any time she needs her mother—here I am, with open arms."

Then Mother drove away to *her* seaside cottage at Hermosa Beach, expressing scorn for the guards patrolling the temple grounds, and the next morning installed a bulldog on her front porch. His name was Jiggs, she said, and he had been given to her by friends who thought she needed protection from "Angelus Temple fanatics" who might try to force their way into the house. Said she, stroking the bulldog's neck:

"Jiggs can beat any of their old temple guards with their popguns. If any halfwits go to strolling around my yard, they are going to buy a new pair of pants—Jiggs bites first and thinks it over afterward."

For another month Sister remained invisible, except once when she distributed diplomas to the Bible School's graduating class of one hundred and thirty. She went through the drill brightly, but afterward collapsed. Late in December, Winters was informing attorneys who were pressing litigation against the pastor that she was so ill the slightest sudden noise, even the rustle of a paper, caused her to faint. She was spending most of her time at an unidentified beach resort, he said, with her children (Roberta Semple had returned from Ireland), a nurse, and Miss Waldron.

So New Year's Day came and went, and in January, 1931, the temple flock was told that their pastor was at sea—on a trip around the world—with no date set for her return. The name of the ship on which she had sailed was not disclosed in order to safeguard her privacy, Winters said. He specifically denied that she had left Los

Angeles because of threats or demands for money.

"We know where she is going, and so do members of the temple board. There is no mystery about it," he insisted.

Her current attorney (she changed attorneys almost as often as she changed costumes, and not a few of them were forced to sue for their fees after being dismissed), Joseph W. Ford, also denied that there was any mystery.

"I have a pile of letters a foot high," said Ford, "which Mrs. McPherson has received from cranks and would-be blackmailers from all parts of the world, but there has been no letter received lately that differed from the usual run."

Among Aimee's friends a story was circulating about a "Hungarian baron," for whose benefit she supposedly had pawned an ermine coat in Budapest, but Ford was unperturbed.

"Hungarian barons sometimes write, too," he winked, "but they get nothing, either. We pay little attention to such letters. I understand barons are quite common in Hungary." Then, his tone changing, he said, "Mrs. McPherson is kind to people, and some misconstrue her kindness as offers of employment or financial aid. She certainly is paying no attention to any threatening letters from anyone."

Interest was added to the disclosure of Sister's secret departure in quest of health because it came only four days after the revelation that Mae Waldron was out as a temple official. Winters confirmed the fact:

"Yes, it is true that Miss Waldron is no longer vice-president of the Echo Park Evangelistic Association, nor is she acting in the capacity of secretary to Mrs. McPherson. Miss Waldron tendered her resignation and it was accepted by the association. Miss Semple has succeeded her as vice-president of the association, and is acting as private secretary to her mother."

So Roberta Semple, whom Aimee had been training from childhood to be her successor, had been taken into the family holding company, as it were, and was with her mother on the world cruise. Was Aimee Semple McPherson nearing the end of her ministry?

Miss Waldron attached no special significance to her retirement.

"I stepped down when we decided that Roberta was competent to handle the work," she explained. "There is no unexpectedness or surprise in the situation. I will not cease to be an active worker."

Minnie Kennedy was suspicious. "I don't *know* Mae Waldron is out," she grumbled. But she confirmed that the changeover had been planned for at least five years. Roberta's half-brother, Rolf McPherson, was expected to assume the business management, Minnie said.

Nevertheless, public speculation regarding Aimee's true condition continued rife. The nerve specialist who had been treating Sister said that she was indeed "a very sick woman."

"In August, at the beach, we thought she would die," he revealed. "She had acute acidosis, would not take food or water. Her people didn't know it, but we had to resort to saline solution injections to pull her through. Then came dilation of the heart. When I first saw her, last August, and again in November, her pulse was fast and not good; her respiration was twenty. She came near dying twice. Upon her return from the Caribbean trip she weighed a hundred and twenty-eight pounds, a loss of forty pounds. Her blood pressure was below one hundred—much too low. There are no organic disturbances, just a general letdown. She is a woman who has been through a complete collapse and is still very weak."

The doctor did not believe any face-lifting operation had brought the once vital, dynamic evangelist to death's door; in his opinion, it was simply the accumulated strain of "four terrible, tempestuous years." As for the reported face-lifting, he doubted that: he had examined her many times, he said, and "I am sure I would have noticed the scars, if this had been the case. She is suffering from what might be called a reflex breakdown under the accumulation of great nervous strain over years. All those fusses she had, and all the troubles that followed, all told on her. I told her she would need complete rest, and she was not getting it. The picture is the same."

This verdict of physical and moral exhaustion seemed conclusive, yet public doubts revived when, a few days after she had shipped secretly out of San Francisco aboard the liner *President Wilson* (it was established), a Los Angeles newspaper published a portrait photograph of her under the caption:

"Aimee Finds Secret of Eternal Youth!"

In the photograph, the forty-year-old evangelist might have passed for thirty or less. The picture, it was stated, had been taken just before her sailing.

Public cynicism suggested that Sister's secretive departure (no singing farewell, no flowers, no band, no pompoms) might have been to elude process servers, rather than to avoid excitement and display. Litigation against her had been piling up formidably. The miscarriage of her plan to make a talking-picture film had provoked a major storm, and her associates in that ill-starred venture were suing her for hundreds of thousands of dollars. The scenarist, Harvey Gates, was demanding ten thousand dollars for work already performed; the director was suing for four hundred thousand; and Sister's former lawyer, Cromwell Ormsby, wanted a quarter of a million. These were only the largest of many claims pending as a result of the ill-considered promotional schemes to which she had lent her name and prestige. Minnie Kennedy had said over and over again that Aimee's business judgment was unsound and her gullibility extreme.

II

All in all, time seemed to be running out for Aimee, and not only the temple, but all Los Angeles, and the world beyond that, seemed duller for her eclipse. Her people prayed and trusted, but the light and liveliness at Echo Park were dimmed. Even the irreligious thought the joke in poor taste when a Panama saloonkeeper mailed out postcards advertising a "Hallelujah Cocktail" that he said he had invented in honor of Sister's visit to his bar during her trip to the Caribbean. Ma Kennedy was outraged.

"If I were within shooting distance I would start in on that scoundrel," she sputtered. "I'd make him eat the words he has directed against my little girl! The nerve of him! I don't believe she was there, and if she was, no harm done! Besides, it's nobody's business! Somebody is always picking on her! I often wonder why Aimee doesn't fight back. But as long as I'm alive I'll fight for her! It certainly looks like the hand of the Evil One!"

The news received from Sister's wanderings was fragmentary. At Hong Kong she placed a wreath on the grave of Robert Semple, inscribed: "To Robert, to whom I owe all the best in me." At Singapore, Roberta Semple was married to the ship's purser, William Bradley Smythe; the bride was twenty, and the bridegroom twenty-three. The wedding was held in the Wesleyan church of Singapore, with cruise passengers serving as matron of honor and best man. Aimee gave the bride away and beamed on the love match.

Minnie, too, approved the marriage. Reporters found her drinking

Around the world cruise was broken in Shanghai, where Sister McPherson
conducted services in one of her Foursquare Gospel mission stations.

an orange juice toast to her granddaughter, with Roberta's photograph
propped up before her.

"I was married when I was fifteen," Minnie recalled, "and Aimee
was married when she was seventeen; so Roberta waited three years
longer than her mother. I hope she is happy! I practically raised
Roberta, you know—from the time her mother brought her to me in
New York. She called me 'Bonnie.' I know *she* loves me still."

From Singapore the evangelist and the newlyweds pursued their
way around the globe. At Marseilles the party was joined by Charles
Walkem, the temple's music arranger, who had come from Los
Angeles at Sister's bidding; according to wireless reports from the
ship, Aimee was working on several "sacred operas." And on May 12,
1931, Sister sailed into New York harbor.

The newsmen were waiting. Brother Walkem informed them that
Mrs. McPherson was too ill to stand the fatigue of an interview;
that she had by no means fully recovered her health. But they kept
up their demands to see her, and at length Aimee came on deck,
looking wan. She whispered that she was glad to be home and had
lost forty-three pounds. Then she retired to the captain's cabin and
remained out of sight.

Her companions were more talkative, saying that Sister had ridden

In her flat by the temple, Minnie Kennedy drinks a toast to her granddaughter's marriage in Singapore. "I know *she* loves me still."

a camel in the Egyptian desert, had played deck games, and had spent much time in her cabin with a camp organ, composing Biblical music dramas.

But as she crossed the continent toward home, vitality seemed to flow back into the evangelist. Her languor disappeared. At Chicago she laughed merrily at the rumor that she had been married secretly to a count or a baron.

"It wasn't a count or baron," she quipped. "I married the Prince of Wales!"

At Omaha she fired off a long telegram of instructions to the temple about the pulpit setting she wanted for her first sermon. The theme would be "Lost at Sea," and she wanted a ship's prow built out over the rostrum, and the choir must wear white robes with flowing sleeves that they would wave, on cue, to simulate the tossing ocean. Sister, in nautical regalia, would preach standing at a ship's wheel. But the next day, from Salt Lake City, she wired a change of program: she had decided to preach on "Attar of Roses," and she wanted the temple to be banked with roses, roses, roses everywhere.

What Helen Morgan could do Aimee felt she could do better. Here she poses sitting on the piano with her musical arranger, Charles Walkem, composing one of her numerous "sacred operas."

The temple workers scurried to do Sister's bidding. Garlands were woven, palm branches were distributed, choir and bands were rehearsed, and reception committees were formed. At the Santa Fe Railroad depot a flatcar was shunted onto a siding near where the train would halt and was decorated with bunting and flowers. Harriet Jordan had new locks fitted to all the doors of the temple.

In her nearby flat, Minnie Kennedy overheard the joyful preparations. She had no part in them; Mother was shut out. The window shades were drawn, and an occasional friend, crossing from the Bible School, rang the bell in vain. Mother, her secretary reported, had taken to her bed, and she wanted to die.

"Mother devoted the best years of her life in building the temple and the work," was the mournful explanation, "and now she is a stranger. It has just been piling up and piling up. She says over and over she wants to die, now that Aimee doesn't love her any more. When she heard the Bible School students singing 'In the Sweet Bye-and-bye,' she sighed, 'Maybe it will be different then,' and turned over and went to sleep."

But the next morning reporters found Ma very much alive, sitting up in bed toasting her granddaughter's photograph again, this time in ginger ale.

"She's my baby, God bless her!" Minnie beamed.

That rumor that she had collapsed was nonsense, she said; she had just had a cold, that was all. She had picked it up a week before, on a four-hour climb up Mount Rainier, near Portland, and that and just plain weariness had got her down for a few days. Those goings-on over at the temple? That was no concern of hers.

"I never intend to enter that building again," she declared. "But I hope Aimee will come back and take up the work."

When the Sante Fe's "Chief," bringing the nation's most glamorous preacher, slid into the railroad yard, ten thousand cheering, singing, frantic followers jammed the area and spilled for blocks around. Thousands more of curious onlookers were wedged in the throng. On the decorated float, the fifty-piece Bible School band played, and the Silver Band, also fifty strong, competed. The train rolled to a stop, and there on the rear platform stood Sister. A roar went up. Behind the evangelist stood Roberta and her husband Smythe, smiling shyly; then Rolf McPherson, who had joined the party at Chicago, and in the rear, Brothers Walkem and Winters. Sister, natty in a green silk sports suit and knit white silk turban, very blond and slim—slim enough for Hollywood—lifted an arm impulsively, and with a dramatic, all-encompassing gesture and a "God bless you!" took the crowd to her heart. "Oh, how I love you!" she breathed into a microphone. Then, as a born leader to whom nothing came as naturally as leading, she took charge of her own reception.

Welcomed home with bands, crowds, flowers, and cheers, "Oh, how I love you!" she told the throng from a decorated flatcar. Then she marshaled her own triumphal procession to Angelus Temple.

Stepping along an aisle kept open by thirty policemen linking arms, she mounted the flatcar, around which tossed a sea of hats, flags, palm branches, and the inevitable pompoms in temple colors of blue and gold. She pepped up the band, then signaled for silence to permit a member of the city council to extend a civic welcome. She waved to friends, and told the throng and radio listeners she had gone away because "I had been forgetting to rest, so God punished me. But I expect to be preaching for another twenty years!"

Then she ordered the line of march to Angelus Temple, where thousands more of the curious and the faithful overflowed into Echo Park. "Sister's home again!" was the chant, and under a triumphal arch Aimee and her family entered the parsonage, as little children pelted them with flowers. Buffeted by the throng, Smythe walked beside his wife in an apparent daze.

Up Lemoyne Street, the blinds of Mother Kennedy's flat remained pulled down.

Sister declined to comment on her mother's absence from the crush of welcomers.

The next day Aimee was back in her pulpit, and the press reported that she scored one of the greatest triumphs of her career. Few who sat through that service ever forgot it. Her reentrance into the temple was not merely a resumption of an accustomed role, it was the rebirth of a personality, brilliant in virtuosity and irresistibly magnetic.

Two hours before the doors opened, streams of people were converging on the park. After every inch of seating space had been filled—in the temple and in the Bible School next door, where loud-speakers would carry Sister's voice—ten thousand, by newspaper estimate, remained outside.

The temple was a bower of roses. On the platform Sister's throne-like pulpit chair was wreathed with flowers. At the side, two smaller thrones were set for Roberta and her husband, and over these swung a white satin wedding bell. The choir, banked in tiers on either side, wore white robes, with red roses pinned over their hearts. A second civic greeting was offered by Acting Mayor Sanborn; and after more hymns and band music, a door high up at the top of the right-hand ramp, at the first-balcony level, opened, and Sister came down the ramp half-running. Long-stemmed American Beauty roses spilled from her arms, and on her breast glistened a cross of brilliants. Behind her came her son, Rolf McPherson.

The crowd stood up and applauded. A xylophone virtuoso sprang into action with a dazzling solo. A woman drummer stood on the steps of the platform and thudded and rolled. People squeezed out of the aisles and climbed up and squatted cross-legged on the ramp. While Aimee prayed, a trombonist on the platform moved his lips in silent fervor, while from all over the auditorium came muted hallelujahs and amens.

In her sermon, Sister was a dynamo of energy. Every word was decisive, every gesture told. She traced the inspiration for her theme to her stay in India, where she said she had learned that a rose lasts only a few hours, but the attar, if captured, may endure for centuries. Jesus, she said, was the Rose of Sharon, and just as only by breaking the rose (here she tore a petal from a rose and held it up, lying like a drop of blood in her palm) is the perfume obtained, so the blood of the Lamb was shed to produce the attar of life everlasting. In her altar call she cajoled and pleaded, her voice alternately rasping and passionate. Children cried, a score of women

Sister Aimee preaching on "The Rose of Sharon" in one of the most vivid displays of virtuosity in her career.

fainted and were carried out by ushers. In front of the building the crowds stood raptly under the loudspeakers. Now and then a "Halle-lujah!" or a long, descending "Pra-a-aise His name!" broke the silence.

At last she finished, and, pale and drained of emotion, sank into her garlanded chair. While an elder solicitously handed her a glass of water, an assistant pastor sprang to the rostrum. Aimee drank the water greedily, while another elder fanned her. But in a moment she waved him aside and was once more at the pulpit, exhorting, with arms flung out, blue cape aswirl in the spotlight, calling on sinners to be saved. Sister had come back!

In a darkened room up the street, Mother Kennedy sobbed, "Oh, Aimee, Aimee!" and recounted her latest rebuff:

"I bought a little card. It had a picture of a rainbow on it, and a golden sun, and there was a blue sky. The blue sky meant 'love' and the rainbow meant 'hope.' I put it in a little envelope and wrote on it, 'To my darling, darling Aimee.' With my own trembling hand I wrote at the bottom, 'Always Mother, when you need me.' Kharvina [Minnie's secretary] took it over to the temple and tried to give it to Sister. They told her they would give it to Harriet Jordan, but not to Sister—they wouldn't even take it in!" Tears coursed down Minnie's cheeks. "Mother helped to build the temple, but now—not one word of love or forgiveness in the hour of Aimee's triumph!"

The next morning Ma and her secretary moved out to Hermosa Beach permanently; and there Minnie received, by ordinary letter post, her daughter's cool acknowledgment. On a printed "get well" card, Aimee had written, in her angular, schoolgirlish script:

"I have been advised of your illness, Mother, and I am sorry for you and hope that you will soon recover. May God bless you. Aimee."

For Minnie this was the final cut. While Sister plunged into a whirlwind of activity, Ma stamped the dust of Angelus Temple from her feet for good and cocked her eye toward a brighter future.

"Whataman" and Wedding Bells

~⌖~

"To her go I, a jolly, thriving wooer."
—*Richard III*

The news that came from the city of Longview, Washington, on June 28, 1931, seemed hardly more credible than had been Sister's vanishing in the ocean, in 1926. At 11 P.M. on that night in June, Minnie Kennedy, aged sixty, was married by the light of the moon on the banks of Lake Sacajawea, in the city park. The knot was tied by a religious co-worker of the bride, the Reverend J. G. Gay, who read the Angelus Temple double-ring service. As Minnie promised to "love, honor, and serve" the man who had captured her volatile heart, the officiating minister thought she made a very pretty picture against the shrubbery.

The name of the bridegroom was Guy Edward Hudson. Brother Gay had never seen him before. Immediately after the ceremony, the couple had driven away in Ma's big blue automobile, with Hudson at the wheel. Their destination was not disclosed.

The newspapers scrambled to shed some light other than the rays of the moon on this unexpected culmination of an unsuspected romance. The Reverend Mr. Gay was able to give them little assistance: the bridegroom he described as middle-aged, slender, of medium height, with smooth black hair—pleasant-spoken and apparently somewhat younger than Minnie. Mrs. Kennedy (that is, Mrs. Hudson) had told him, the minister added, that it was practically an elopement. Her words, as quoted by Brother Gay, had been:

"He just appeared and carried me off. He said, 'Get your bags and grips, we are going to be married.' It was just like love at first sight!"

Minnie also had said, Brother Gay recalled:

"Living alone was simply awful. But now, with someone to love and live with, I'm going to forget all about my trials and tribulations in Los Angeles."

Brother Gay had gathered that Hudson was an evangelist, but churchmen in the Northwest could recall no religious activist named Hudson. Inquiries at Angelus Temple brought the terse statement from business manager Winters:

"Mrs. McPherson never heard of Mr. Hudson."

The marriage license application stated that Guy Edward Hudson had been born in Missouri, his last previous address had been New York, his age was forty-six, and he was divorced. Mother's age had been entered discreetly at fifty-two.

For three days the honeymooners evaded all search. Then a reporter in Seattle stumbled upon them lunching in a coffee shop.

At first Ma tried to cajole the newsman into forgetting that he had seen them.

"Let's keep it a secret and you pretend you haven't discovered me," she suggested, digging into her meal.

Hudson offered nothing, and made such play before his face with his napkin that the reporter could hardly see what he looked like. The newsman did gather that the bridegroom was slightly built, had dark, slicked-down hair, and a watery smile. But Hudson waved aside all questions, explaining:

"You see, I have a bad cold and can't talk much. I must have got it staying indoors so much. This is the first day I've ventured out in daylight since our marriage. After all, Mrs. Hudson and I are both free and over twenty-one—that is, we *were* free."

At length Minnie, realizing the cat was out of the bag, consented to say a few words.

"This honeymoon," she sighed, "is the happiest moment of my life! You can tell the folks in Seattle I'm in a daze—I'm soaring in the clouds—I could travel on and on like this forever!"

She gazed fondly at her spouse, who was trying to get past the reporter and out of the booth.

"Reverend Mr. Hudson!" she sighed gustily again. "What a man!"

By this time Hudson was inching toward the door, the reporter sticking with him.

First sight of the wedded Hudsons, surprised in a Seattle restaurant. Guy
Edward kept his face covered with a napkin. The Rev. Theodore H.
Osborne, a friend of the bride's, looked startled. Minnie sighed, "What a
man!" and christened her husband.

"How long have you known Mrs. Hudson?" the newsman asked.
"For many years. I'll call you later and tell you all about it."
And he was out the door and away.
Ma, occupied with her dessert, crooked a finger.
"Boy," said she, "Pa's got a cold, but I can talk. I can tell things—
but I won't!" She winked.
How did she happen to marry Mr. Hudson? Her answer was
straightforward:
"Because he is the first man who ever came to me and didn't pull
that line about 'a little cottage with roses all around'—you know the
rest. I told him I wanted to carry the Gospel. 'Fine!' he said. 'Work!'
Then I got interested."
Would she call herself Mrs. Kennedy-Hudson? Ma was undecided: maybe she would get "Gee" ("that's my loving name for
him") to change his name to Kennedy. She regarded the debris of
her cantaloupe and sighed again:
"What a man!"
Then she picked up the check.

From that day on, in the nation's press, from coast to coast, Guy Edward Hudson was known and headlined as "Whataman."

The couple celebrated their first week of wedlock by appearing at a "costume rodeo" in Longview—Minnie in a powdered wig and satin knee breeches as "Lord Chesterfield," and Hudson as a cowboy, ambushed behind furious false whiskers that he refused to take off for photographers. Then rolling down the coast, stopping now and then to let Minnie preach to the inmates of jails, the honeymooners arrived at Hermosa Beach, where some of Ma's friendliest antagonists of the press were waiting.

These interviewers found Hudson apparently overcome by shyness.

"I had no idea what I was letting myself in for when I married Mrs. Kennedy," he exclaimed, but added gamely: "However, being married to her is worth it."

Said Ma:

"He's a brick! He hasn't failed me once! Poor boy! He can't understand why anyone should be interested in him. They gave us a lovely banquet up north, and he was miserable all through it. Why, do you know he has lost a lot of weight—just from worrying about having his picture taken and having people point him out. Everywhere we've been, somebody would recognize me and pass the word. And how poor Gee would shrink from it all!"

Ma shooed the reporters out the door with a parting word:

"Boys, just say we'll be on our honeymoon for the rest of our lives. And, oh, yes, now that we're married, I do hope folks will stop referring to me as 'Ma Kennedy.' I'm afraid somebody will hit on the idea of calling Mr. Hudson 'Pa Kennedy'!"

The next day, to escape from the sightseers who were hanging around the cottage, Ma and "Whataman" drove away to "ramble around a bit" and enjoy some privacy. First, Minnie took her husband on a tour of Angelus Temple. They drove up to the entrance like any tourists, marveled at Sister's residence glowing under multicolored lights, and then went through the great building that Minnie's energy and shrewdness had helped to erect from dome to basement. That was the last time Minnie's footsteps would ever resound inside that structure.

Then the couple drove away—as the newspapers phrased it, "fleeing into the land of flowers" somewhere south of the City of the Angels.

Unlocking her honeymoon cottage by the sea, Minnie lets "Whataman" in for a long stay.

Hardly had they dropped from sight when a woman living in Beverly Hills, a self-styled widow with a twenty-year-old son, announced through attorneys that Guy Edward Hudson was her husband, from whom she had never been divorced. This claimant to Ma's Gee was Mrs. L. Margaret Newton-Hudson. She said that she and Hudson had been married in Las Vegas, Nevada, in November, 1929. He had called himself a traveling salesman then, had given his age as thirty, his birthplace as Salt Lake City, and had listed a divorce from a previous wife in Bellingham, Washington, obtained in 1925. Mrs. Newton-Hudson further averred that Hudson had shown himself averse to gainful labor and that she had put up with this for four months and ten days, until he walked out on her in San Jose, in April, 1930. The manner of his leave-taking had been particularly distressing, she claimed, because he had stuck her with their hotel bill.

This was not the only irruption of that day. Simultaneously, from the opposite side of town, Mrs. Ethel Lee Parker Harbert was telling her lawyers, and the world, that Guy Edward Hudson had left her waiting not at the church but at the marriage license bureau in Los Angeles in 1929.

"He just rushed me off my feet," Mrs. Harbert recalled, "and we filed an intention to marry. It's still there. He was always telling me how he would make a lot of money and we would have a glorious honeymoon. He was a wonderful salesman, all right! But he kept postponing the date for our getting married, and my money was going fast. Then he made some excuse that he was going to make more money, and left. I didn't see him again until just a week before he married Mrs. Kennedy. Where did I meet him? Of all places—Angelus Temple! I had been there to hear Mrs. McPherson's sermon, and behold, who should I see in the congregation but Jack—that was how we knew him, he hated that name Guy. He was all nervous and confused when he saw me. I said, 'I hear you are married again.' 'Oh, yes,' he said, 'but that's all over.' I said, 'What are you doing here? Have you been converted to religion?' 'No,' he said, 'I'm not converted, I just came with a friend who wanted to see Mrs. McPherson.' I'm sure Jack is not a minister. When I knew him he never went inside a church."

Mrs. Harbert (she had herself been married since the shattering of her idyll with Hudson) produced a souvenir that she said she treasured—a snapshot of herself and "Jack" taken on the amusement pier at Venice.

"Everything was roses and moonlight for *us* then," she sighed.

And the same day, a Mrs. Guy Edward Hudson of Denver, Colorado, telegraphed to the Los Angeles police her suspicion that Ma's mate was the husband who had deserted her; she said the photographs in the newspapers looked like him. But this Mrs. Hudson proved to be mistaken.

In the midst of this cascade of accusations, "Whataman" and Minnie returned to town and notified the newspapers that they had come back to face the music.

"We were on our way to San Diego," explained Ma in a downtown hotel, "when we saw a newspaper. 'Gee,' said I, 'what about this?' Said he, 'Let's go back and find out.' So we turned around and here we are. This matter is going to be cleared up right now. You don't notice Mr. Hudson running away from anything, do you? He is here with me, and he is here because he has nothing to fear. Why, last night he said to me, 'Darling,' he said, taking my hand in his, 'if there is any question in your mind about this, we'll live apart until it is cleared up.' I said, 'My husband, I'll stick with you till hell freezes over, and don't you forget it!' You can tell the world—all of you—that Mother Kennedy-Hudson has got her fighting togs on and is going to battle for her happiness!"

Standing in the background, "Whataman" pushed out his chest proudly as Mother spouted on.

"That beach photograph!" she sniffed. "Let 'em show their pictures! I don't care how many women are after him! You say it's only three? There ought to be three thousand! I'm going to hire a lawyer for my husband tomorrow morning, and I announce right here and now there will be no tribute paid to anyone! A Las Vegas marriage! Well, I have my opinion about that, too! Bring 'em on! We're not afraid! He's my man and I'll fight for him! All for love, but not one cent for tribute!"

As for that slur about "Whataman" not being an ordained minister, Minnie snapped:

"Of course he's ordained! I ordained him myself! Just before our marriage!"

Then she snatched up the telephone and called a lawyer.

And the next morning she held another press conference while breakfasting in bed at the same downtown hotel. Hudson was not on hand, and Minnie suffered a spasm of hysterics when a callous reporter suggested that he had run out on her.

"He is too noble!" she gasped between sobs. "I pressed him to stay here, but he said we would live apart until this thing is settled. I was alone—and oh, how I missed him!"

It transpired that Gee had checked into a hotel two blocks down the street.

Her purpose in resummoning the press, Minnie at length got down to saying, was to issue, through the newspapers, a challenge to all self-styled Mrs. Hudsons, whoever and wherever they were, to come out in the open and fight for their man.

"Gee is just like any other popular man," she said spunkily. "There are plenty of Janes following him around—but he is mine and I am going to keep him! I'll scratch the eyes out of any woman who tries to take him! It's just like Aimee's affairs—I've settled a dozen and one cases for her. Certain wives of certain men thought she had money, and made all sorts of charges, and I had to quiet them down. I'm serving notice again—all for love, but not one cent for tribute!"

As for concrete plans, she said she was going to get her marriage annulled, thus freeing "Whataman" to get a quick Nevada divorce from Mrs. Newton-Hudson—provided that marriage had really been on the up-and-up. Then Ma and Gee would remarry and live happily in their cottage by the sea.

Spurred on by incessant telephone calls, her lawyer drew up the petition for annulment within one hour and brought it to the hotel. Hudson had been summoned, and cameras recorded the poignant scene as Minnie and Guy sorrowfully signed the document. Slowly Ma slipped the wedding band from her finger and handed it to Hudson, who dropped it into his vest pocket with a doleful air.

"It's off temporarily," sighed Minnie, "but when this is settled we'll be married again—and what a wedding!"

Then she hustled the lawyer away to file the papers that very day, while "Whataman" dissolved out the door.

Disengaged for the afternoon, Ma improved the time by issuing a pronunciamento to the public on the subject of love, life, and the hazards of matrimony. It was one of the briefest statements she ever gave out.

"Marriage," she proclaimed, "is in the heart, the most delicate, tender, and thrilling of life's varied experiences. To me it has come in an unexpected moment and mode. The public have been informed (and misinformed) of various and sundry aspects of my love-union with Mr. Hudson. Before this reaches you, dear friends, I will have signed with my heart's blood the application for annulment of my wonderful marriage to the only man in this big wide world for me. For my part, I would never say 'separate,' for our hearts are welded in the sunlight of love."

Then Minnie drove into the sunset, back to the honeymoon home, hinting that "Whataman" was already Reno-bound. But wherever he might be, she was sure he would be thinking of her because of the pocket Bible she had pressed into his hand as they parted.

"I'll be hugging my lonesome pillow tonight," she murmured mournfully, then brightened: "But it won't be for long!"

That day in Cowlitz County, Washington, where Longview is situated, an unsentimental district attorney disclosed that he was drawing a complaint against Guy Edward Hudson, charging bigamy, and he wondered whether Mrs. Margaret Newton-Hudson—if expenses were paid—would be willing to come to Washington State and testify. On those terms, replied Mrs. Newton-Hudson, she would be charmed to assist justice.

In Seattle, where she was presiding over a Foursquare Gospel Bible School commencement, Mrs. McPherson held aloof from her mother's marital dilemma.

"Mr. Hudson is just a newspaper headline to me," she said. "Our paths didn't cross. Anyway, that is strictly Mother's business." As for her stepfather's reported plurality of wives—"That also is Mother's business. But I do read the newspapers!" Her eyes flashed and her laugh was jolly.

Closer to home, Minnie's plight was winning unlooked-for sympathy. The *Los Angeles Times*, a staid and at times severe journal that more than once had been denounced by the Angelus Temple pair as among their detractors, made handsome amends in an editorial headed "Ma's Mix-ups." Exuding good nature, it read:

"Whatever else may be said about Ma Kennedy, it must be

admitted she takes the slings and arrows of outrageous fortune like a good sport. In her courage, in her willingness to face facts, and even in her *joie de vivre*, Mrs. Kennedy sets an example that might be followed by other grandmothers—in spirit, of course, not in detail. Ma has had enough happen to her in the last five years to discourage almost anybody. The drowning, the kidnaping, the return from the desert, the discovery of Carmel, the quarrels, bashes in the nose, the breach of promise suit, and now this crowning indignity, have not, however, made her down-hearted. Her irrepressible spirit bounces like a rubber ball—the harder it is hit, the higher it rises. What a woman!"

Ma could use a little friendly encouragement, for her woes were increasing. The day after Minnie petitioned for an annulment, Mrs. Newton-Hudson filed a suit in Los Angeles for divorce from the vanished "Whataman," optimistically asking the court to award her five thousand dollars alimony and five hundred dollars for attorney's fees.

Minnie was pleasantly sarcastic:

"I'm glad to know Mrs. Newton [sic] places a fairly high price on Mr. Hudson. If it had been me, I'd have made it five hundred thousand dollars, at least. The photographs of the ladies now attempting to associate with Mr. Hudson show that he has excellent taste and discrimination. But needless to say, there will be no money forthcoming from me."

But her fortitude was shaken when her lawyer advised that should Mrs. Newton-Hudson divorce "Whataman" in California, a whole year must elapse before he could remarry. To Minnie a year meant a year closer to eternity, and she gave up.

"All right," she surrendered. "I'm through, all washed up. From now on my life is my own. If the other lady considers herself his wife, I'll gladly relinquish him to her and perform a new marriage ceremony for them myself—and give them our rings and my blessing. And it won't be a Las Vegas ceremony either!"

A few hours after thus bowing out, she was hostess at tea in her cottage to some very special guests—two examiners and the secretary of the Los Angeles Lunacy Commission, who had been sent to determine whether there were any grounds for certifying Minnie as mentally awry.

The action had been brought by a watchman at Angelus Temple, one B. F. Clearwater. He had appeared at the office of the lunacy commission and requested that a complaint be issued against Mrs. Kennedy-Hudson. He denied that he represented Mrs. McPherson or any temple official and said his action was being taken solely because of the "hundreds of telephone calls" coming to the temple, demanding that "something be done about Ma."

He presented a prepared affidavit, to which he swore, and which stated that, to his knowledge, Mrs. Kennedy-Hudson was:

1—Senile;

2—Suffering from lapses of memory;

3—Subject to delusions of persecution;

4—Addicted to dressing fantastically in short skirts in an effort to appear youthful;

5—"Likely to be imposed upon by other persons!"

The commission thereupon dispatched two alienists and its secretary to Hermosa Beach to conduct an official examination.

It is a long drive from central Los Angeles to Hermosa Beach, and Minnie had plenty of warning from a friendly reporter. She slipped around to the beauty parlor to have her hair curled, then changed into a severe black chiffon with velvet. When the delegation, accompanied by her lawyer, arrived at 4:10 P.M., she opened the door smilingly and invited them to step inside; perhaps they would join her in a cup of tea?

The door was closed, and two policemen stood guard outside. In the street, reporters and several hundred spectators stared and fidgeted.

One hour and twenty minutes later the door opened, and one of the psychiatrists stepped outside to give reporters a written statement that nothing in Mrs. Kennedy-Hudson's behavior or mental processes warranted her commitment to a psychopathic ward.

Minnie graciously bade her visitors good-bye, then turning to the impatient newsmen, informed them:

"The examiners acted like gentlemen. I had a real nice chat with them. I enjoyed it."

She would not hear of anyone blaming her daughter for the occurrence; she put it down to a "general temple campaign" against her.

After being visited by the Lunacy Commission, and convincing them that she was saner than some of themselves, Ma said a prayer for "Whataman," who was somewhere dodging bigamy charges.

"I've been expecting it since 1927," she confided. "I haven't been afraid of it either, because I'm as sane as any of them."

Of course the press tried to find out whether Aimee had known about the maneuver, and in Portland, on her way back to California, Sister denied all responsibility.

"If Mr. Clearwater or anyone else connected with Angelus Temple thinks my mother is insane, and if they wanted her committed to an asylum, it is only because they wish to protect her and me. I am desperately sorry about the whole situation."

As Ma thought over this disclaimer, she became indignant.

"Angelus Temple had better attend to its own loonies before trying to put me in the squirrel cage," she announced. "There are plenty of them over there, and it's always best to start the good work at home. That fellow Clearwater—he's only a monkey on a stick! Somebody told him to sign that complaint. As for that statement the papers say Aimee made, that it was an act of kindness and only done to protect me—pooh! Pooh! And a couple of more poohs!"

She said she was going to sell her cottage, because she couldn't sit on her front porch without people gawking at her; and she put up a big "For Sale" sign on the lawn.

"I've been in such a whirl," she exclaimed, "I haven't even had time for a good cry!"

What effect would all this have on her program to remarry "Whataman"? Ma whispered into the ear of a reporter, "I'm not going to hang my harp on the willow!" and waltzed into the house.

When the Los Angeles County sheriff received a telegraphic request from Longview to arrest Guy Edward Hudson (whom the telegram identified as aged thirty-seven) on a charge of bigamy, the elusive "Whataman" was not to be found. He was, among other things, dodging process servers in the suit brought against him by Mrs. Ethel Lee Parker Harbert for breach of promise to marry. Her optimism was even greater than that of Mrs. Margaret Newton-Hudson, for she was asking a quarter of a million dollars as heart balm. During their association, her complaint asserted, "Whataman's" dominant characteristic had been that same repugnance for gainful employment that had annoyed Mrs. Newton-Hudson; in fact, she had been obliged to keep the romance afloat financially by pawning her rings.

The newspapers were having trouble keeping the several Mrs. Hudsons distinct, and they became further confused when Mrs. Margaret Newton-Hudson and Mrs. Minnie Kennedy-Hudson entered the courtroom of Superior Judge Sproul arm-in-arm for the hearing on Ma's annulment petition. The proceedings were marked by brevity.

Attested Minnie: "He mentioned a woman named Margaret, but said his marriage to her had been either annulled or she had got a divorce."

Swore Mrs. Newton-Hudson: "I married that man in Las Vegas on November 22, 1929. He is my husband."

Said the judge: "Annulment granted."

In Los Angeles Superior Court, Mrs. Minnie Kennedy-Hudson and Mrs. Margaret Newton-Hudson join forces to enable Minnie to get an annulment of her marriage to "Whataman" and let Margaret get a divorce.

Ma's ready tears overflowed as, with an arm around her predecessor in "Whataman's" affections, she offered a prayer for them both. They left the courtroom chummily. Minnie had been married—or almost married—just three weeks and four days.

The next morning her Gee (who, it developed, had never left Los Angeles) was the star attraction in another courtroom when he appeared for arraignment on the bigamy charge. He had surrendered the night before and had spent the night in jail, after declining to tell the booking clerk whether he was "single" or "married." (The clerk had concluded that in view of the circumstances it would not be too far off to list him as "married.")

When he was brought into court, there in the front row of spectators sat Ma, on her lap a handbag bulging with banknotes to provide his bail. She blew him a kiss as he entered, and after he had pleaded "not guilty" and bail had been set at fifteen hundred dollars, she posted the necessary. A few minutes later she posed for the newsreels in front of the Hall of Justice, fondly shaking hands with her liberated ex-consort.

All this activity, however, went for nought when the governor of Washington refused to sign an extradition warrant to bring "Whataman" back for trial. Times were hard, said the governor, and the state's extradition fund would be used up fast enough "in caring for Class A criminals." Mrs. Kennedy and Hudson he considered merely "a couple of careless performers." So the bigamy prosecution lapsed by default.

Next—while Minnie's lawyer was letting it be known that in spite of that display of cordiality at the annulment hearing, inquiries were being made into the validity of Mrs. Newton-Hudson's divorce from a husband who antedated "Whataman"—Ma relaxed by composing her memoirs at the beach cottage. Attired in floppy blue pajamas trimmed with pink and white, she wrote for hours—doing for "Whataman," she said darkly, what she had once done for Aimee— "using my brains. We'll save him yet. I'll prove that Mr. Hudson has been crucified." Then waving her fountain pen: "I'm not buying a husband. Not one cent on the line from me for anybody or anything!" And she returned tirelessly to her beneficent task.

Friends who were privileged to peruse snatches of Ma's outpourings said they were a paean of poetry and love.

"I shall always be satisfied that Mr. Hudson thought himself free when he married me," read one passage. "He treated me as he would a piece of fragile china. He loved me for myself alone."

II

This was the year of jubilee, the year of wedding joys and griefs for the Angelus Temple family.

When Sister McPherson returned from the Northwest, she assembled reporters and told them she had hastened home to preside at the marriage of her son, Rolf McPherson, to Miss Lorna Dee Smith, a Bible School student. Both were eighteen.

The interview took place at the parsonage in the midst of preparations for the wedding rehearsal in the temple next door. Dressmakers

Arraigned on a bigamy charge, "Whataman" Hudson shakes hands with his bailbondswoman, Minnie herself, who plunked down $1,500 to restore him to temporary liberty. "Attaboy, Jack!" she cried. "You are absolutely right when you are absolutely wrong!"

were darting about, musicians were receiving instructions, telephones were ringing in a happy confusion. Aimee said she had been told of the engagement on her return from the world cruise, and at first she had felt that Rolf was too young to marry; but after thinking it over she had given her consent. The wedding was to be held in the temple, with five thousand invited guests, and in a setting of Hollywood splendor.

Sister's interest in her mother's current difficulties seemed to be minimal. Asked about that attempt to have Minnie Kennedy-Hudson committed, Aimee thought it all very foolish.

"There never was the slightest suspicion of insanity in our family," she said. "Naturally, the whole thing is very tragic. All I know about it is what I have read in the newspapers."

"What disciplinary action, if any, do you propose to take against Clearwater?"

Sister studied her reflection in a long mirror, eyeing the fit of her pulpit uniform of white satin.

"I don't know," she replied. "I would have to make a thorough investigation."

"If Mother should come to you with open arms and suggest that you both agree to let bygones be bygones, how would you act?"

Aimee's eyes flashed.

"I don't think it is fair to ask that!" she shot back. "The relations between Mother and myself are our own affair, and I am determined no longer to have them aired in print! It seems to me that you have all delighted in taking one of us in one hand and the other in the other hand, as you would two little bulldogs—and hissing, 'Sic 'em!' There will be no more of that!"

And out of the room she swept, to direct the rehearsal.

The crowds on the wedding day brought out police reserves; four thousand persons were shut out. The pageantry lasted almost two hours, starting with a hundred and twenty members of the temple choir singing "Semper Fidelis" and a musical program that included grand opera, light opera, vaudeville, and popular airs. Sister McPherson, queenly in white, was mistress of ceremonies. As four bridesmaids and four groomsmen arranged themselves below a flight of steps, at the top of which Aimee waited radiantly, and the choir sang "Ah, Sweet Mystery of Life," the bride and bridegroom slowly descended the ramps along either wall, and ascended the stairs until they stood just beneath Sister. With just a suspicion of tremolo Aimee read the service, while violins softly played "Honest and Truly." At the close she bestowed her maternal blessing with an abandon that brought deafening applause. The wedding cake on the platform, four feet high and shaped like Angelus Temple, was cut up and passed among the guests, and then the newlyweds drove away to honeymoon in Aimee's mountain cabin at Big Bear.

Minnie had not attended the wedding, but she sent her blessing.

"So Rolf is getting married," she said. "Tell him his grandmother wishes him well."

Rolf McPherson's marriage occurred in July. Roberta Semple's marriage had been in March. Minnie Kennedy had been married (she thought) in June. All in 1931. Of the temple family, only Aimee remained unwed.

She had no time to devote to thoughts of romance, for the burden of her work was increasing from day to day. The Depression held the country in a starvation grip. Los Angeles had been hit hard; it was not an industrial city, and a large portion of its population was made up of retired farmers and tradesmen, whose savings had been wiped out by the crash. Thousands of formerly well-to-do persons found themselves reduced to poverty and many to total destitution. Such facilities as existed for coping with a crisis so grave were utterly inadequate, and their resources were rapidly used up. Aimee threw herself and the energies of her church membership into the emergency.

When the city and benevolent agencies could no longer provide free hot lunches for schoolchildren, Aimee did. She expanded the temple's commissary department again and again and, continuing to run it on a policy of "give first and investigate afterward," brought at least the basic means of subsistence to thousands of hungry, homeless people.

Coincidentally with this extra activity, Sister's legal harassments piled higher. She was sued for various sums, always on the same general grounds—services allegedly promised and not performed, failure to remit, misrepresentation, expectations unfulfilled, bills not paid. The federal government claimed twenty-one thousand dollars in unpaid income taxes for the years 1926, 1927, and 1928. It was the government's contention that large sums that she had collected and credited to church revenue in reality had been devoted to her personal expenses, mainly legal, and therefore were taxable. Replied Winters, the temple manager:

"Our attorneys believe one way and the government officials believe another. If the Board of Tax Appeals determines Mrs. McPherson has to pay her tax, she will pay it the same as anybody else."

But despite the harassments, Sister bustled through her tasks with

Aimee officiating at her son's wedding in Angelus Temple before five thousand invited guests.

vigor and good humor. To snatch a brief rest now and then she would retire to the villa she had built in the hills some sixty miles southeast of Los Angeles, overlooking picturesque Lake Elsinore. This structure attracted sightseers: it was an oriental fantasy, a stucco palace with flat roofs and minarets and domes, altogether an odd sort of home for a Christian minister, some carpers thought. Actually, the building was modeled on the Near Eastern architecture that Aimee had seen on her visits to Palestine. Stories were told of the villa's lavishness: the ceiling of Sister's bedroom was said to be covered with gold leaf and that of Roberta's room with silver; the door knobs were silver, and the lighting fixtures exotic. There was a garden and a swimming pool, but no telephone, and heavy gates shut out the curious, providing Aimee's only place of real seclusion. That was a luxury to which she clung.

Throughout the hot summer, meanwhile, Minnie Kennedy-Hudson continued to pursue her happiness in the person of Guy Edward Hudson, who in early August had popped up in Las Vegas—not seeking a divorce, he protested, just "escaping the heat." Mrs. Newton-Hudson was holding steadfast in her determination to get a California divorce unless she was reimbursed one thousand dollars, which she said it had cost her to square the bills "Whataman" left behind when he vamoosed. Guy Edward Hudson's impecuniosity was apparent to all, and Minnie declined to fork up.

"I want the world to know I'm friends with everybody," she proclaimed, "but I am not going to pay back bills, and I am not going to buy a husband."

She waved a telegram just received from "Whataman," cooling himself in the shadow of Boulder Dam. It read:

"THIS WILL SURELY SURPRISE YOU TO HEAR THAT I AM NOW RESIDING IN NEVADA. HAVING COMPLETED OUR PRESSING BUSINESS AND BEING UNABLE TO BE WITH YOU I AM ATTENDING TO IMPORTANT BUSINESS HERE."

Back wired Minnie:

"ATTABOY! YOU ARE ABSOLUTELY RIGHT WHEN YOU ARE ABSOLUTELY WRONG! REST ASSURED AND BE CONFIDENT OF MY LOYALTY AND SUPPORT. AS TO PARTIES HARASSING YOU FOR MONEY, YOU DO NOT NEED TO ENTERTAIN THE SLIGHTEST ANXIETY. MY DEEPEST LOVE, GOOD LUCK, AND GET RID OF THAT COUGH."

Forty-eight hours after this exchange, a Las Vegas attorney arrived in Los Angeles with information that when Guy Edward Hudson and Margaret Newton applied for a marriage license in 1929, she had listed a previous husband (an army colonel) as deceased and herself as a widow, whereas in reality the colonel had been no more dead than any other ex-husband; she had merely divorced him in Panama. Upon receiving these tidings, Ma threw a couple of dresses into a suitcase and headed for Las Vegas, shouting as the train pulled out:

"We're wearing our wedding rings again!"

At the Las Vegas railroad station she jumped off the train, picked up the waiting "Whataman" in her arms and took the "great big kiss" she said she had been promising herself all the way from California. A crowd of several hundred had gathered to witness her arrival; they cheered. Bowing to this well-disposed gallery, Ma stepped into one of the automobiles Gee had become a salesman for, and was driven to a comfortable house placed at her disposal by a city commissioner; Las Vegas intended to do right by its famous visitor.

In 1931 Las Vegas had none of the tourist glitter that would gild it later. It was a raw, brawny, brawling construction camp, a throwback to such rowdy outposts of half a century before as Virginia City, Tombstone, Gold Hill, and "bold, bad Bodie." Its population was largely the construction workers who were building Boulder Dam, a swashbuckling, devil-may-care, unruly crew. The prohibition law was a dead letter, there being a saloon every fifty feet, and gambling went on everywhere without hindrance. Ma suited the frontier spirit, and wherever she went she was warmly welcomed. At the Boulder Club, one of the flashier bars and gambling rooms, she jumped up on a crap table and preached a red-hot revival sermon, and the boys yelled for more.

After a brisk overnight stay, she traveled back to Los Angeles with a photostatic copy of the Newton-Hudson license application in her purse. Twenty-four hours of palaver ensued. Although Minnie was present at the legal huddles, she insisted it was only as a spectator; but soon word got out that Mrs. Newton-Hudson had decided not to press her divorce action; that she would, in fact, withdraw the suit and allow "Whataman" to get an annulment, or a divorce, or whatever he could, in Nevada.

Nevada law required six weeks of residence before Gee could file an action, and during this lull Ma found herself with nothing to do. Rather than fiddle the time away, she graded her front yard, driving a team of horses hitched to a road scraper and mowing the grass to help out the news photographers. Then she painted her house.

After six weeks, Hudson applied for a divorce in Las Vegas. The story he told the court was commendably concise. He said that one evening Margaret and he were "sitting peacefully at home, when my wife looked out the window and exclaimed, 'Why, there's my husband!' He came in and I went out."

The court waited for him to continue, but his tale was told.

Said the judge, "Divorce granted."

Minnie was on hand, and she had not forgotten to bring a chiffon bridal veil. Thirty minutes after the court ruled, she and "Whataman" took out a license to marry. A girl reporter offered to press Ma's dress and crimp her hair, but Ma cried, "I've got something better!" and out of a bandbox lifted a wig.

"One of Aimee's old ones!" she smirked.

In the excitement the wedding rings could not be found; Hudson had sent them to a jeweler to be polished. But at length they were retrieved, and a long procession of automobiles led by the mayor and the district attorney (the hero of the hour because of his securing the first conviction for murder in the town's violent history) and bearing the flower of Las Vegas, escorted the reunited couple to the site of Boulder Dam (later Hoover Dam). On an observation point a thousand feet above the rushing Colorado River, the ceremony with the shined-up rings was performed by a justice of the peace. When the two were pronounced one, Ma shouted, "He's mine again!" and six hundred construction workers set off a dynamite blast.

The bridegroom signed the visitors' book, "Pa Hudson."

A cottage at the edge of town had been prepared for the honeymoon, and that night a tipsy parade straggled down the road from the saloons, blowing horns, banging pans, letting fly with sixshooters, in an old-fashioned shivaree. But the canny lovebirds had decamped. With "Whataman" at the wheel of Ma's automobile, they were tooling westward toward a honeymoon stay as the guests of Death Valley Scotty, in his desert home on the floor of the valley that he advertised as "the hottest place this side of Hell."

The day after the wedding, a reporter drove out to where the knot had been tied. Hundreds of cars were parked on the plateau above the dam site, and the path leading down to the observation point on the rim of the canyon was crowded. The reporter heard scores of sightseers ask to have pointed out the rock on which Ma and "Whataman" had stood, but not one asked about the engineering marvel rising under their feet, Boulder Dam.

III

During the latter days of that August, while Mother was plotting strategy to retrieve her Gee, Aimee had been immersed in the staging of her latest Biblical oratorio, "The Iron Furnace." She had been working on the book and score, she told the press, for a year and a half, and in the production she would function as author, composer, scene designer, costumer, producer, director, and advance agent.

The first-night performance—before a capacity audience in the temple, with four hundred and fifty costumed actors—was in the supercolossal style of filmland. Aimee led the orchestra and between acts doubled as narrator. She was alluring in a shimmering green gown with a girdle of gold; a red-and-gold embroidered headdress covered her blond hair. The action dealt with the delivery of the Israelites from bondage in Egypt, and critics approved the fine voice of the singer who took the part of Moses. They paid little heed to the booming baritone who sang the role of Pharaoh, and this was not perspicacious on their part, because three weeks after that opening-night performance, Aimee Semple McPherson eloped with Pharaoh. Offstage, Pharaoh was known more prosaically as David L. Hutton, Jr.

The elopement was carried out with utmost secrecy. At 3 A.M. on Sunday, September 13, two closed automobiles sped from the parsonage to an airport in Burbank, twelve miles away. In the cars were Aimee, Hutton, Rolf and his wife, Winters and his wife, and Harriet Jordan. The party boarded a chartered plane, which three hours later set them down at Yuma, Arizona. The county clerk was routed out of bed, and issued a marriage license; Hutton gave his age as thirty, and Aimee hers as thirty-eight. (She was within less than one month of forty-one.) Back at the airport, the couple stood on the steps of the plane while Harriet Jordan read the marriage service handed to her by Sister. Both Aimee and Hutton spoke their responses quietly, Aimee looking tense and pale, but not otherwise nervous. She was wearing the newest of the current Eugénie hats and a modish blue suit trimmed with fox fur, set off by blue shoes and handbag. She appeared even younger than her stated age, and surprisingly small beside Hutton.

As the service ended, a patter of rain lashed across the field, there were kisses all around, handshakes for the bridegroom, and the plane took off. It landed at Los Angeles at 10:30 A.M.—at a different airport to elude crowds—and at 11 A.M. Sister was in the pulpit at the temple preaching a sermon on the love story of Ruth and Boaz, "Ruth and the Gleaning." Husband David lent his baritone to the choir. No announcement was made to the congregation at that service.

But the news had been flashed from Yuma, and immediately after the service, Aimee faced reporters in the parlor of her home next door.

"Who is he?" was the first question.

"The finest man ever!" responded Aimee. They had met casually six years before, she said, but the romance dated from his being engaged to sing the role of Pharaoh. Proudly she flashed her wedding ring and diamond solitaire. "I've been taking voice lessons from him and he has been helping me with my musical work," she went on breathlessly. "Maybe that's how the romance began. Anyway, he is a splendid man and I know we are going to be happy—gloriously happy! I've been lonesome for sixteen years, but now God has rolled away my lonesomeness!"

Would she be known in the future as Aimee Semple Hutton? She laughed and disclaimed having any extreme views in that line.

"In my work I will still be known as Aimee Semple McPherson, because all of my organizations are incorporated under that name. But in private life I'll be Mrs. David Hutton."

Up to this point she had stood alone, dressed in her pulpit uniform of blue cape and white silk gown.

"Now," she smiled happily, "I want you to meet the fine man who is my husband, while I get fixed up for photographs."

Hutton stepped into the room. Practiced eyes took in swiftly that he was tall, heavy-set, and broad-shouldered, had dark hair, blue eyes, a jovial smile, dimples, and a rich, rather high-ranging baritone voice. He walked with a slight limp as a result of an attack of polio when he was a child, and was proud of having overcome the handicap to the extent of becoming a good tennis player. He was pelted with questions. Was it love at first sight? Hutton grinned.

"You figure that out for yourself," he advised. "You can say it is a real love affair, first sight or otherwise." They had not planned to be married so soon, "but Mrs. McPherson—I mean, Mrs. Hutton—is going north on an evangelistic tour and we decided we could go together and combine a honeymoon with our work."

The evangelist returned, hair smoothed and dress freshened, and snuggled up to her husband for the flashlights. Picture-taking over, she went across to the temple to conduct the afternoon service. Hutton took a seat on the platform, among the assistant pastors and elders. Reporters watched intently to observe the reaction of Sister's followers to this dramatic abandonment of her oft-stated belief that divorced persons should not remarry as long as both partners were living. Again and again she had said that she would not remarry, or at least "Mr. McPherson would have to cash in first," and had usually added that there was no man around whom she wanted to marry. Nevertheless, an accepted attitude of her church was being challenged.

The feeling of Sister's congregation was quickly made apparent. Hutton was asked to lead in the singing of a hymn, and when he selected, "There Is Sunshine in My Soul Today," the throng applauded. Then Brother Arthur, by right of seniority and his years of devotion to his church and pastor, formally gave the marriage the temple's blessing.

"We elders approve of Sister's choice mightily," he declared.

Sister stepped forward on David's arm and told her followers of her glowing happiness.

"It hardly seems real yet. I've been alone for sixteen years, and I've hated every day and every night!"

Hutton added that "we are sure, after much prayer, it was ordained by the Lord."

Mother Kennedy (who was just departing for Las Vegas and reunion with her quicksilver Gee) was tickled by the news.

"My darling deserves the best in life, and they have my deepest love and best wishes, both personally and for God's work," she exclaimed, and wired her blessing.

The Los Angeles newspapers gave whole pages to this latest of the temple family's marriages, all occurring within six months. The radio was no less taken up with the event, and on Monday morning

First picture of Aimee Semple McPherson as Mrs. David L. Hutton, Jr. Aimee and her husband posed for cameras in her home, the Parsonage, next door to Angelus Temple, on her wedding day, September 13, 1931.

a broadcast was piped directly from the bridal boudoir in the evangelist's home.

Beside Sister's canopied bed a microphone was planted, and an announcer described the sumptuous setting—thick purple carpet, draperies, a dressing table cluttered with feminine toiletries—while Aimee, slim and elegant in a clinging negligee, smiled from a divan. Hutton, wrapped in a bathrobe, told the listeners about the inexpressible happiness of his bride and himself, and thanked everybody for the telegrams, flowers, fruit, and other gifts pouring in for "the most precious girl in the world. . . . Now you will hear my wife."

He passed the microphone to her, and she quoted Scripture to explain why she had married, then handed the microphone back to her husband, who quoted Scripture to the effect that his path had been directed from above. Then over the air came the smooch and smack of a long-drawn kiss.

Downstairs, lawyers were waiting with a prenuptial agreement that had been drawn up, but not yet signed, under which Aimee and Hutton mutually waived all claims to each other's property. These papers being signed and the lawyers dismissed, the bridegroom made a trip to his parents' home in Pasadena to collect his clothing and got a foretaste of what being married to a celebrity meant when he found a police motorcycle squad waiting at the Pasadena city line to escort him the rest of the way. His parents were not at home, having gone to a Long Beach hospital where Hutton's aunt lay ill; so back to the parsonage sped David, reporters pounding him with questions all the way.

"I shall make it my business," they quoted him as saying, "to see that Aimee is hindered by no more carping critics. I shall be pleased to smack on the nose anyone who persecutes my wife by making slanderous remarks about her."

From the parsonage, Hutton drove with Aimee in the evangelist's sixteen-cylinder coupe to Long Beach, where Sister carried out divine healing rites for the recovery of Hutton's aunt. Then home for more interviews and photographs, until Hutton rebelled.

That evening, at the final performance of "The Iron Furnace," Sister told her audience the reason for the secrecy of her elopement.

"Always my slightest move has been flaunted before the public," she said. "Much of this publicity has been of a sort to cause mental anguish—I don't have to be more explicit. Since the nervous breakdown I suffered a year ago, the sound of newsboys in the street below, calling out their headlines, has given me cold chills of apprehension. I was in a hysterical state, suffering spasms, when we began our trip to Yuma Sunday morning. I decided to have it all over as quickly as possible, so that the big spread of news would come in one smash."

Then in a rush of emotion she told what this love meant to her.

"You have no idea of how lonesome I have been. I have been alone all of my life except for four years, my previous married life having covered only that period of time. But I am through with being lonesome now! Oh, it is fine at the end of the day, when you are all hot and wet, to know that someone is waiting for you at home! I have seen the young couples whom I have married in the temple as they kissed each other, and I have just stood and wistfully watched. I used to watch Rolf and his bride, and Roberta and her sweetheart, as they came in from evening strolls, excitedly talking about the moon, and they would grab me and say, 'Isn't the moon wonderful, Mother?' But I couldn't find anything wonderful in the old moon. I have been seeing myself home every night with a trip-hammer in my throat. I have stood while loving couples in my congregation would start for home saying, 'Good night, Sister,' and I would force myself to smile a cheery, 'Good night!' Then I would go home and kiss my own hand, and tell myself, 'Good night, Sister.' You remember the word of the Good Book—'It is not good for man to be alone.' Well, it's worse for women. But lonesomeness is gone now and I am singing that song, 'It's All Different Now.' Love came in on silver wings and I don't think I'll ever complain about anything any more!"

But the world's curiosity was not so easily satisfied. The press published fact after fact about Angelus Temple's new consort. Hutton had been born in Dawson, Illinois, and had lived with his parents in or near Los Angeles for years. He was a singer and vocal instructor, maintained a studio in Hollywood, and had served as audition manager for a radio station and a film company. At his Vine Street apartment, friends described him as endowed with a winning, forceful personality. His name had never figured prominently in the news before, although about a year previously he had been mentioned in a copyright dispute over a song for which he had composed the music—a number entitled "My Faith in You"—but the episode had been trivial. His marriage had surprised his own friends as much as it had the temple membership.

In the search for comment, the newspapers tried even "Whataman" Hudson, but he ran true to form and declined to be quoted, saying:

"When I married, I lost the power of free speech. You'll have to ask the better half."

Ma was not reticent.

"After one good look at the picture of that freshie Aimee married," she shook her head dubiously, "I'm stronger for my Jack. There are things that just aren't done—and one of them is broadcasting from one's bridal boudoir."

Hutton's tribulations as the husband of the most publicized preacher in the world began on the very Tuesday after his Sunday wedding. That morning a process server knocked at the kitchen door of the parsonage, bearing a summons in an action instituted by one Myrtle Joan Hazel St. Pierre, charging David L. Hutton, Jr. with breach of promise to marry. Hutton, who was unaccustomed to summonses, appealed to his wife as they sat in the upstairs living room, chatting with a reporter. Aimee knew all about process servers.

"Go down and face him," she counseled. "Show him you are not afraid of this woman's story."

Hutton hesitated, but she encouraged him:

"Don't be afraid, darling. You've got to expect such things when you marry a woman like me. Everyone of prominence has to go through it."

Hutton went downstairs and returned blushing and indignant.

Myrtle Joan Hazel St. Pierre, who described herself as a therapeutic massage nurse, in her complaint asserted that she had met Hutton at a Hollywood party in January of that year, and eight days after they met, intimacies had taken place; after which, she contended, his ardor cooled until he ceased to see, call, or speak to her. The shock of hearing over the radio Sunday morning that her David had married "one Aimee Semple McPherson" had produced such distress of mind and body, the complaint further stated, that Miss St. Pierre could find assuagement only in the sum of two hundred thousand dollars.

"Why," expostulated Hutton, "there isn't a word of truth in it!

This woman has simply taken advantage of my marriage to try to get money from me! I only knew the woman six weeks!"

Aimee listened and smiled.

"If that's all there is to it," she said, "we won't even call an attorney. We'll go on our honeymoon as we planned and forget all about this woman. To consider a settlement," she addressed the reporter present, "would be to encourage every little girl Mr. Hutton ever ate ice cream with or treated to soda pop to file similar suits. She's barking up the wrong tree." She stood up. "Well, breach of promise or not, I'm going to the hairdresser. Stick with it, dear! You've got to expect all that now."

The next day Sister's lawyer, appearing on behalf of Hutton, filed a blanket denial of the accusations made by Myrtle Joan Hazel St. Pierre.

But, as Aimee had predicted, other troubles sprang up around her abruptly acquired husband. Mrs. Roland Neese, a radio entertainer residing in Long Beach, announced that she was looking for a lawyer to file a complaint on her behalf similar to that of Miss St. Pierre. And in Pasadena, a Mary Jane O'Kane instructed an attorney to prepare an action based on the alleged grievance that Hutton's slow fox-trot, "My Faith in You," had been dedicated to her originally, and not to the baritone's Angelus Temple bride, as radio listeners were being told.

These fresh alarms merely caused Aimee and Dave (as the newspapers called him) to laugh as they headed toward Portland, Oregon, where Sister was to conduct an eight-day revival. They passed through San Francisco and motored out to San Quentin prison, where Aimee shook hands with Asa Keyes, who as district attorney had prosecuted her in 1926 and had done his utmost to put her in prison himself. Keyes was about to be paroled, and Aimee expressed the friendliest feeling for him and wished him well. She also shook hands with her former attorney, Cromwell Ormsby, who was doing time for jury tampering—though not in any case connected with Aimee. Ormsby was still suing the evangelist for several hundred thousand dollars over the discarded film project. Aimee bore him no ill will and chatted easily with him before passing along to pray with a notorious "hammer murderess," who was under sentence of death.

All this was startlingly novel to Sister's husband. Standing outside the gates of San Quentin, he mopped his brow and ejaculated:

No time for a honeymoon, the newlyweds took off to conduct a revival in Portland, Oregon. From left, Aimee, Hutton, his mother and father, Mr. and Mrs. David Hutton, Sr., and an unidentified friend.

"Married on Sunday—chased on Monday—sued on Tuesday—in prison on Wednesday—what a life!"

Aimee assured him he would get used to it after a while.

In Portland, she received an offer to preach in Boston—in the Boston Garden, a sports arena seating twenty-two thousand. This was indeed a challenge, for on her "vindication tour" the clergy of Boston had shut her out. The manager of the Garden flew to Portland, and Aimee signed a contract. The opening date was set only three weeks away, and she returned to Los Angeles to prepare. There she told her flock that she and her husband had called off all plans for a honeymoon trip and would carry the Word to Boston instead. After nominating her husband to be one of the temple's twenty-four elders, she retired to her Moorish villa at Lake Elsinore for two days of rest.

When she came back to town she looked bronzed and fit. Curled up in a big chair in the parsonage, she chatted with the press on how it felt to be a bride.

"Really, I know little about that," she said frankly. "I have been married only four years in my life, although this is my third venture."

Was she sure this marriage would last?

"This marriage of mine can never fail—never!" she answered earnestly. "I have all the longing of those empty years to give me realization of what this means. I was like a tree clinging to the hillside, bowed down by the wind, as I built my temple and fought my fight," she went on, dramatizing herself as she dramatized every fact and incident in life. "Now I have someone to shelter me, someone to lean on. Just last night the completeness of our happiness made itself so apparent. It was getting late, and David asked me if I would say evening prayers, with Rolf and Lorna Dee and David's mother gathered around us. I said, 'No, David, you're the head of the house; you say the prayer and let me be just plain wife.' And he did, and I cried and was so happy."

She was full of plans for her Boston trip. Her sermon topics had been selected, she said: for the final meeting, she intended to preach on "Curfew Shall Not Ring Tonight," and swing out over the audience clinging to the clapper of a huge bell. To show that she was in trim for such a feat, she bragged a little that before starting back to the city that morning she had swum across Lake Elsinore, three and one-half miles, paced by a rowboat, and had made it in one hour and twenty-five minutes. She was delighted to tell about it.

On Sunday, October 4, Aimee and David set out for Boston, sped by the cheers of a thousand followers.

"They say I am going into Boston cold," she shouted, "but I'll guarantee you that I am going in there red-hot, to turn that town upside-down with the biggest revival ever seen on the Atlantic seaboard!"

The obstacles she faced seemed insuperable. Times were desperately hard (this was 1931, close to the nadir of the Great Depression), and she could count on little organized support in Boston. The Unitarians, Episcopalians, and Congregationalists were cold or hostile, and she could hardly expect Catholics to turn out to hear a Protestant spellbinder. Her contract called for a daily outlay on her part of twenty-six hundred dollars, in addition to the personal expenses of her party.

The first day in Boston she and David called on Mayor James Michael Curley at City Hall.

"This is my thirty-ninth birthday," she told the mayor, her eyes shining, and introduced her husband.

Off to Boston in happy union to score a resounding success.

Curley, his eyes also twinkling, promptly handed her a shillelagh with the remark, "If you are going to drive the devil out of the people who go to Boston Garden, you had better have this."

Pointedly, the mayor suggested that it would be a fine thing if she contributed half the proceeds of her collections to the city's unemployed, who were daily growing in numbers and were vociferous in their appeals to City Hall.

Countered Aimee:

"I'll give it, if you will take up the collections."

Even before she got back to her hotel, the mayor put out a statement to the effect that Mrs. McPherson had pledged her word to make a fifty-fifty split of her collections with the city's needy.

"Oh, for goodness' sake!" exclaimed Aimee when she saw the mimeographed handout. She suggested that the mayor had "shot over a fast one," and got on the telephone to the Garden. Apparently Curley had taken the first set in the game.

Her opening meeting was on Saturday evening, at the start of the long holiday weekend over Columbus Day. Her audience numbered just under five thousand. In the cavernous Garden they seemed lost. Undaunted, Sister threw herself into her sermon, and reporters present were moved to admire her courage. She joked about the trick played on her at City Hall, but praised the mayor—"one of the best businessmen I have met in a long time. Now let's get hold of a $5 or a $10 bill! It all goes for the expenses of the campaign and the unemployed. It's very old-fashioned and very simple, the way we take a collection," she explained with good humor. "We just pass the plate." But the offering brought only about $500, and at Sister's altar call, only eleven men and nineteen women came forward.

On Sunday she preached to sixty-two hundred persons in the afternoon, and to an announced fourteen thousand three hundred and two in the evening. (The police, with or without prejudice, gave their estimate of the evening turnout as eighty-five hundred.) The collections rose to $700 in the afternoon, and $1,000 at night—still far short of expenses. Quipped Aimee as she led the singing, standing before a huge American flag:

"There are too many curleycues in this campaign!"

But she persisted, and on Monday, Columbus Day, the response picked up further. Her energy, meanwhile, was wearing out the press representatives assigned to report her every move. After she had preached to a crowd of ten thousand on Monday night, she invited the newsmen to come with her on a tour of the night clubs.

"The parable of the lost sheep is on my mind," she said.

Dressed primly in black velvet with lace collar, a jaunty black

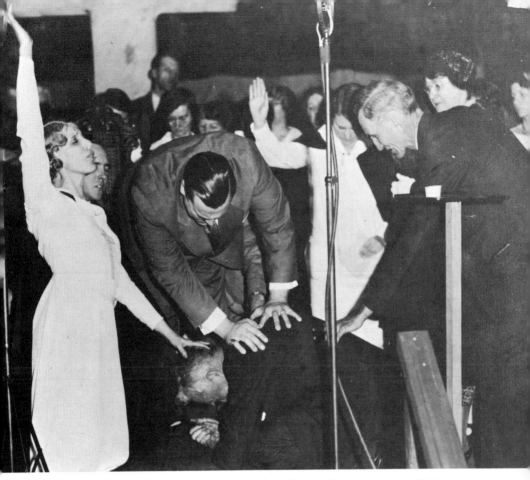

At healing service in Boston, Aimee invokes divine aid to restore a blind man's sight, while Hutton and an elder lay on hands in apostolic rite.

Eugénie hat and smart white jacket, and wearing a diamond necklace that she said was her husband's birthday present, she sallied out with her escort. In the night clubs where hot jazz blared she was neither embarrassed nor forward. When permitted to say a few words, she spoke pleasantly to the patrons, telling them, "The ninety and nine were safely in the fold at the Garden tonight. I hope you folks will come to fill up the top balcony." Flashing a special smile toward the orchestra, she added, "And bring your lovely orchestra, too."

So the week progressed, and tier by tier the Garden filled. For nine days she preached with fire and charm, and on the final night, Sunday, a capacity crowd of twenty-two thousand heard her, and many were turned away.

The evening ended with a surprise. After the collection had been taken, Sister told again about her visit to City Hall. She had only praise for Mayor Curley, and she spoke feelingly of her concern for the unemployed everywhere, not only in Boston, and told about her work for them on the West Coast. Quoting the mayor's observation that religion and charity ought to go hand-in-hand and that she might donate half the profits of the campaign to relieve suffering locally, she turned to Hutton, standing behind her on the platform, and said, "Husband, lend me five dollars." He handed her a $5 bill. She held it up.

"Now," she cried, "I am going to take another collection for the unemployed. It is going to Mayor Curley and the unemployed tomorrow morning. And if the offerings of the week's services show our expenses have been paid, we will split everything left over with the unemployed, too!"

The crowd stirred uneasily, for this was strange to them. Aimee dropped her $5 bill into a collection plate and started the ushers around again. There was a little laughter, then a spatter of applause, and soon all over the immense hall sounded the clink of coins falling into the plates. Before the end of the service Sister announced the total—$908.90. Then she asked the crowd to join in singing "God Be With You Till We Meet Again," made a final bow, shook hands with the ushers, and hurried off to catch the train to New York.

The next morning Richard Dunn, manager of Boston Garden, filed an accounting at City Hall. It showed that at eleven meetings the regular collections had brought in $23,506.30. Expenses totaled $23,441.48. The net surplus—$64.82—was divided equally, the poor of Boston receiving $32.41, and Aimee receiving the same. In addition, the unemployed benefited by the special collection of $900-odd dollars. Total attendance for the nine days was one hundred sixty-five thousand three hundred. Aimee appeared to have taken the match.

Back in Los Angeles, an all but civic huzza was raised for Sister's triumph over Eastern doubters. The *Los Angeles Times*, speaking on behalf of the less Aimee-dazzled elements of the city, editorially saluted "A Good Sport" and judiciously pointed out that "an audience of one hundred sixty-five thousand three hundred in nine days is not to be sneezed at."

Aimee glowed. "I like Boston!"

Heart's Balm, But No Heart's Ease

"Let not the heavens hear these tell-tale women
Rail on the Lord's anointed."
—*Richard III*

Aimee's public relations—and sooner or later Aimee's most private relations became public—seemed flourishing at the commencement of 1932. Happy in her marriage and absorbed in her work, she appeared to have run her wild courses and settled down. Her church was growing steadily, her charitable activities were winning grateful commendation, and Los Angeles took pride in Sister.

As the depression deepened, the temple's resources had been strained and overstrained, and Sister told her people frankly that the church was forty thousand dollars in debt, although no mortgage stood against the temple. Meanwhile, bread lines in the streets stretched longer and longer, "Brother Can You Spare a Dime" became a hit song, and public machinery to alleviate misery on so unprecedented a scale creaked to a halt.

Aimee threw herself into the breach, through her commissary department enlisting scores of workers and by sheer drive and insistence organizing a relief program that embraced the entire Los Angeles area. In November of '31 she had opened her first soup kitchen, where, from 10 A.M. to 2 P.M., stew, soup, coffee, and rolls were served to all comers. In addition, the police and fire departments were pressed into service to distribute food and clothing to the destitute in their homes. At Christmas time, the Bible School students made thirty thousand wreaths and greeting cards and sold them from door to door, bringing in funds to pay for twenty-one thousand five hundred Christmas baskets to the needy. A second soup kitchen was

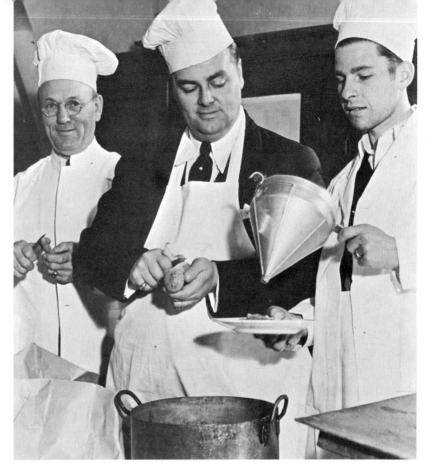

David Hutton, assisted by his father, left, and Rolf McPherson, gives send-off to one of Aimee's soup kitchens, which fed thousands of hungry in Los Angeles in the early days of the depression.

opened, feeding five thousand persons a day. A free medical-dental clinic, staffed by a dozen doctors and dentists, was started. A school of practical nursing trained five hundred women especially in the care of children and elderly people suffering from malnutrition. Aimee flattered, cajoled, and bullied ranchers, meat packers, bakeries, bankers, and business groups of all sorts into donating supplies and talked truckers into hauling the provisions gratis. She prodded the government at Washington to throw open a disused army cantonment at Alhambra, east of Los Angeles, where twenty-five thousand unemployed might be housed and raise vegetables for their partial sustenance.

Amidst these labors her health failed again, and she experienced attacks of vertigo, in one of which she fell and sprained her wrist badly. She had preached her 1931 Thanksgiving Day sermon with one arm in a sling and told the press cheerfully that during that week she and Hutton had turned down stage and film offers totaling half a million dollars, rather than slight the temple's relief work. By the close of January, 1932, the program seemed to be running sufficiently smoothly to enable her to depart with her husband on a rest cruise to Panama. She confessed to the followers who bade her good-bye at the dock:

"We are tired of being goldfish. We want to have a little privacy and do a lot of resting."

Hutton had been given official standing in the church organization, having been appointed business manager, succeeding Winters; he had also been elected vice-president of the Echo Park Evangelistic Association in place of Sister's daughter Roberta.

Roberta had somewhat withdrawn from active participation in church affairs since her marriage; her husband Smythe disliked the superheated emotionalism that prevailed around Angelus Temple, although there was no personal antagonism against his mother-in-law. He was seldom seen at Echo Park. At first there had been talk of his taking a place in the church administration, but he preferred to be independent and had found work selling insurance. He and Roberta occupied a modest flat off Wilshire Boulevard at some distance from the temple and lived out of the limelight. Roberta's replacement in the family corporation by Hutton therefore excited little comment. Hutton's father had been given a place as purchasing agent for the temple, and his mother was serving as "mother" to out-of-town Bible School students as well as supervising Sister's household arrangements.

At the first of March, 1932, the Huttons returned from their cruise, and Sister seemed revitalized. She fairly bubbled with enthusiasm as she outlined her latest project—establishment of a "missionary radio network" to cover the entire Caribbean region and reach into French Equatorial Africa, perhaps in time to girdle the globe.

One week later, while preaching her Sunday sermon, she collapsed, and doctors hurried her to a hospital for a blood transfusion. A medical bulletin said, "She has reached the point of complete physical exhaustion," and once more her followers prayed in relays that she be spared.

Twenty-four hours after the transfusion, the astounded doctors reported that she was improving so rapidly she might leave the hospital by the end of the week. This she did, and on Sunday she preached twice, telling the crowd in the evening:

"Now I am going to take it easy—I won't preach again until Thursday."

In this crisis, a rumor sprang up that Sister McPherson was about to sell Angelus Temple and retire from public life. Her followers were thrown into dismay, and all the city took interest, for Angelus Temple and Sister had become civic institutions.

The proposed sale of the temple was an episode that would always remain murky. The would-be purchaser, according to his account, which later was supported by statements made by other parties, was the Chicago evangelist who had substituted for Mrs. McPherson during her absence in 1926, the Reverend Paul Rader. In 1932 he was preaching independently in Los Angeles. He said he was approached by an emissary purporting to be speaking for Sister McPherson. This go-between alluded to the precarious condition of Sister's health, which would probably force her to give up active work, and said that in view of this she might be willing to sell Angelus Temple. Rader maintained that he had been shown a draft contract, containing interlineations and corrections in a handwriting that he recognized, for the purchase of everything—temple, Bible School, parsonage, radio station, and real estate holdings. The down payment was to be fifty thousand dollars, another three hundred thousand was to be paid within ninety days, and the total price, one million dollars, was to be remitted over a period of six years.

Rader consulted bankers to find out whether he could get backing for a deal of this magnitude and was promised financial support, he said. He added:

"Then I waited for further overtures. They were not long in coming, through another agent, who represented himself as a temple business manager."

By this time both Rader's headquarters and the temple offices were buzzing. In response to expressions of alarm from her membership,

Sister assured her flock that she would never desert them. With newspapermen, however, she was more direct.

"Well, I can't go on forever," she pointed out. "I've been able to preach only about five months during the last three years because of my health. I might take a long vacation—that's not improbable. And while I will not say that Dr. Rader has opened negotiations, I will say that he is a good man and would be an excellent evangelist for this work."

What would she consider a fair price for the temple?

Aimee whispered to Hutton, who was sitting beside her, and scribbled figures on a pad, then said:

"Oh, it represents far more than a million dollars. In times like these, when almost all churches are in the red, Angelus Temple is an alluring proposition, inasmuch as it continues to show a profit. . . . I will not say that I am negotiating with anyone for the sale of Angelus Temple," she hedged again, "but if the right sum is named, I won't say that I would refuse it."

Then instantly she added:

"However, should the temple ever be sold, I will continue in similar work, after a rest. It is my life."

The contradictions and cross-statements kept up for several weeks. Aimee's attitude veered erratically. At one time she said:

"Angelus Temple is not for sale. The properties are worth at least five million dollars. We put three and a half million into them in hard-earned cash, and the developments should add another million and a half dollars."

And at another time:

"Whether there ever has been a contract, or whether it is a figment of somebody's imagination, the temple is not for sale. Furthermore, you can't buy it with peanuts!"

But only forty-eight hours later she was admitting that certain of her associates ("well-meaning if overzealous") had in fact been negotiating with Rader, and "while thought of selling Angelus Temple had not entered my mind before, should the condition of my health reach the point where I could not continue my work here, I believe Mr. Rader would be the logical person to take up my burden. If Mr. Rader has sufficient capital for such an investment, any proposal he chooses to make to me personally will receive every con-

The Huttons relax on a Caribbean cruise while trouble builds up at home.

sideration from me and the Angelus Temple board of directors, to whom I will submit it."

Mrs. Kennedy-Hudson gave her opinion of the matter by saying that her daughter would be justified in selling out while she was still on top.

"Aimee's no Methuselah," said Ma. "She has to quit some time. Walking down the aisle with a bunch of roses is a bit different from attending to the million and one details of the temple organization—that job is killing. If my daughter sees a chance to be free, I hope she'll be happy. I told her once there was no need to be chained to her burden. If my little girl feels she wants a change, I hope she gets it. If she sells Angelus Temple and wants to buy an airplane, I hope she gets that."

Would Ma be interested in taking over the temple? Minnie laughed good-naturedly.

"Me? I'm divorced from that temple! If they took it down brick by brick, it would be of no interest to me. Its work has been done."

The shillyshallying (as he saw it) tried Rader's patience beyond endurance, and at length he made his story public and bowed out.

"I did not seek the temple," he insisted. "I was approached by its agents. Details of the contract were gone over thoroughly and the negotiations progressed favorably with one exception—I failed to receive assurance from Mrs. McPherson-Hutton that when I took over the work of the temple I would have a congregation as well as a building. I was not assured that I would not be interfered with in my work at the temple."

Aimee hurried out a counterstatement that Angelus Temple positively was not for sale—"It is my past, my present, and my future."

That closed the episode; but Aimee's nerves were obviously on edge, and her doctors tried in vain to diagnose the cause of her recurrent prostration. She was plagued especially by outbreaks of carbuncles, such as had beset her during her legal troubles in 1926.

In April, the agitation over the possible sale of Angelus Temple having subsided, she left Los Angeles to conduct a revival in Kansas City. Hutton went with her, and from Kansas City they proceeded to take a sea voyage to Central America. A coming event that preoccupied them both was the trial of the breach of promise suit instituted against Hutton by the therapeutic massage nurse, Myrtle Joan Hazel St. Pierre. There had been no compromise, and the case was calendared to come to trial in a few weeks.

II

The faithful at Angelus Temple received spotty advices from the travelers, but they all indicated that Sister was benefiting from the sea air. Therefore it was a shock when, early in June, announcement was made that Sister was home again—taken off the train on a stretcher—and secluded in an apartment in the Wilshire district.

The medical report was that Sister had contracted tropical fever in Guatemala, and "frequent hemorrhages and the fever, with worry, have caused her condition to become serious. She needs complete rest."

At the temple, Hutton told the congregation that Sister had suffered a general collapse and was very weak.

Just at this juncture the lawsuit brought against the evangelist by Harvey Gates, the scenarist for Aimee's abandoned moving-picture film, came up for trial. Sister's physician warned the court that "a grave attack of neurasthenia and . . . internal complications . . . make it impossible for her to attend to any business or court matters," and reluctantly, in view of numerous previous delays, the judge set the case over to a date four days after the scheduled start of the Hutton-St. Pierre trial.

Aimee was insisting that when her husband's case came up she would appear beside him in court, but the medical advisers forbade it; they doubted that she could survive such an ordeal. It was decided, therefore, to tell her that the trial had been set over, and she was taken in an ambulance to her fantasy castle at Lake Elsinore, in charge of a nurse. At Elsinore there were no telephones, and she would not be disturbed. She was there, cut off from the radio and newspapers, when the trial did start.

In a courtroom packed to suffocation, mainly with giggling women, Myrtle Joan Hazel St. Pierre took the stand to relate the events that she alleged had culminated in her seduction by the husband of Aimee Semple McPherson. The weather was warm, but it was not as warm as the testimony. The trial fascinated the public, both because of its lubricity and because over everything hung the unseen presence of Angelus Temple's pastor.

Discreetly guided by her counsel, Miss St. Pierre, demure in mourning black relieved by a froth of lace at the throat, testified that, on the very first night they met, Hutton told her, "I was lovely, adorable, and wanted to know where such a gorgeous creature had been kept all this time." She described with histrionic effects her alleged downfall:

"He seized me in his arms and crushed me to him, raining kisses on my hair, my eyes, my mouth, my neck. I pushed him from me and he fell from my divan to the floor and pulled me down on the floor with him. He told me marriage is a man-made convention that can be ignored at times. . . ."

At this point, choking with sobs, she clutched at her attorney and slumped to the floor, almost pulling the lawyer after her. The judge ordered the room cleared, and the disgruntled crowd shuffled out muttering and remained stubbornly standing in the corridor outside while the nurse's testimony continued in camera.

Myrtle Joan (she pronounced it Jo-ann) Hazel St. Pierre said she had been married twice, but preferred to use her maiden name. She testified that some of the "passionate interludes" had occurred in the massage establishment where she was employed, and on a blackboard she drew a diagram of the place's layout, indicating its various facilities with "MT" (massage table), "HB" (health-building room), and "SG" (salt-glow table). It was on one of these tables, she said, that (as a newspaper put it) "two-hundred-fifty-pound Dave went in for body-building in a big way." Myrtle recalled that he had arrived late that night for his regular treatment.

"He told me he loved me dearly and asked me to be his wife, and I told him I would marry him," she testified. "But he said it couldn't be right away. He said he would have to wait until some oil wells near Santa Barbara came in, or until he began making records of his voice, or cashed in on songs he had written. He said he would be making a thousand dollars a week when this took place. I believed him implicitly."

As she recounted this she gazed fixedly at an autographed photograph of Aimee's husband she held in her hand. Said Hutton during a recess:

"They're not trying Dave Hutton in this case; they're trying poor Aimee, who lies flat on her back in the hospital."

Essentially, it seemed that this was true.

Neither of the nominal principals was accorded any dignity by the newspapers, and readers who had a taste for pruriency were abundantly gratified. Hutton was characterized as "the former choir boy who espoused the front pages when he wed the Angelus Temple pastor," as "the corpulent chorister," as "the overstuffed playboy," and was depicted as "cringing under the blasts from the witness chair, where sat, reclined, or crouched the pretty nurse who charges he practically wrecked her with his off-tackle rushes, which ended unsatisfactorily for her in a homemaking way."

Miss St. Pierre battled a withering cross-examination, which was reported tongue-in-cheek, the news accounts crediting her with ability to "out-talk, out-argue, and out-yell all opponents, including the judge"—who, in addition to the vocal irritants, was victimized by an ulcerated tooth and swollen jaw.

Three times she was admonished by the suffering bench to stop trying always to get the last word. Should an attorney interject, "I withdraw that question," she would swiftly cap it with, "And I withdraw my answer!" She wrangled with Hutton's lawyer over the pronunciation of the word "salon," and finally consented to have it called "saloon-salon." When the same attorney spoke of her "masseusing" patients, Myrtle corrected his French haughtily. Much of the testimony was salacious, more was scandalous, and all was broadly reported by the press, which also published numerous photographs of counsel, plaintiff, defendant, and spectators (the public having been readmitted); among the last appeared Rolf McPherson and his wife glancing at each other, giggling and looking embarrassed.

Miss St. Pierre was forced to admit that she was thirty years old, and although she professed to have been utterly prostrated by grief and humiliation after Hutton's ardor cooled, she had not been too ill to give "a few salt glows and magnetic massages" in a Glendale hotel.

"I was in and out of bed," was her description of her condition.

A violent dispute developed over how much weight she claimed to have lost in consequence of her mental anguish, and the record finally stood that she had dropped from one hundred fifty pounds to one hundred forty-eight.

She denied that after the breakup she had told a friend that Hutton was "a puddinghead and a mamma's boy" and he "could go to Hell." And the press made sport of her inability to recall whether, on a certain evening, Hutton had "popped the question or merely popped a few more bourbon corks." Asked why recently she had been using the name Jean de Ville, that, she replied, was because of Peeping Toms. She also charged that attempts had been made to bribe, discredit, or get her to leave the state.

The crowd tensed when the famous name that hovered over the proceedings was spoken for the first time. Hutton's attorney was pressing Miss St. Pierre, and he asked:

"Did you or did you not say to Dr. Marshall, of the Marshall Health Institute in Hollywood, in October, 1929, that it would be

Myrtle Joan Hazel St. Pierre holds photograph of David Hutton in court-room during trial of her heart-balm suit against Aimee's husband. Empty candy boxes in front of her were intended as exhibits of the gifts he allegedly showered upon her.

a good idea to have a doctor get Mrs. Aimee Semple McPherson into a compromising position and shake her down for some dough?"

The response came blazing:

"I did not, and that looks like a stunt to frame me!"

When at last the witness stepped down, she was overheard to mutter, according to published reports:

"All I want now is to show up that man in a big way!"

What was transpiring could not be concealed from Aimee indefinitely; trouble was erupting on too many fronts. The suit over the unfulfilled scenario contract had come to trial, and the court, exasperated by so many postponements, had entered judgment against the evangelist for ten thousand dollars. Aimee knew nothing about this until the day after it occurred.

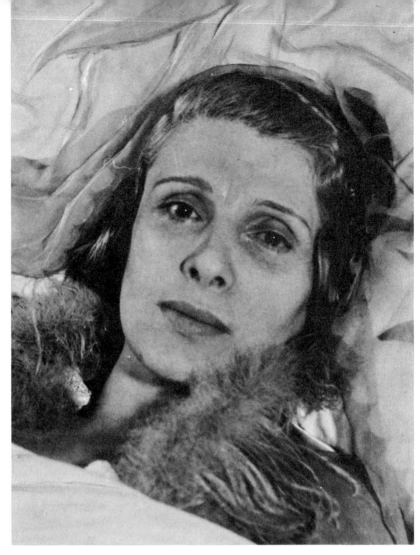

While Hutton sweated through the St. Pierre trial, Aimee was carried from hospital to hospital, deathly ill, unable to find rest. News photographers, finally admitted to see her, found her haggard.

For better care she had been taken to a desert sanatorium at Palm Springs, and halfway through the first week of her husband's trial she asked to see a newspaper. The doctor was hesitant, but decided that the risk must be accepted. Several papers were brought, and Aimee read the detailed accounts of both court actions—against herself and against Hutton. Both events were related in terms galling to a proud spirit, and Aimee was proud. She said nothing while she read, seeing her husband caricatured in text and photographs as a bombastic figure of fun.

After she had finished, she lay silent for a while. Then she said only that she was certain David would exonerate himself and requested that the news cameramen who had tracked her to the hospital be allowed to come in; since her return from the Caribbean, no photograph of her had been published.

The photographers were admitted; they found Aimee looking wasted and feeble, but she spoke calmly. And that evening, seeming in an unusually docile mood, she told the doctor:

"Now I feel better. I guess I'll have to stay here six or eight weeks longer, but I'll stay until I'm well again; then I'll go back to my work with as much pep as ever. Watch and see."

Her confidence was the more noteworthy because the newspapers had informed her also of another attack made against her prestige and public esteem. In a speech before the Los Angeles Bar Association, a judge had charged that Angelus Temple solicitors were working a political shakedown, offering the support of temple radio broadcasts in return for a cash "donation." Roy A. Watkins, whom Hutton had appointed head of the temple's commissary department, was implicated in the judge's statements.

Regarding this, Aimee told the press that she was out of touch with affairs at the temple, but she was sure that nobody was trying to sell radio time politically.

"This will come out all right," she smiled brightly. "Wait and see."

But that night her condition deteriorated, and the St. Pierre trial went into its second week of frazzled lubricity. Over the weekend, Hutton had assured reporters that his wife was "only amused" by the testimony of Miss St. Pierre.

"She thinks it is something of a joke that anybody should bring such a suit against me," said he.

During the following days, Hutton's counsel paraded more than thirty witnesses through the box in a massive attack on Myrtle Joan Hazel's character, her actions, and her intentions. She wept and objected as the transcript took on the tone of a bedroom farce. She fainted and was carried out of the courtroom, and the judge ordered that she be kept out until she had regained self-control. And the testimony continued in a riot of ice cubes, gin bottles, nightgowns, miniature golf courses, Arabian rug dealers, hand-kissing, midnight spankings, Lotharios in spats and cane (in July), "treatments," "treatments," "treatments," and a male witness who testified he had visited Miss St. Pierre's bungalow at late hours and "played with her goldfish and a three-legged duck in the yard."

In vain did the judge plead with counsel to wind up the testimony, reminding them that the trial was costing the taxpayers heavily. He received anonymous threats for his pains. And the storm of words continued.

A former friend of Miss St. Pierre's testified that Myrtle had told her, after pouring "a couple of drinks," that David was "a liar, a sissy, a mamma's boy," and a "big fat slob," and Myrtle Joan Hazel's sister recounted discussions that she said they had held concerning the chances of Myrtle's collecting heart balm, after hearing about Hutton's marriage to the temple pastor. The sister also said that once, during an argument over one of Myrtle's husbands, "she knocked me cold" with a single blow.

The climax came when Hutton himself took the stand. He had been the target of innumerable cameras in court and according to one account had been "also touched, poked, and prodded by the fingers of innumerable women among the spectators, until he must have resembled a pot roast after a hard Saturday at the market."

The newspapers outdid themselves in describing "Dave's" manner and language. One reporter wrote that the Angelus Temple baritone "lifted up his voice in a three-hour oratorio entitled 'The Great Denial,'" while categorically spurning every suggestion that he had committed any improprieties with the plaintiff. It was this same reporter's opinion that, if "Dave's" version of the matter were true, "Miss St. Pierre had every reason to feel love-starved during the period of their acquaintance." The transcript bristled with his "I did not!," "I certainly did not!," and "Absolutely no!" Other witnesses had entered their denials even more vehemently: "Incredibly no!" and "Absolutely and indelibly no!"

"Did you ever kiss Miss St. Pierre's knee?" counsel demanded. "Ever take any liberties with her? Ever enter a bedroom with her alone?"

Hutton's voice boomed in refutation of each and every charge, and he was still on the stand when the second weekend recess intervened.

During that weekend Hutton received a death threat, and Aimee was

Testifying in his defense, Hutton vehemently denied every charge preferred by the therapeutic massage nurse. One reporter said the baritone singer "lifted up his voice in a three-hour oratorio entitled 'The Great Denial.'"

thrown into hysterics when she saw what she believed was a prowler outside her hospital window. An Angelus Temple guard was posted at her door, and police detectives fanned through the grounds vainly searching for an intruder. But the incident so unnerved her that she was transferred to a resort in the San Bernardino Mountains, completely isolated.

The next day she spent two hours in the sun and seemed cheerful when the trial was mentioned.

"The charges made by this girl are ridiculous," she told friends. "I can't believe David would ever say the things she says he did."

She felt so well that evening that she had dinner with her husband, the first meal they had enjoyed together since their return from the Caribbean. Aimee reclined in a steamer chair and teased David about the testimony; she was confident he would win the trial.

"The idea of David being guilty of such charges! It's absurd!" she exclaimed lightly.

But the new week produced new ribaldries for the public's delectation, when Hutton's cross-examination provided the press with a carnival of slapstick comedy. He showed up on Monday morning armed with a tear-gas fountain pen and produced an illiterate letter threatening him with death or dismemberment. The court quickly disarmed "Big Boy," as the newspapers were calling him. The weather was sizzling hot and the courtroom became an emotional oven. At times waves of uncontrollable laughter swept the spectators, relieving the tension, and in vain the toothache-racked judge attempted to preserve decorum. In vain he urged opposing counsel to terminate the questioning. Hutton's denials of any and all misbehavior rolled on.

"You are sure you never kissed Miss St. Pierre, never failed to drop her hand immediately after shaking it, and never placed your hand on any part of Miss St. Pierre's anatomy during your evening automobile rides together?"

"I am absolutely sure!"

"Then you were the great unkissed David?"

"I was!"

At this three defense counsel arose and cried in unison:

"I object!"

Again the banging gavel of the judge was drowned by laughter.

Once, Hutton said, when he was ill and failed to call "Miss Pierre" (he pointedly omitted the "Saint" from her name), she telephoned him and told him he could "go straight to Hell." And he was positive that he had never called her a "gorgeous creature."

Although professing to be sanguine as to the outcome, he admitted glumly to reporters during a recess, "It's anybody's ball game." The press was undecided which of the litigants was ahead in the race; all they were sure of was that the public was the loser.

That the action was spreading discord at Echo Park became apparent when a delegation of well-wishers, identifying themselves as members of Angelus Temple, handed Miss St. Pierre several baskets of flowers as a symbol of their sympathy on the steps of the Hall of Justice. The temple elders hastily repudiated the group, and to head off any more floral demonstrations sent guards to patrol the courthouse corridors with the special bailiffs assigned by the court.

In a florid summation, Miss St. Pierre's counsel read the story of King David and the prophet Nathan from the Bible and implored the jurors to "send this sweet, old-fashioned girl back to society; she might have been a virtuous wife." The defendant's boisterous denials the attorney scorned as "Huttonian mouthfuls."

Hutton's lawyer retaliated by reciting "The Shooting of Dan McGrew."

Saturated with eloquence, the jury of seven men and five women deliberated six hours and returned their verdict. From the start, they said, they had been unanimous in finding for Miss St. Pierre, but it had required eight ballots to reach agreement on the amount of damages they would award her. They settled on five thousand dollars. Cheers greeted the verdict.

Hutton was at the temple when the result became known. He was stunned.

"They can't be telling the truth!" he wailed. "Why, it's rank injustice! Oh, it's all a nightmare!"

In Sister's twelve-cylinder limousine he sped to Lake Elsinore, to be the first to break the tidings to his stricken wife.

III

It was shortly after seven o'clock on Saturday evening when Aimee, relaxing on a sun deck of her minareted villa, saw the car turn into the driveway. In it she espied her husband and Roy Watkins of the commissary department. Rising, she called down:

"What is the verdict?"

Hutton shouted back:

"It isn't so bad after all, Betty! It'll cost us only five thousand dollars!"

Aimee swayed, and before the attending nurse could reach her, she fell, striking her head on the concrete floor. She was unconscious for forty-five minutes. Her doctor was summoned urgently from Los Angeles.

The newspapers were informed of the mishap, but for the most part dismissed it as a mere "bump on the head." Nevertheless, reporters were sent to Elsinore to investigate.

They found the gates of the villa locked and watched by scowling guards.

"Where's Aimee? We want Aimee!" they called, until Hutton appeared, pulling on trousers over a wet bathing suit. His weekend guests could be heard splashing in the garden pool.

Hutton told the deputation that Aimee was too ill to see anyone. Would his wife help him out of his financial predicament, they wanted to know; there had been rumors at the temple that "the ball is rolling" to get rid of him. He offered to get a statement from his wife ("from her own lips") attesting her unshaken devotion to him and trotted away.

Returning shortly, he pushed a slip of paper through the bars of the gate. On it was scrawled:

"Certainly I am for my husband—and always will be, $5,000 or $50,000."

To the reporters the handwriting looked like Hutton's. They asked him again about those temple rumors.

"I've heard them for months," was Hutton's answer. "I defy them to put me out. Aimee is boss down there. She is president and pastor, and we are very much in love. At least, I love her dearly. Darn it all!" He clasped his head in his hands. "Can't a fellow go for a drive with a girl without being accused of everything under the sun?"

The laughter of the swimmers disporting themselves in the pool carried clearly to the open window of an upper corner bedroom where Aimee lay. She had suffered a basal skull fracture in her fall, her physician said, and "she is an awfully sick woman."

Aimee McPherson's "Moorish castle" on Lake Elsinore, east of Los Angeles, where she received word of the result of the balm trial, fell, and was injured.

In the midst of her woes, a scandal about graft in the temple's relief program had broken into print, and the city's Social Service Commission had ordered an audit of the commissary accounts. Large contributors of supplies, notably bakeries and packing houses, thereupon had suspended their cooperation while the matter was being threshed out.

The allegations included lurid yarns about a police raid on a still being used by solicitors for the commissary to make liquor out of donated apricots, and about a leakage of sauerkraut and salad oil from the commissary supplies to neighborhood groceries. At a hearing in City Hall, Hutton as temple manager, and Roy Watkins as head of the commissary, were questioned. They denied any irregularities. But violations of a city ordinance regulating the solicitation of charitable gifts were uncovered, and the commissary's permit to operate was suspended pending a reorganization. And Roy Watkins was dropped as the commissary head.

This assault upon an activity close to her heart impelled Aimee to strike back in defense, and from her sickbed she dictated a statement:

"They have clashed loud their cymbals and blown their trumpets about a still and some sauerkraut, but although they speak with the tongues of angels, they have no charity. So long as suffering is in our midst, our work is still before us, in spite of all the clamor. I am sorry that things have not been altogether smooth down there. If anyone made a mistake, it is to be regretted, and if anybody abused his trust, it must not happen again, but the needy children and mothers depending on us for sustenance must not be forsaken. . . ."

At this point she fainted and remained unconscious several hours. When she revived, her mind wandered, and she continued in intermittent delirium for several days. The doctor described her condition as precarious, saying:

"She has periods when she regains almost her full mental and physical powers, between spells when she is in a comatose state—but these periods of strength are far less frequent now than when she returned from Central America. She is in extremely exhausted condition. When she attempts to use her eyes, she suffers severe headaches. Any disturbance, such as a sudden shock, might possibly kill her."

A cordon of temple guards—adherents of long standing, fanatically devoted to their pastor—was maintained around the Lake Elsinore grounds to block process servers as well as to keep out the curious who milled outside the gates. Even Hutton was barred from the sickroom, and at Echo Park, Sister's flock filled the air once more with moans and ululations. After one Sunday service, the entire congregation volunteered for day and night duty in the Prayer Tower.

Sister's legal antagonists, however, gave her no respite. Gates, the scenarist who had won the ten-thousand-dollar judgment, attached the villa in which Aimee lay. Her lawyers disposed of this, but then the parsonage was attached. Other litigants were demanding cash from the evangelist, and attorneys for these claimants charged that she was play-acting, that her illness was far from being as grave as reports would have it.

At the same time, discord was spreading in her Church of the Foursquare Gospel. A convention of the churches in Ohio passed a resolution deploring Sister's recent activities and expressing disapproval of her marriage. Thirty-two ministers in Iowa and Minnesota severed their connection with the evangelist because of "certain widespread publicity and policies of the international church which have brought undue reproach on the work."

In the midst of this turbulence, Aimee returned, at the end of August, to the parsonage, and announced, surprisingly, that she would preach her first sermon in nearly five months the coming Sunday. She met reporters alone; Hutton was traveling in the East on church business, she said. Photographers were permitted to snap her seated at a typewriter, looking rested but still wan. She said she had requested that there be no special celebration of her return, explaining:

"If the congregation isn't too demonstrative, I'll get through the beginnings of it nicely, but I won't be able to stand much excitement."

As for the events of recent months:

"I want to forget all the turmoil during my absence from my flock. I hope I won't be reminded of it. I don't bear anybody any ill will."

She seemed frail and underweight, but the fire gleamed in her blue eyes as she tossed her blond (once auburn) locks and exclaimed:

"I'm back to stay! My head is all healed up and my nerves are as calm as a mill pond when the wind has been turned off. I'll preach eighty-three sermons in the next ten weeks—eight a week and three thrown in for good measure—and I'm sure I'll be the same old Aimee. I'll be so glad to see my flock again I'll probably try to kiss every blessed one of them! So turn on the radio, so the world can hear that Aimee has come back!"

That Sunday evening, the familiar scene was reenacted: every seat in the great auditorium, every available space in the aisles and on the platform was filled when Sister came superbly down the ramp. The congregation went wild. At first she seemed not strong; during the morning there had been a report that she had collapsed again, but she explained that she had merely become overtired while working up her sermon and been forced to lie down.

The meeting opened with a greeting to "first nighters"—persons who were attending a temple service for the first time. This was a practice with her: a special section was roped off for newcomers, and they were asked to stand up and identify themselves by their home states. Often every state in the union and several foreign countries would be represented. This evening Sister called the newcomers to the platform for a personal welcome, and scores filed past, each of the women receiving a hug and each of the men a handclasp. Then came hymns, with choir, orchestra, and organ joining in, and Sister proceeded to take up the collection. Here she showed her old-time verve, joshing the crowd, admonishing them to "make those plates rustle." All irregularities in the commissary department had been rectified, she said, and the poor were being fed—so "never mind what's done with the money you put in the collection plates—you're getting your money's worth!" It was apparent that the response was generous.

In her sermon—her topic was "The Son of Pharaoh's Daughter"— she started shakily, seeming to fight off nervousness. But gradually she kindled and acted out the story with her usual panache. Now and then her face would blanch, and assistants on the platform would start up in alarm; but she hurled herself along and at the closing altar call filled the aisles with sobbing penitents. Then she walked off, surrounded and supported by half a dozen solicitous attendants, too weak to remain and make the customary announcements.

Newspaper reporters, who had come there to observe without any predisposition to applaud, voted that performance the greatest exhibition of "sheer grit" in Aimee's career. And they were certain that she would never carry through the ambitious schedule to which she had committed herself.

But the next evening she was back on the platform in high spirits.

"Am I back?" she crowed. "I'll say I am, and I'm full of vim, vigor, and vitality as I haven't been for years! I expect to preach in my temple until January 15, after which I'll rest up a bit and prepare for a trip to the Holy Land in the spring!"

Opening a telegram from her husband in Boston, she cried radiantly:

"And are David Hutton and I still very much in love? He has sent me at least five telegrams, three special-delivery airmail letters, and half a dozen phone calls since yesterday morning!"

And she carried out her program just as announced—eighty-three sermons in ten weeks—meanwhile resuming her multifarious life. She did not cease to be surprising otherwise, either, and gave newspaper offices a jolt by notifying them that she would issue no state-

The first anniversary of the McPherson-Hutton wedding was celebrated by a family dinner. Around the board, left to right: Mrs. Margaret Hutton, David's aunt; Rolf McPherson; Lorna Dee McPherson, Rolf's wife; David Hutton, Sr., and Mrs. Hutton; Aimee and Hutton.

ments to the press unless they had been approved previously by her board of elders. This incredible about-face led one newspaper to headline:

"Bottom of Depression Has Been Reached—Aimee Goes Silent!"

When Hutton got back from the East, he was hauled up by lawyers for Miss St. Pierre bent on collecting the five thousand dollars awarded to their client. Hutton cheerfully told them he would be glad to pay, but he was broke. He was examined under oath as to his assets, and testified that though he had a job at Angelus Temple, it carried no salary. He possessed absolutely nothing of value, he said, adding:

"No, I don't own any stocks or bonds, I have no bank account, no safety-deposit box, and I have no automobile. I did have a diamond ring, but my attorney, Willedd Andrews [who was present, and who was also Aimee's lawyer], now has that as part of his fee."

Aimee was subpoenaed in the matter and rose, she said, from a sickbed to appear. Her son Rolf McPherson helped her to the witness chair, where she looked chic in furs and orchids, as slim as a film star.

"Believe it or not," she confided in an aside, "I only weigh one hundred and twenty-five pounds—and three years ago I tipped the scales at a hundred and seventy-five!"

She was not amused by the questions put by Miss St. Pierre's counsel. She cited the prenuptial agreement she had signed with her husband, relieving her of his obligations. She did say that she received no salary from the temple; that she had acquired no real estate, bonds, stocks, or mortgages since her marriage; that she had no bank account and no safety-deposit box; that the church paid her expenses, but not in cash to her, all bills were sent to the church board and paid by them, including such items as tires, food, and necessities for her household. Offhand she could not give the names of all the board members and reminded her questioner that "you must remember I have been ill for three years."

Having demonstrated that she could be of no help to her husband's creditors, she moved along to another courtroom. She was in three courtrooms that day, wearing a different costume in each—which caused one newspaper to caption its photograph of her: "Her Life's Just One Suit After Another."

Meanwhile, Hutton encountered more grief when Roy Watkins sued him for nearly two thousand dollars—money that Watkins contended he had laid out while engaged in a secret assignment during the time he had headed the temple's commissary department. This confidential assignment, he explained, was a sub rosa attempt to head off the trial of Myrtle Joan Hazel St. Pierre's heart-balm suit.

To back his claim, Watkins placed in the record letters and telegrams that had been sent to him by Hutton during the latter's absence with Aimee on the Caribbean trip, just before the trial. The messages, usually opening with "Dear Ole Pal," contained the plainest instructions. Samples were:

"Sister wants to know what you have done in regard to the St. Pierre case, as it worries her very much."

This had been sent from Kansas City at the commencement of the Huttons' trip. It continued:

"Now, Roy, you know we have given you full charge of this matter. The case must be killed. Cannot she leave the state, or, better yet, mysteriously disappear, eh? We are both banking on you. It is not enough to get evidence against her—she must not appear in court, as it would kill Sister. We have left the entire matter in your hands and we trust you, ole pal, to do the job right. Yours, Dave."

Subsequent messages were more urgent:

"Understand Pierre case set June one. . . . Be a pal and quash case at once. . . ."

"Roy, you must get the case dropped at once. I know Sister could not stand a trial. If necessary give the gal a couple hundred, only get it settled once and for all. Do it up, Roy, as you said you would. So it will never get any publicity. . . ."

"Do your stuff on St. Pierre and pray for us. . . ."

"Sister very tired. Needs sleep and rest. Roy, be sure of everything and get that case dropped forever. . . ."

"Roy, I hope you can settle it, as it will be too much for Sister to go through. . . . If a few hundred would settle her it would be better for the papers. Better still, she might look good in a frame, eh? Leave it to you. . . ."

Despite all the ructions, on September 13 Aimee and David celebrated their wedding anniversary at a dinner party in the parsonage. Around the festively appointed table were gathered Rolf McPherson and his bride; Hutton's parents, and his aunt, Miss Margaret Hutton, for whose recovery from grave illness Aimee had prayed in one of her first actions as David's wife.

On October 9 Aimee celebrated her forty-second birthday by leaving Hollywood Hospital, where she had been confined with a fever and had undergone clinical tests, and thereafter throughout the autumn her health fluctuated. Several times she was reported to be seriously ill, as she drove herself to the utmost, but always she reappeared. The swarm of litigants gave her no rest, while inside the temple, as outside, tensions built up.

At last, on December 30, she told her flock that she would be

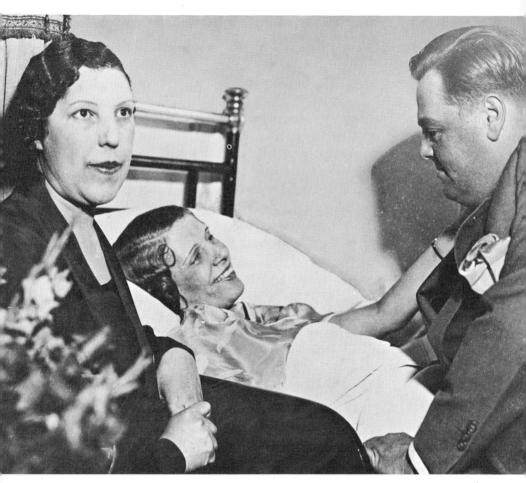

Carried aboard a ship at San Pedro, the port of Los Angeles, Aimee, attended by her nurse, Bernice Middleton, bids Hutton good-bye and sails into a raging Pacific storm, leaving a hurricane brewing at Angelus Temple.

compelled to lay down her responsibilities as pastor for an indefinite length of time. She planned to sail around the world, inspect her mission stations, and rest, she said.

"I shall remain away as long as necessary to regain my health," were her words. "I don't know how long I will be gone."

She would travel with a nurse-companion, she said; her husband would remain at his post in the temple.

The board of elders feverishly collected funds to defray the cost of her trip, and in January, when a settlement had been reached in regard to the most pressing of the lawsuits against her (the several actions arising out of the abandoned motion picture), she was free to sail.

On January 19, 1933, without fanfare or public announcement, she motored to Los Angeles harbor and boarded the Italian freighter *Fella*. The ship had accommodations for fifteen passengers, and Mrs. McPherson-Hutton had been given an outside stateroom. Hutton, his father, two of his friends, and Sister's nurse and traveling companion, Bernice Middleton, went on board with her. While the nurse tucked Sister into her berth, David stood guard at the head of the gangplank to repel any last-minute process servers. A few reporters were on hand.

Stricken with mystifying illness again, Aimee says good-bye to her people in Angelus Temple on January 18, 1933. On the platform she was supported by her husband and Bernice Middleton, a nurse-companion.

"The only purpose of my trip is to get well and see the Holy Land again," Aimee told them. "Mr. Hutton may join me on the French Riviera next fall."

During her absence, she added, her husband would be in executive control at Angelus Temple as general manager. Aimee looked very ill and forlorn.

At noon Hutton came down the gangplank and the *Fella* cast off. The worst storm in eight years was lashing the California coast, huge waves dashing against the breakwater and sending spume skittering through the air. Aimee's ship steamed into the teeth of the gale.

Hutton watched the vessel move away; his eyes were red from weeping. Getting into the temple limousine, he was seen to jerk down the rear shade and fling himself back on the seat, sobbing, as the big car rolled away.

"Love Is a Wonderful Thing, But Marriage—Jamais Encore!"

~⟡~

> "Doth any man doubt, that if there were taken out
> of men's minds, vain opinions, flattering hopes, false
> valuations, imaginations as one would, and the like,
> but it would leave the minds, of a number of men,
> poor shrunken things, full of melancholy and indis-
> position, and unpleasing to themselves?"
>
> —BACON, *Essay on Truth*

But what of Ma? And what of "Whataman"?

While Aimee and David and Myrtle Joan Hazel St. Pierre were demonstrating that two can be company but three's a disorderly assemblage, the Kennedy-Hudsons had been taking the bumps of their roller-coaster spin over the dips and curves of matrimony in relative privacy. Now and then Minnie's name popped up in the news in some minor connection: as when she answered a traffic citation and annoyed the Gardena police chief by presenting a driver's license from which her age had been erased. Ordered to restore it at once, she blandly wrote in "56."

"Whataman" seemed permanently enrolled among the unemployed, and in time this condition grew irksome to his helpmeet of threescore years and one. Now Ma, in the flush of their honeymoon, had promised the press that should she ever decide to dispense with "Whataman," she would tell the world, no coyness and no hush-hush; Ma was never coy about admitting a cast-iron fact. Thus in fulfillment of this pledge, on the Fourth of July, 1932, she summoned reporters to Hermosa Beach to proclaim her independence of conjugal obligations. The news was imparted at the height of the perfervid antics of the St. Pierre-Hutton trial; nevertheless, Ma got a good press.

To the reporters gathered in her modest parlor Minnie emptied her heart. Guy Edward Hudson was not present; his wife said he had been staying in a downtown hotel for several days.

"Boys," she opened, "you can say for me that after a year of fruitless attempts at establishing Jack, as I call Mr. Hudson [the reporters remembered when it had been Gee], I have decided that it would be to our mutual advantage if he went his way and I went mine."

Did this mean a divorce? No, Ma said, it just meant that things couldn't go on as they were.

"It isn't that he hasn't found a job; I don't hold that against him. And it's true that I have carried the financial load throughout the year we've been married, but—"

An impending soliloquy was interrupted by the entrance of "Whata-man," who announced as he walked in:

"You can say for me that if there's a separation or divorce in this family, it's not because I want it. All I want is a chance to work."

He stomped into the kitchen to get a drink of water, being dry, he said, after his long ride from downtown.

"As I was saying," resumed Minnie, "I have only good wishes for Mr. Hudson, and will do anything I can to start him on his way— wherever he wants to go."

"I only want a chance to work at my profession," said "Whataman" between gulps. "I'm a salesman . . . could get into a good line . . . can't do it broke. Imagine letting a man go downtown without a dime in his pocket!"

Ma intimated that Hudson couldn't sell her anything, dime or no dime.

"I used to cry," she confessed, "but not any more. It's just a comic strip, this life of ours—funny and getting funnier. And I want it understood that I am not responsible for any debts or other obligations he has incurred."

"I say again," interrupted "Whataman," "all I want is a job."

"Jack's trips to various places in search of employment have cost me a lot of money," was Ma's comment. "If I have a crust of bread, Jack is welcome to it any time. But when a person runs out of money, that person is broke."

As the press straggled out, "Whataman" shouted after them, "This is by no means final!"

But final it was, although accusations, rebuttals, and surrebuttals would spangle the air for weeks. "Whataman" blamed his hard luck on having married a famous woman.

"I can't get a job without letting people know who I am," he protested, "and every place I go people want me to do something that would exploit her name and fame. I don't want to make money out of our romance."

"Romance!" sniffed Minnie. "When we got married it was understood that each would do as he liked. I hope he gets a job soon. How long can this thing go on, anyway?"

The question of a divorce she fended off, saying:

"Nobody has a right to ask me point-blank what I am going to do. Do you think I'm sap enough to tell? We're still battling to reach a decision."

Two days after this pronouncement, she personally deported "Whataman." She took him in her car to Santa Barbara, bought him a one-way ticket to Portland, Oregon, a thousand miles to the north, and saw him get aboard the train. On the drive back to Hermosa Beach, she told two traffic policemen, a waitress, and three friends along the way:

"Yes, I've packed him up and packed him away. Gone but not forgotten! I gave him ten dollars, bless his heart, so he wouldn't be hungry on the train ride. I hope he gets a job soon."

She was understandably nettled, therefore, when she discovered that her Jack had backtracked and reached Los Angeles even before she got home. That settled it. Minnie said she would get a divorce.

"I'm signing off," she broadcast. "I've paid for two marriages, one annulment, and one divorce, and now I'm going all the way and try for a fifth and final decision. I've tried my best, but I've come to the point where I feel it is useless to go on. Why, he threatened to get in the bread line and have his picture taken by the newspapers if I didn't give him money! These eternal trips of his—this continual asking for money—I've almost gone broke in the year I have been with him. It's no use trying to make myself believe things will get better," she wound up realistically. "If I had married 'Whataman' sooner, I might have had a chance to prevent him from being 'Whataflop.' But I'm just a little girl trying to get

Minnie displays her romantic souvenirs—$4,500 in IOUs signed by "Whataman." "My sock just wasn't long enough," she said.

along, and I can't stand the strain any longer. I want peace and happiness."

In her action for divorce Minnie charged her luckless mate with excessive drinking, abusive profanity, mental cruelty, and indebtedness to herself to the tune of four thousand five hundred dollars. All of this debt, except three hundred dollars, was secured, so as to speak, by Jack's handsomely autographed IOUs; Minnie posed for photographs sheepishly holding these expensive souvenirs.

"Mind you," she said, "I have no ill feeling for Mr. Hudson.

If he were here right now I'd even buy him a dinner. My sock just wasn't long enough."

"Whataman" had betaken himself to Las Vegas again, and his first communiqué from there was chivalrous:

"If Mrs. Kennedy wants a divorce, I won't stand in her way."

But later, standing up to a bar, he informed the other barflies:

"Ma's got a sweetie! One of those Salvation Army officers. Ma's no gilded lily! I'm not saying who her sweetie is, but I'll have plenty to say later, and it may be tough on some of the kidnaping shenanigans in her family! I'll rattle family skeletons! I'll fill her whole backyard with the family wash! Evidence can be introduced to show that she indulged in a petting party in my presence!"

This iced the cake for Minnie.

"Oh! The terrible things, the terrible things he has said about me!" she exploded. "After all I've done for him! I even bought him hair tonic for his bald spot! The idea of me having another sweetie—a Salvation Army captain from Buffalo—how absurd! I have been a member of the Salvation Army the greater part of my life; I know many members of the organization intimately. I expect two Salvation Army officers to call at my home this morning, but it has to do with leaving some of my property to the Salvation Army when I die. If 'Whataman' doesn't want a more serious complaint against him, he had better keep his nose clean!"

And she put in an indignant call to the district attorney in Las Vegas demanding that he prosecute "Whataman" for libel.

"It's going to be nice to be a free woman again, believe me!" she exclaimed as she hung up. "This time I *am* going to hang my harp on the willow and call it a day! No more weddings for me! I know when I've had enough! What a man!"

Hudson waved a flag of truce. Writing from Boulder City, on the stationery of Laubach's Recreation Palace and Pool Hall, where he had obtained work behind the cigar counter, he begged Minnie to send or fetch his clothes, which were impounded in a Los Angeles hotel as security against an unpaid bill.

"Am working but can't keep clean," he wrote. "It is 108 here today and stays hot all night."

He proposed that Minnie forget everything and come swelter with him. He told customers:

Ma repels a reporter who asked her about those terrible things "Whata-man" was saying, including "Ma's got a sweetie—one of those Salvation Army officers." Fumed Ma, "If 'Whataman' doesn't want a more serious complaint against him, he had better keep his nose clean!"

"She always said if I got a job and went to work she would come to me, no matter where. I have a job. Now is her chance to make good."

Responded Ma:

"Enough is enough! No!"

But she did bail out his clothing and then was infuriated when he refused to accept service in her divorce action and thus obviate a ninety-day delay.

"Instead," she cried, "he called me by long-distance phone—at my expense—and wanted me to move over to Las Vegas and let the world slide by! What a man!"

So she filed a civil action in Los Angeles, charging her spouse with slander and asking one hundred thousand dollars to compensate for the damage done to her reputation as an evangelist and a preacher of the Gospel. This suit she accompanied by a belligerent manifesto:

"I have no sweetie nor do I want one. I want to be left alone in peace and I am going to be left alone and I am going to have peace! That is what I am fighting for!"

By this time a month had been used up, and "Whataman," having proved inadequate to the temperature and tedium of steady work, had wandered to Denver, Colorado, where he went into vaudeville. Billed as a "Noted Sexologist," he starred in a "lecture" surrounded by "beautiful living models." The skit was entitled, "Delicate Secrets of Love."

Minnie's robust frame quivered with laughter when she first heard about this extravaganza over the radio.

"Can you imagine anything funnier?" she gasped. " 'Whataflop' in a Don Juan costume doing a maypole dance with a 'bevy of beautiful girls!' The name of that lecture ought to be, 'What I Have Done to Women and What Women Have Done to Me.' He spent all his time with me going over that speech! It's all he talked about!"

But as she thought over the outrage, she became angry.

"It's too abominable for words!" she sputtered. "The whole thing is disgraceful and I can't stand it any longer! To think of his putting out thousands of circulars as *my husband!* He's no husband! He's a has-been!"

Forthwith she instructed a law firm in Nogales, Mexico, to start proceedings there to obtain an annulment of her marriage; she wouldn't wait for a California divorce, it was too slow.

In Sante Fe, New Mexico, where his act was booked for a week's run, Hudson at last had signed an answer to his wife's Los Angeles suit, denying all her allegations and accusing her of extreme cruelty. Ma couldn't be bothered: she withdrew her divorce suit and also her action for slander.

"No practical point in getting a judgment against a man who has nothing," she shrugged, "and I don't want to give any more publicity to an almost forgotten man. He's still using me for a meal ticket."

Just as she was making up her mind to this conclusion, Minnie received a social call from Myrtle Joan Hazel St. Pierre, fresh from her courtroom victory over David Hutton. The two women chatted cozily over tea and afterward said they had had a lovely time.

It was Thanksgiving Day, 1932, when Ma received word from Nogales that the Mexican court had granted her a divorce from Guy Edward Hudson. She read and reread the telegram, rocking on her front porch.

"For the first time in my life," she said, "I have something *big* to be thankful for on this day. It's worth anything to be free again. Now don't ask me if I'm ever going to marry again. I've had my lesson! Freedom is too sweet. My friends are all congratulating me—and they can't all be wrong!"

She fingered a sheaf of handbills sent to her from cities where "Ma Kennedy's Husband" had been expounding his "Delicate Secrets of Love." Suddenly she flung them down.

"I'll hear no more of an actor called 'Whataman—Ma Kennedy's Husband,' " she cried. "What a man!"

II

To Aimee Semple McPherson, 1932 had brought reverses other than the total collapse of her health. That year she was dropped from her regular listing in *Who's Who in America*, the reason stated by the editors being "inability to verify the biographical data." But just before she steamed into the gale of January, 1933, she had made one gain that gave her much satisfaction: Roberta, her daughter, had returned to the parsonage to live and take charge of the temple's bookstore. Roberta's husband Smythe had been unable to adapt himself to the kind of perpetual turmoil in which everybody connected with Angelus Temple seemed to live. He had gone back to sea, and in due course Roberta would bring an action for divorce. Her complaint would cite that "within a short time after the marriage and ever since [he had] humiliated her by speaking disparagingly of her mother and of the religious purposes of plaintiff." Also that on many occasions

Smythe had "curbed the enthusiasm of the plaintiff about her mother, her religious work, and her desire for church activities," and had "criticized the activities of the church, its organizers, members, and personnel."

There were no children of the union, there was no community property, and no alimony would be asked. The suit would not be contested, and the divorce would be granted, with restoration to Roberta of her maiden name. The decree would become final in 1935.

This full reunion of mother and daughter, however, lay in the future.

In January, 1933, while Aimee was tossing on the Pacific, another hurricane was gathering force at Angelus Temple. This one centered around her husband.

Hutton's position in the church organization was becoming untenable. Aimee had told reporters on the eve of sailing that David would be in executive control of the temple as business manager. But Hutton quickly found out that his authority was not recognized once Sister was away from the scene. The temple's "old guard" resented his intrusion; he was not "of the church"; and the heart-balm scandal had fed a prejudice against him that had long been festering in the ranks of the workers.

He was to discover, moreover, that his authority was entirely illusory, for his wife had given a power of attorney to act for her in all official matters to Harriet Jordan and Willedd Andrews, her lawyer. When Hutton protested against being thus sidetracked, the board of elders enlightened him that he had not been the temple's business manager for almost a year, although he had assumed he was. The minutes of the board showed that for months David Hutton, Jr. had been carried on the church records as simply head of the music and radio departments. The elders told him that Harriet Jordan was the business manager and that he would take his orders from her.

Hutton had strongly suspected that there was a cabal intent on easing him out of temple affairs. Now his suspicion widened to wonder whether his wife's elimination was not also intended.

In this atmosphere of mutual suspicion and hostility, several months elapsed, until in June, Hutton brought the conflict into the open. He told the press:

"I have been shorn of all authority as business manager since my wife left. But I am Aimee Semple McPherson's husband and I intend to look out for her interests. I have cabled her to come home at once."

Aimee was then in Paris.

The ill feeling at Echo Park grew more intense. The elders objected to Hutton's entertaining as a house guest in the parsonage a theatrical acquaintance, a male dancer. Other annoyances and frustrations harassed him, until he decided to withdraw from all official connection with the temple administration. Resigning his positions in the church, he dropped Willedd Andrews as his attorney, retaining other legal counsel, engaged a press agent-manager, and announced that he was embarking on a theatrical career.

"I am going to work as David L. Hutton, Jr.," he told the press. "I am not going to drag my wife's name around in an effort to cash in on it—I'm no 'Whataman!' "

Thereafter events exploded with dizzying rapidity. Not since the publicity-furious days of 1926 had there been such fireworks—accusations, denials, mystifying messages, contradictions, and even a hint of a miracle.

First, it was remarked that Mrs. McPherson-Hutton's daughter Roberta had left Los Angeles suddenly and at New York had sailed aboard the liner *Berengaria*, tourist class, for Cherbourg, France.

Next, on June 23, a cablegram arrived from Paris, carrying no signature but addressed to "David Hutton, Angelus Temple, 1100 Glendale Boulevard, Los Angeles, California." It read:

"DARLING DAVE. NINE-POUND BOY. DOING NICELY. UNDERSTAND PRESS INQUISITIVE BUT KEEPING QUIET. ADORINGLY, WIFE."

Reporters learned the wording of this startling message even before it was delivered to Hutton.

"Why, it's impossible!" he exclaimed. "Utterly impossible! Ask her—why, just ask me! It's ridiculous! If she said she had adopted a son, it would be different—but this business of 'doing splendidly!' "

Immediately he wired to his wife, in care of the American Express Company in Paris:

"MY DEAR. YOUR ASTOUNDING AND UNSIGNED TELEGRAM RECEIVED. PLEASE CONFIRM. HUSBAND."

Hutton was not aware that his wife at that moment was a patient in the American Hospital at Neuilly-sur-Seine and that the newspapers were about to publish a report that Aimee had entered the hospital to undergo a "monkey gland" rejuvenation operation.

In Paris, Dr. Charles Bove said yes, Mrs. McPherson-Hutton was his patient in the hospital, and she had undergone surgery; but the operation had been to remove an intestinal obstruction. He described her as very ill and forecast that she would be invalided for several weeks.

This news sent the temple's prayer battalions into action again. Hundreds of the faithful gravitated to Echo Park, crediting a miracle on behalf of their pastor, although Miss Jordan was issuing categorical denials that a child had been born. Not by any human agency, maybe, the devout insinuated—but miracles were not unknown.

Hutton got no immediate acknowledgment of his frantic inquiry from his wife, at least directly. Messages purporting to be from her were relayed to him through the temple office, but he was at a loss to know whether he could trust these or not.

Then, in Paris, Dr. Bove told newsmen that he had sent the "baby cable" at his patient's request; the reason being that private messages that she had sent had been leaking to the press; so she had sent a message so preposterous she knew her husband would never believe it, just to see whether this would be betrayed to the newspapers also. A cablegram to Hutton himself followed this elucidation:

"DAVID. YESTERDAY'S ASTOUNDING WIRE TAPPED AND POSITIVELY PROVED PRESS INTERCEPTED PRIVATE CABLES. THEIR OPERATIVES KNOWN HERE. LONGING FOR YOU EVERY MOMENT. WIFE."

A second message crowded this, reading:

"YOU ARE MY HUSBAND WHOM I WORSHIP AND OBEY. IF YOU ASK ME TO I'LL COME HOME RIGHT NOW."

Hutton wrote and told his wife to come home as quickly as she could and in reply received a batch of letters from Paris, breathing love and tenderness. But Aimee did not start home. The arrival in Paris of her daughter Roberta was noted, and thereupon Sister walked out of the Neuilly hospital without bothering about a formal discharge. Her doctor was embarrassed.

Meanwhile, the temple office continued to relay to Hutton conflicting and mysterious messages, which he was told had come from his wife. One cablegram, signed by Sister's nurse, Bernice Middleton, said, "IMPERATIVE DAVID COME." Hutton could not understand why he should go to Paris when his wife presumably was traveling toward home as rapidly as possible. Nor could he understand the apparent eagerness of temple officials to have him go. He floundered in conjectures and was further astonished when he learned, on July 12, that Aimee was still in Paris and cabling for money. A message received on that date read:

"DESIRE TO RETURN IMMEDIATELY. . . . SEND TELEGRAPHIC MONEY ORDER TO ME HERE FOR $400. ACT QUICKLY. . . . LOVE AND AFFECTION. WIFE."

This requisition Hutton turned over to the temple office, which cabled the money the same day. But three days later another cable reached Sister's baffled husband:

"ARE YOU COMING OVER OR WILL I RETURN? I AM VERY ANXIOUS TO HEAR FROM YOU. WIFE."

All this while, Hutton's mother, Mrs. Joyce Hutton, was receiving telephone calls from people at the temple urging her to persuade David to leave for Paris at once and saying that the church would pay his expenses. But Hutton stood firm.

"I am tired of having temple officials relay to me the desire of my wife for my presence in Paris," he said finally. "And I fail to see the wisdom of adding to the number of globetrotters being financed by the temple. She has never requested me to go over and join her."

To Aimee he cabled:

"IT IS VERY IMPORTANT THAT YOU RETURN AT ONCE. I AM NOT COMING OVER. DAVID."

Throughout all this, there had been open speculation that a divorce was impending. Hutton indignantly denied a rumor that he planned to seek a divorce in Mexico. But meanwhile the suspicion grew in his mind that the reason behind the pressure to get him to go to

Paris might be in order to enable Aimee to serve papers on him in a divorce suit there. The solicitations continuing and being himself unable to obtain any satisfactory clue to the intrigue that he felt was victimizing both himself and his wife, he took the initiative and on July 16 made public his intention to apply for a divorce in Los Angeles. For him the situation had become intolerable.

"I am sorry to take this step," he said, "but I really believe it will be to the advantage of the genuinely sincere followers of the temple work, as well as to my own advantage, if this marriage is dissolved. The really well-meaning folk of the temple need a rest from hippodrome publicity."

The complaint, filed in Los Angeles Superior Court, summarized the accumulated vexations of months past. His wife, he charged, had humiliated and embarrassed him by allowing intimate details of their married life to be discussed in public; she had made their marriage "ridiculous" by "perpetrating a hoax as to the birth of a baby, [which was] bandied about in the press of the world, when in fact no baby was born." He further charged that his wife, "shortly before her departure for Europe, displayed a total lack of faith and confidence in the plaintiff, and delegated to persons hostile to plaintiff all of the authoritative positions having to do with management of the temple, well knowing that said persons would conduct the temple in such a way as to humiliate the plaintiff."

When Hutton had advised her of a "system of intrigue to embarrass and humiliate" him, the complaint further alleged, Aimee had "failed, neglected, and refused" to protect him. Moreover, her trip abroad had been undertaken without his consent, and she had subsequently misled and left him in ignorance of her condition, advising him repeatedly by cable and letter that she had undergone a major operation, although "plaintiff is now informed and believes that the said operation was a minor operation, undergone for purposes of beautification." His wife had compounded his humiliation, Hutton concluded, by having "third persons come to him and give him information" concerning her, her plans, and her wishes, at a time when he was kept in the dark even as to her address. The technical charge that all these allegations boiled down to was "extreme cruelty."

Hutton said he would not ask alimony: he could pay his own way.

"Married life for me has been no bed of roses," was his valedictory observation. "But I am going out of temple affairs and the life of the pastor with a clear conscience and a closed mouth. I am not going to do a lot of talking—provided I don't find it necessary in order to defend myself at any time."

III

Aimee was at sea, on the way home, when a wireless bulletin from Harriet Jordan brought word of her husband's action. At the last minute she had boarded the Baltimore Mail Line steamer *City of Havre,* booked as "Miss A. Hutton, lady's maid, of Hendaye," traveling with "Mrs. R. Smythe" and "Miss B. Middleton." Reporters in Paris were not even aware that she had left the city.

Jordie's dispatch Aimee refused to believe.

"It's preposterous!" she cried. "Why, it's unbelievable!"

Back she wirelessed:

"DAVID. SWEETHEART. REASSURE ME OF YOUR CONFIDENCE."

But a second message from Jordie, giving details and asking for instructions, dispelled her disbelief. Nevertheless she radioed to the Associated Press in Paris:

"Never have I considered divorcing Mr. Hutton. I still completely love him. . . . I console myself that with faith, and the business tangles adjusted, the cloud will quickly pass and we will live happily ever after."

Angelus Temple threw itself into a veritable state of siege to exclude any persons who might be unfavorable to Sister, in anticipation of their pastor's homecoming.

At Hermosa Beach, Ma Kennedy held aloof.

"I'm not interested, not interested in the least," she told inquirers. "I'm through with temple affairs. I'm living quietly down here minding my own business, and I don't care what happens to their marriage. I just am not interested—not at all."

As an entertainer, Hutton faced what he called his "first paying audience in nearly two years" in a vaudeville theater at Long Beach. The town had been plastered with posters advertising "The Famed Angelus Temple Baritone." His act combined song and patter. The curtains parted to discover him leaning against a piano, in white flannels and blue blazer with a boutonniere, singing "Wanting You."

He followed with "My Faith in You" and a medley of operetta songs. In his running chatter he told the audience that "it is good to be back in the theatrical profession—although of course I have never really been away from it: I have been playing a continuous performance in Los Angeles for the last year and ten months." And there were quips about his marital difficulties.

The applause was generous, and he took five curtain calls. But while he was on stage, three temple elders, armed with a writ of replevin, seized and drove away the sleek temple limousine he had been using. Harriet Jordan had issued an edict that "no temple automobile is going to be used by anyone in the theatrical profession."

The same day Willedd Andrews flew east with a copy of Hutton's divorce complaint to meet Sister at Baltimore.

Her arrival at that port brought a swarm of reporters aboard the ship, bent on interviewing the about-to-be-divorced evangelist. Aimee was a reporter's dream, always good for copy.

She received the delegation in the captain's cabin, lying down, staring at the ceiling. Her dress was beige, of woollen crepe, and a mesh scarf was twined around her head turban-fashion. On her left hand was neither wedding ring nor diamond but a large aquamarine. Her lips were red, her cheeks were pink, her fingernails scarlet, and her face was an expressionless mask.

In response to an intimation that she might be just as discouraged about their marriage as Hutton evidently was, she murmured:

"Of course I am still in love with my husband. I know nothing about the suit except what I have read in the papers. I don't want to discuss it."

"Your husband has charged that you humiliated him by announcing the birth of a baby that was not born," ventured a reporter.

Aimee replied nothing.

"Your husband said if people didn't stop criticizing him for his divorce action, he would blow the lid off Angelus Temple. What do you say to that?"

"I can't believe he said anything like that. . . . People get so mixed up. I don't want to talk about it until I know."

"Is your husband in charge of the temple now?"

"No, he never has been in charge. I am pastor, you know, and no one else can have charge of the temple."

Several times during the interview she collapsed (the newspapers printed the word in quotation marks—"collapsed") and the ship's doctor was kept on the trot fetching ice packs and smelling salts. When the questions reverted to the "baby" telegram, Aimee's lips twitched and she appeared to faint, and the newsmen were hustled outside by Miss Middleton and Roberta. But Aimee shortly appeared on deck for photographs and spoke a few words for the newsreels. Then she was led back to the captain's suite, where she "collapsed" again.

"The poor woman is really sick," said the captain, and the newspapers published his words, but kept "collapsed" in quotation marks.

The entire affair was being treated by the nation's press in a manner at best flippant and at times verging on the scurrilous. Hutton was called "dimpled Dave of the cherubic countenance," "rotund baritone," "Big Boy," and "Aimee's delight"; and the evangelist was guyed scarcely less crudely at every stop in her progress westward across the continent.

Her changing moods baffled interviewers. The one question people wanted to have answered was whether Aimee would counter Hutton's suit with one of her own; but on this point she was noncommittal.

"I have never said to this minute that I will divorce David," she repeated over and over. "I don't know."

At times she seemed crushed and would sit with her expressive eyes staring into vacancy.

"I only knew him six or eight weeks when I married him," she would sigh wistfully. "He had a beautiful voice. . . ."

Then the vivid eyes would flash and she would snap:

"What's this latest report I get from Los Angeles? David appearing in a film short carrying a nine-pound baby and the picture called 'Aimee's Tearful Eyeful!' He is merely getting this publicity because of my reputation! But David is on the slide, he can't last. He ought to slay 'em in vaudeville! Only last night I received an offer of twenty-five thousand dollars for a few weeks of vaudeville, but the price is too dear—especially when I think of the twenty-two thousand persons in my temple who look up to me."

Hutton was experiencing the shifting fortunes of popularity. On the stage of the Warner Theater on Hollywood Boulevard he told the audience that he was glad to be back in the City of the Angels— "You know, I married one of them." Whereupon a young woman in

Aimee breakfasts on the train nearing Los Angeles on her way home from Paris to find out whether David really means the divorce action he filed— "whether he is the gentleman I married, or just a vaudeville singer." She was slim and her eyes were hauntingly expressive.

the second row stood up and lobbed four eggs at Sister's husband, scoring three bull's-eyes on his white, double-breasted jacket.

Taken in charge by the police, this bit of truculent femininity said she was Jane Jones and would say nothing more. At her hearing the next morning she corrected her name to Jane Thomas. She denied that she was connected with Angelus Temple, although detectives identified her as a follower of Aimee's. Her action had been impulsive, she said, provoked by "his slandering the place that gave him a start. And another thing, judge—those eggs were fresh!" Pleading guilty to a charge of disturbing the peace, she was fined twenty-five dollars, and the fine was paid immediately by two men who stepped up from the spectators. They refused to give their names.

Hutton took the attack like a trouper.

"At least," he remarked as he scraped the scrambled criticism off his chest, "we have something to be thankful for—they might have been ostrich eggs!"

But he requested, and was given, police protection to and from the theater.

All this was less than edifying, nor was it instructive to see Sister Aimee aborded by reporters at Chicago demanding her reaction to this egging of her "eggs-asperating" mate.

"I don't know what to think," she said cutely. "I thought he was an angel, too, when I married him. I hope he's not a fallen angel!"

Later she said she would like to meet the young egg-hurler. She also suggested that she might not contest the divorce suit.

"I might sue David for nonsupport," she suggested, "but that's not a Bible reason. I am going to find out whether David is still the Christian gentleman I married, or just a vaudeville singer."

Always wiser in the ways of the public than any of her advisers, she posed graciously for photographs whenever a request was made. Her attorney, Willedd Andrews, thought she ought to remain in her stateroom and tell the reporters she was too fatigued to appear.

"Heavens no!" she protested. "If I did that, there would be head-lines in Los Angeles tomorrow saying I was dying or something!"

It was August 1 when she reached Los Angeles. A committee of temple dignitaries headed by Brother Arthur and Miss Jordan had boarded Sister's train well up the line, at San Bernardino, and were closeted with her before the arrival in the city at 8:30 in the morning. There was a crowd on hand—temple workers, Bible School students, brakemen, red caps, idlers, reporters, and camera crews. The evangelist cast a smile across the uplifted faces, bowed, posed for newsreels cuddling Rolf's baby (a girl, born during Aimee's absence, and named Sterling Kay McPherson—the "Kay" being explained as "an initial of our family;" Aimee had unsuccessfully proposed "Evangeline"), and it was generally agreed that Sister had never looked more charming. She was slim, very slim, and her features seemed refined by an inner glow that had not been apparent before. Her eyes, in repose, were hauntingly expressive of suffering, and she bore herself with dignity. There were no visible evidences of the Paris surgery, though her beauty certainly seemed heightened.

The temple limousine (the same retrieved from her husband) wafted her luxuriously to the parsonage, where, to reporters pushing into the house, she said her plans were "chaotic"; that if David was serious about a divorce, all she wished to do was "work, work, work," and forget it all.

"But he will have to take me in his arms and tell me with his own lips that he no longer loves me," she added emotionally. "If he doesn't want to, so be it. I wish him well."

Hutton declined to meet her.

"Why should I make myself ridiculous by helping to stage a scene?" he wanted to know. "I don't wish to hurt her or her people, I only want to be left alone to follow my career."

He was rehearsing with a night club orchestra and dancers, and gave the reporters a sample of his singing style with "Baby Shoes," followed by "Tell Me It Isn't So."

At the parsonage, all through the day Aimee clung to hope. At times she wept quietly.

"I'm sure he'll call me," she insisted. "He shouldn't let money come between us. Maybe we can separate my private life from this temple life. I'm sure he doesn't like the stage."

But the hours dragged by, and by evening she was resigned. Drying her tears, she said brusquely:

"Let it go by default—I guess he means it all. I don't want to take any action that will injure him in any way. Really, I cannot adjust myself to the realization that I have lost his love." Her lips trembled. "It is going to be hard to stay in this house tonight with the memory of him clinging close. But I guess I'll just have to plunge into my own work, which I have neglected since my marriage."

Twenty-four hours later, Aimee announced that the church elders had approved a plan for her to appear in vaudeville houses across the nation—strictly as an evangelist.

"It will be the most important evangelistic enterprise I have ever attempted," she said proudly.

Furthering his career required night club publicity shots like this, Hutton contended. They shocked Aimee.

A salary of five thousand dollars a week was mentioned. Aimee said she wanted it paid directly to the church. And that night, speaking in the temple and over the radio, she thrilled her listeners by her opening words, delivered with the old familiar lift and verve:

"This is radio station KFSG—Aimee Semple McPherson speaking."

It was the first time in nearly two years that she had omitted "Hutton" from her name. The applause lasted five minutes, while the preacher smiled gratefully.

"With such a demonstration of loyalty I feel I can go on through life without anything else to lean on," she purred. "Now I am going to get right to work."

IV

Twice during the next several weeks David and his estranged wife met and a reconciliation was looked for; but Hutton was not to be persuaded.

"Mrs. Hutton is a fine woman," he said repeatedly, "a splendid woman, an excellent friend. I am tremendously fond of her and wouldn't hurt her for the world, but I am sick and tired of being married to Angelus Temple. She still has no idea what was the basic cause of our separating."

But as time passed their public exchanges grew less friendly.

Said Aimee in Kenosha, Wisconsin:

"If David wants a divorce, why doesn't he serve me with the papers? Barking dogs don't bite, and I rather think he is using the divorce threat as a publicity stunt for his cheap theatrical venture."

Retorted Hutton in Chicago:

"You know, the one thing Aimee cannot do is to do something for somebody without boasting about it. When I married her, I married the whole Angelus Temple—Brother Arthur, Sister Hattie Jordan, the Bible School, the rest. I'm tired of being dictated to by a bunch of nincompoops, and down in her heart Aimee is, too. Why, the elders even told her whether to get married! And another thing." He pointed to a newspaper headline reading, "Aimee Was Kidnaped?" "That's very disgusting to a husband. That and a lot of other things I won't mention—baby wires and all that stuff! Why, she never trusted me at all! She won't stick to what's what! Still, I wish her every good. I hope she slays 'em!"

Aimee made her bow as a bigtime stage evangelist at the Capitol Theater in New York City, sandwiched between a team of adagio dancers and a drill by the chorus of pretty girls dressed in devilish costumes—and devilish little at that. Sister, in a luminous, ankle-length, white satin gown, wore the most complete costume in the show.

"Brothers and sisters—or should I say ladies and gentlemen," she began in her husky, rasping voice, perfectly at ease, "there are seventy thousand persons on their knees in the United States right now praying that God may give me courage and wisdom. I am preach-

In a "raid" on the Temple Bible School, Hutton and his father retrieved his personal piano, while Bible students buzzed around and the Temple elders got a court injunction against his making "loud and unusual noises" in the neighborhood.

ing the Gospel in a theater, an unprecedented thing, and I need guidance and strength."

A couple of blocks down Broadway, at the Palace Theater, David Hutton was placarded as "Big Boy, the Baritone of Angelus Temple."

But in spite of the exploitation, both acts met with less than instantaneous success. Aimee, in fact, proved so monumental a frost that the critics thought she actually kept customers away from a lively film that topped the bill.

For once Aimee had misjudged her public. Her perception of the mistake was swift and her recovery immediate. Giving up the idea of preaching to theater crowds, who when they paid to be entertained didn't want to be preached to, she went on with her barnstorming tour, appearing before revival-hungry throngs.

Hutton was the first to get back to Los Angeles, and he said that the papers in his suit would be served on Sister at once, to counteract rumors that he was holding out for alimony. He caused a near riot at Echo Park when he and his father rolled up to the Bible School in a moving van and personally trundled his piano out of the building. Bible students buzzed around like angry bees, and a watchman, aroused from slumber, ran out wearing his badge but no shoes; but the Huttons drove away with their prize.

The next day temple officials obtained a court order enjoining Sister's husband from trespassing on church property or disturbing the peace of Echo Park by making "loud and unusual noises."

Hutton was wroth.

"Loud and unusual noises!" he cried. "Here's one of those loud and unusual noises for that gang right now!"

His anger boiled up again when from Fort Worth, where she was preaching, Aimee said that David was withholding service in his suit until she agreed to pay the five thousand dollars heart balm awarded to Myrtle Joan Hazel St. Pierre; she pointed out that service outside California would bar Hutton from seeking a property settlement.

Exploded Hutton:

"If she must talk, talk, talk, let her come to town here and talk in court, where we can both talk together!"

Aimee arrived sooner than he or the temple expected—on December 20—and her revitalized appearance astonished the home-towners. She had not seemed in such glowing health for years. Her eyes flashed eloquently as she recapitulated her tour—fifteen thousand miles; one hundred and fifty days; preaching in twenty-one states and forty-six cities—three hundred and thirty-six sermons to a total of more than two million listeners, not counting the radio audiences reached by forty-five broadcasting stations.

While she described all this, she toyed animatedly with a silver cross hanging from a silver chain looped over her striking black crepe gown; on her shoulder was the customary immense orchid. Roberta beamed at her mother's side.

On train nearing Los Angeles in March, 1934, Aimee recounted her breathtaking barnstorming tour through twenty-one states—150 days, 15,000 miles, 336 sermons, audiences totaling 2,000,000, not counting millions reached over forty-five broadcasting stations. She glowed with health, belying her forty-four years of age. Roberta Semple beamed at her mother's side. Aimee had just filed her own countersuit for divorce against David Hutton.

"I've preached as many as five sermons a day," said Aimee triumphantly, "and I was the first woman ever to open the state legislature in Iowa. I feel stronger and better than I have at any time since the breakdown I suffered more than three years ago. I have been able to recover from the shock of David's action simply because I have completely lost myself in my work. I have just opened seven new churches, and during the next year I expect to open two hundred and fifty more."

Just before her train reached the city, the papers in her cross-complaint requesting a divorce from David Hutton were filed in Los Angeles Superior Court. Her complaint contained many explicit allegations against her husband. She asserted that he had interfered with the operations of Angelus Temple by demanding that he be put "in complete charge and control of its affairs," thereby damaging its work and causing her to become ill. On many occasions, she alleged, he had awakened her and "insisted that she had money hidden away and that she disclose its whereabouts," and had demanded that he "be willed all the furniture, silver, and other personal property" in the parsonage. Especially, she emphasized, he had demanded that she pay the St. Pierre judgment, alleging that she was responsible for it, and by inference had threatened to publish stories of a scandalous nature unless she complied. The skull fracture at Lake Elsinore she laid to David's account, asserting that he had "cruelly, rudely, and deliberately . . . rushed to her side, stating that a judgment in only the amount of five thousand dollars had been secured against them"; and that this sudden shock had caused her to faint, fall, and suffer "a permanent disability from which she has not recovered."

After their separation, the complaint went on, Hutton had humiliated her by appearing in night clubs with insufficiently clothed women, whom he permitted to caress and kiss him for newspaper photographs, pleading in extenuation that such publicity was necessary for his stage career. She averred that Hutton had used her name for "cheap publicity, permitting headlines on the outside of theaters such as 'Aimee's Man,' ridiculing her from the stage, and letting his managers book him into cities where she was conducting revival services, in an attempt to wreck her meetings." On her part, she said, she had been a loyal and dutiful wife, and though she "abhorred the thought of divorce," she had found it "impossible to carry on her religious work in a dignified and successful manner."

Aimee had signed the complaint weeks before in Cleveland but delayed filing it until she returned home.

"When Mr. Hutton first sued me for divorce, I was stunned and amazed," she said. "When I returned to America and he continued his inexplicable attacks on me, I was first mystified, then crushed, then brokenhearted. Finally the cat came out of the bag and he asked for money to pay the judgment placed upon him by a jury which found he had stolen another woman's love. As I have said before— not one cent for tribute!"

It was Mother Kennedy who had said that; but at Hermosa Beach the by no means inarticulate Minnie nodded vigorous approval. That was her girl speaking—late, but at last!

Hutton met his wife's accusations with a smile and, using Aimee's pet name, he responded:

"If the public expects a lot of dirty wash to be aired on the courthouse line, now that Betty has filed her action, they're going to be sadly disappointed. We are going to have a quiet, dignified little divorce. Sorry we aren't going to put on a show, everybody, but the curtain just won't go up."

This attitude was a relief to Aimee, who had been nervous about David's reaction.

"I knew he would be nice about it," she sighed. "Really, I don't feel any acrimony. He's just a big, clean, overgrown boy, easily led and impulsive."

And she posed for a publicity photograph in Echo Lake Park demonstrating that she would be able henceforth to paddle her own canoe.

Cheers, handclapping, and a mountain of flowers greeted her at the temple that evening as she threw her energy into organizing a gigantic Christmas party for disabled war veterans at Sawtelle Hospital. Temple trucks scoured the city for clothing and comforts, American Legion posts and fraternal groups pitched in, and on the gala night twelve chartered suburban trains and scores of ambulances and private cars brought twenty-five hundred guests to the temple. The Police Department's drum and bugle corps serenaded the crowd, the platform was thronged with civic leaders, lodge officials, and hospital representatives grouped around a huge Christmas tree, and hundreds of gifts were handed out. Afterward Aimee visited more than a thousand bedfast veterans unable to make the trip, distributing roses gathered by her followers.

And 1934 she ushered in with a church parade through downtown Los Angeles. There were floats, a band, and dozens of automobiles in line, even a humorous entry—a float labeled "Atheism," drawn by a trained mule that stopped every few paces and let fly a kick at "Old Nick," the driver. At City Hall, Mayor Shaw stood beside Sister in the reviewing stand.

Her other activities did not lessen. There was a multiplicity of lawsuits hanging fire, and in spite of their domestic disagreement, Hutton supported her in this litigation, readily giving testimony when called upon. And Aimee appeared in Hutton's behalf when the lawyer who had handled David's defense in the St. Pierre trial sued to collect his fee.

Having filed her countersuit, Aimee demonstrated that thenceforward she would be able to paddle her own canoe by doing so in Echo Lake Park, across the street from Angelus Temple.

Toward the end of January, the press of business had been cleared up sufficiently to allow Aimee to resume her restless travels; and while she was on tour, on the last day of February, 1934, her attorneys in Los Angeles filed a stipulation that permitted Hutton to obtain a divorce by default. This step had been made possible, it was explained, by the conclusion of a property settlement, although neither party would disclose its terms. (At a later date, under oath, Aimee testified that she had paid Hutton twelve hundred dollars to obtain his waiver of further claims and that she had had to borrow on her life insurance to raise the cash.)

Hutton's action coming to trial, he testified that "parties interested in the temple influenced my wife against me—folks who didn't like the changes I made while I was business manager. They didn't even like the way I dressed."

"You might have expected, in marrying a woman of your wife's fame, that you would be expected to play second fiddle," advised the judge.

"Yes," assented Hutton, "but I wasn't even playing second fiddle; it was less than that."

Mrs. Joyce Hutton, his mother, testified that soon after the marriage, Aimee had informed her that she wanted to make David her business manager. "She said she would have to pay someone a tremendous salary, and Dave could do it just as well." But later, just before Aimee had left for Europe, said Hutton's mother, "she called me to her apartment one morning and said that she and David had quarreled bitterly. She said it would have been better if they had never married, and she could see no way out except to get a divorce. She said David resented having Harriet Jordan dictate to him all the time, but after all, Miss Jordan had been at the temple before him and would be there after he was gone. She also said that David could run the temple no better than the switchboard operator."

When she relayed these remarks to her son, said Mrs. Hutton, David broke down and cried.

David's father testified:

"Yes, it was just about as Mom said. Mrs. Hutton said he wasn't any more capable of running the temple than the switchboard operator was."

On March 1 Hutton left the courtroom with a provisional decree of divorce, which became final one year later.

Aimee received the news in Columbia, South Carolina, and the next day, in Charlotte, North Carolina—where she was the guest of a wealthy woman whose home and rose gardens were a showplace of the state—she made her only comment:

"When I heard of the divorce, I was despondent and blue; but the Lord softened the blow by letting me hear it in the Carolinas where Southern hospitality is so kindly."

Shaking her curls vivaciously, she added:

"I don't believe in marriage after divorce, but even if I did, I'd still say *jamais* to the idea of another husband. Love is a wonderful thing, but marriage—*jamais encore!*"

War in Heaven

⟨❦⟩

"... like one lost in a thorny wood
That rends the thorns and is rent with the thorns,
Seeking a way and straying from the way,
Not knowing how to find the open air,
But toiling desperately to find it out ..."
—*Henry VI, Part 3*

The Angelus Temple welfare program in Los Angeles continued to be carried on at top pressure, if not at top efficiency. Friends cautioned Aimee that the commissary's organization was slipshod, but her justification was:

"I know there is laxity. I know there is waste. I know there are imposters. But far better that twenty fakers should get past us than that we should miss a single individual who honestly needs our help."

A sympathetic observer of Aimee's one-woman determination to alleviate, to the best of her ability, the Depression-caused distress, was the woman who, years before, had been moved to admiration by the sight of the evangelist pounding in the stakes of her tent beside a Florida road—Rheba Crawford. Now Miss Crawford (as she was known professionally—in private life she was Mrs. Bachelder Splivalo) was California's director of welfare, having been appointed to that position by Governor James Rolph in mid-1931.

Rheba Crawford was not alarmed by Mrs. McPherson's direct-action methods. Her training had accustomed her to think and act along much the same lines. She had been born into the Salvation Army, of which her parents were members. They had been married in Stratford, Ontario. Rheba's mother died while she was an infant, and the child had been brought up in the Army's stern school of self-sacrifice and rigid discipline and imbued with its concepts of practical humanitarianism.

"I learned what it means to go hungry; hungry people can't wait," she would say in explanation of her impatience with red tape and bureaucratic procrastination.

In her early years, as a cadet officer in the Salvation Army, she had made headlines in New York City by preaching in Times Square and tying up traffic there, causing her arrest. Some newspapers had dubbed her "The Angel of Broadway." Evangeline Booth, who was commander of the Salvation Army in the United States, frowned on publicity-getting by subordinates. Rheba's temper and temperament were fiery, and soon she was encouraged to seek outlets for her dynamic energies elsewhere.

She tried numerous things, including revival preaching in the South, and in Florida met and married Harold Sommers, a man of wealth and idle pursuits. Rheba hoped to convert him to some useful purpose but was not successful, and after five years she packed up and went to her father, Colonel Andrew Crawford, in San Francisco, where he was in charge of the Western division of the Salvation Army. Sommers soon obtained a divorce on the same grounds on which Harold McPherson had obtained his from Aimee—disinterest in home life and an "incurable propensity for engaging in evangelistic work."

Just before the stock market crash in 1929, Rheba arrived in Hollywood, energetically promoting a scheme to erect a hotel and social center in the film capital for the young girls who flocked there in pursuit of fame, mink, and money—some of them settling for the last two. The economic collapse scuttled that plan, and Rheba married a San Francisco broker and polo player, Bachelder Splivalo. Her concern for the Depression's victims was still keen, and she had persuaded Governor Rolph to appoint her welfare director of the state. In her rush to get things done, she had offended much of official Sacramento. Legislators were jarred by her demands for action, and bureaucrats resented her "unprofessional" approach to relief problems. Yet she got California's relief program, or at least a stopgap program, under way months before Franklin Delano Roosevelt as President brought national resources to bear. Free-swinging in her speech, she was tiny, dark, and spunky, and she got things done.

Rheba Crawford and Aimee McPherson, two pulpit spellbinders, preach from the same text, which Aimee points out when announcing that Sister Rheba had become associate pastor of Angelus Temple.

Her position had brought her into sympathetic touch with Mrs. McPherson; their similar backgrounds were a bond. Shortly after Aimee's divorce, Miss Crawford began to appear occasionally at Angelus Temple as a substitute preacher (she was a licensed Congregational minister), while continuing to hold office as state welfare chief. This ambiguity was commented upon, and the newspapers found out that Miss Crawford had a definite contract with Mrs. McPherson. This interested the press: was Rheba Crawford perhaps being groomed to succeed Sister McPherson as temple executive when, as must sometime happen, Aimee retired?

At first both women had denied the existence of any contract between them, but later they confirmed it and made known its terms. Some of these were unusual.

Rheba was to receive six hundred dollars a month from the church, unless the temple's monthly income fell below three thousand dollars; in that case her payment would be reduced proportionately. (Rheba's salary from the state was only three hundred and thirty-three dollars a month.)

The contract stipulated that while Aimee was in the field on tour, Rheba would occupy the pulpit at Echo Park, at such times controlling the temple radio station. When Sister returned to her pulpit, Rheba was to go on tour (in other words, efface herself from the local scene). She also engaged to go into the field whenever either Roberta Semple or Rolf McPherson should be called to fill their mother's pulpit.

The oddest provision of all in this agreement was a protective clause reading:

"In the event that this contract is terminated by mutual cancellation, neither party will release to the press or otherwise any publicity adverse to any of the parties hereto."

The contract was to run for four years.

The year 1935 was ushered in with another grand march of the Foursquare Gospel Church through downtown Los Angeles, and Rheba marched just behind Sister McPherson at the head of the procession. Both stood on the steps of City Hall taking the salutes of the marching units.

Later that month, Aimee sailed for China on another round-the-world cruise, leaving the business management of the temple in the care of Harriet Jordan and Roberta Semple. (Roberta had procured her divorce by now and had resumed her maiden name.) Rheba Crawford was left as associate pastor and pulpit fill-in.

At once Rheba began drawing attention to herself by a blistering attack on city officials for allegedly condoning vice and gambling. Her outbursts, naming those whom she held responsible for the conditions she described, were broadcast over KFSG, and they raised a commotion at City Hall.

Sister McPherson returned home in June, bringing a new book she had written, *Give Me My Own God;* a new sacred opera, "The

A Foursquare Gospel Church parade through downtown Los Angeles was Aimee's New Year's Day salute to 1935. Aimee, in white cape, heads the march. Rheba Crawford, in dark cape, steps right behind.

Rich Man and Lazarus"; and costumes from every country she had visited. Rheba Crawford then left the city on an evangelistic tour.

To celebrate her homecoming, Aimee dedicated a neon-lighted cross seven feet tall atop the temple dome, climbing up like a steeplejack for photographers. Then she preached a sermon on "Little Red Riding Hood" dressed in a scarlet cloak and hood, assisted by a ferocious "wolf" impersonated by a student from the Bible School.

Meanwhile, administratively she was adroitly consolidating her position as executive head of the church and all its dependencies. The Bible School had become officially the L.I.F.E. (Lighthouse of International Foursquare Evangelism) Bible Training College. The work at Angelus Temple was the Church of the Foursquare Gospel. The top holding company controlling everything remained the Echo Park Evangelistic Association.

Of all these corporations, Aimee Semple McPherson was president, and through them she exercised absolute sway over her church, its policies, properties, and income. Her monopoly was challenged more than once, but each time the challenge was turned back and Aimee's powers were upheld.

While testifying in one of these lawsuits, she expounded her sense of trusteeship, saying:

"All that I have I hold for the church, in my mind at least, although legally it stands in my name."

Her only personal asset, she stated, was a deed of trust (a form of mortgage) secured on Angelus Temple, which she believed would bring her an income of one thousand dollars a month should she quit preaching.

So matters stood in August, 1935, when Miss Crawford returned from her preaching tour, reporting immense success, and Aimee departed again for the Midwest. Again the temple radio carried scorching attacks by Rheba on alleged official condonation of vice in Los Angeles. When she threatened to start a recall movement against Mayor Shaw and the City Council, it was whispered around the temple that Sister McPherson was not pleased by her associate pastor's behavior.

There were other matters that grated on Aimee. One had been the appearance in the newspapers of a photograph of a Bible School student, Vivian Denton, posing in a pulpit costume just like Sister's, holding an open Bible, with one arm uplifted in a travesty of Aimee's well-known pulpit gesture. The caption read, "Bible Calls to Chorine."

Miss Denton told reporters she was the daughter of "an Australian diplomat" and a famous artists' model of London and Paris named Dolores. Her parents were dead; they had not been married, she said, because of objections by her father's relatives. Vivian herself had lived in a whirl of worldly vanity, she professed, until she was converted by Sister Crawford's preaching. They had first met, said Vivian, when she was a dancer in Texas Guinan's New York night club. Now she was training to carry the Word to the Barbary Coast—the one in Africa, not the one in San Francisco, she explained.

To Aimee this looked like a suspicious buildup of a Crawford protégée, and Aimee shared Evangeline Booth's dislike of personal

At a pageant entitled "Cavalcade of Christianity" held in Los Angeles'
Shrine Auditorium in January, 1935, Sister Aimee appeared in this
tableau. More than a thousand players took part in the performance and
the huge hall was thronged.

publicity for the underlings of her organization. Still, she gave no sign of impending friction when she returned to Los Angeles in September, and Rheba and her husband sailed for a vacation in Hawaii.

On Sister Crawford's return, two hundred temple followers and the temple band welcomed her at the dock. Nimbly climbing a pile of baggage, she delivered a homecoming speech in the familiar manner of Sister, saying that she had made arrangements for Aimee to conduct a revival in the islands.

"I've tentatively engaged a boxing ring for her to start in," she laughed. "She'll love that!"

The newspapers called Rheba pert and petite, if not very respectful. Aimee was not sure she liked the tinkle of Rheba's laughter.

However, it was not until February of the following year, 1936, that the first rumbles were heard denoting serious internal dissension at Echo Park.

Again the New Year had been greeted by a downtown parade of temple floats and marchers that snarled traffic. Rheba had taken the salute at City Hall, all smiles, standing just below the grand marshal, Aimee. Shortly after that, Miss Crawford entered a hospital suffering from an intestinal malady.

While she was there, on February 10, an incident occurred that set off a train of violent events.

Late that evening, a man who occupied the apartment above that of Vivian Denton, at 1630 Temple Street, heard groans, and upon investigating found Miss Denton on the floor of her bathroom, gasping that she had swallowed poison. Taken to a hospital, she was pumped out and sent home. In the morning she received the press, lying in bed, seemingly exhausted, and told them the story she already had told the police.

She had wanted to die, she said, because of grief and chagrin caused by the harsh treatment she had received from Aimee Semple McPherson.

For the last six months, Miss Denton related (interrupting herself twice to make sure the newsmen got her age correctly—she assured them she was twenty-six), she had been helping as a volunteer in the temple's publicity office. Three weeks ago, she had been put on the payroll by Sister Crawford as publicity director.

Vivian Denton, ex-chorus girl converted by Rheba Crawford (she said), whose nose was put out of joint by Aimee's abusive language (she said), "swallowed poison while looking at my reflection in the mirror."

Yesterday, she went on, in the absence of Miss Crawford, who was in the hospital, Mrs. McPherson had called her in and upbraided her for supposed shortcomings in her work—and also for her "loyalty to Sister Crawford." She said the harangue started in the morning and lasted until after noon.

"Sister accused me of having made some untrue statements about her; and despite the fact that I denied them, I was fired."

At the termination of the scene, she charged, Mrs. McPherson had given her a shove, causing her to fall down a flight of steps and injure her nose. (Noses again, thought the reporters. Shades of Ma Kennedy!)

"After I had gone through four hours of torture from Sister," Miss

Denton concluded, "I came home and became moody. I paced the floor of my apartment until after midnight, and then of a sudden I could restrain myself no longer. I walked into the bathroom and swallowed the poison while looking at my reflection in the mirror."

To this accusation Aimee vouchsafed no reply.

Roberta Semple, however, put out a statement to the effect that her mother had talked with Miss Denton only about fifteen minutes and had mildly criticized her for statements she had made to temple workers, but that Mrs. McPherson had not pushed or laid hands on Miss Denton, and Sister Crawford's name had not been mentioned.

Reporters cornered Aimee at the close of the noonday service. The evangelist scoffed at the suggestion that she had pushed Miss Denton down a flight of steps.

"Why," said she, "that would be impossible, because I talked with Vivian right here in this room. Afterward she went out through this door."

Opening the door, she stepped outside and stood in pouring rain to show that there were no stairs.

"As for my dismissing Miss Denton because of jealousy for her publicizing Rheba Crawford Splivalo, that is ridiculous. There is no ill feeling between Sister Crawford and myself. She has been ill for three weeks in Glendale Sanatorium and Hospital, so there is no publicity Miss Denton could have given her."

That was correct, Rheba confirmed. There was no rift between her and Mrs. McPherson:

"If there were, we would mutually terminate my contract, which has two years yet to run."

But Vivian Denton was not to be talked down: she sued Aimee Semple McPherson for slander and asked four hundred thousand dollars' damages.

Aimee thereupon referred all inquiries to "my attorney, Jacob Moidel," thereby introducing a new name into the boiling pot of temple affairs and setting off speculation as to why she was not handling this matter through her long-trusted lawyer, Willedd Andrews.

Amid a welter of rumors, Aimee and her daughter left the city for New Orleans and an avowed rest. And Harriet Jordan joined Rheba Crawford in the hospital.

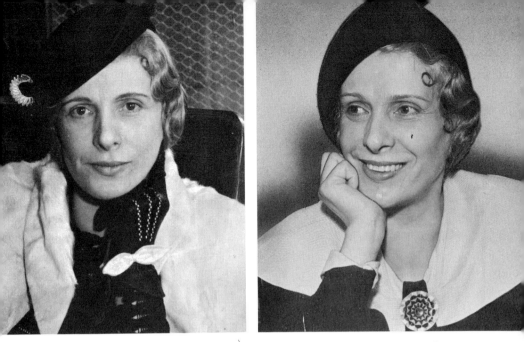

Two photographs of Aimee keeping her own counsel regarding rumored discord at the Temple, when appearing in court in connection with her continuous litigation.

The crisis left simmering at Echo Park was destined to produce a series of shocks and embroil Aimee McPherson in one of the most startling chapters of her career; certainly the wildest since the upheaval of 1926.

When the evangelist left Los Angeles for New Orleans in the spring of 1936, she was a woman mentally obsessed—haunted by fear that she would lose Angelus Temple. Without the temple, all justification for her life would be gone. To it she had given her strength and vitality; it had absorbed her will, her thoughts, her being. Also, there was the gnawing self-knowledge that she was forty-five and growing old.

The previous year had brought a heavy misfortune in the death of Brother Arthur, the mild-mannered, devoted servant of her interests and her church. His passing had snapped her last link with the years of the temple's founding and early struggles. He was accorded a spectacular funeral under the dome of the great auditorium, and Aimee preached the sermon with tear-filled eyes. Not as long as she lived would another person receive the tribute of a funeral in the temple itself.

Pictures such as this, of Rheba Crawford and Harriet Jordan, dean of the Temple Bible School, whispering chummily, fed Aimee McPherson's suspicions of a conspiracy against her.

Estranged from her mother, all her marriages miscarried, Aimee felt desperately alone. The steadying influence that she always needed was lacking. Around her she saw only jealous, envious rivals, eager to supplant her and strip her of her possessions.

A definite suspicion had taken root in her mind that a conspiracy to despoil her existed among her closest temple associates, and gradually Rheba Crawford became the focal point of this supposed conspiracy. Rheba was plotting against her, Aimee felt sure. Rheba's very success told against her. Was she not drawing crowds almost as large and as enthusiastic as those that turned out to hear Sister herself? Rheba was popular with the younger element in the church, and this was another sore point. And hardest of all to take, Rheba was younger—eight years younger—than Aimee. Everything pointed to the conclusion that Rheba was the instigator and leader of the plot to steal the temple, Aimee's imaginings told her. Rheba must be stopped.

On the train ride to New Orleans, Aimee told her daughter things that startled Roberta Semple. She talked about the conspiracy to wean the temple away from her, saying it had been hatched and was being directed by Rheba Crawford and Harriet Jordan.

"Rheba and Jordie have something on me and are blackmailing me to keep their jobs," Aimee said.

The "something" so imagined, later testimony indicated, was a letter or letters that Aimee had written to David Hutton from abroad before their disagreement, containing, or said to contain, "dirty stories."

The evangelist went on:

"Rheba has a secret society in which all the younger women in the temple are banded together for the purpose of stealing the temple. The organist plays a certain piece of music to call their meetings, where ways and means are discussed. Their password is, 'Woe to the one who breaks the link!'"

Aimee could not help dramatizing a danger, real or fancied, and this was how she talked to her daughter, while back in Los Angeles the newspapers were making hay with the billingsgate of the bill of particulars that Vivian Denton had introduced into her suit for slander.

The complainant alleged that during her supposed tongue-lashing, Sister McPherson had called her "a brat" and "an imp of Satan," as well as "a coarse and common woman." Within earshot of two other women, Sister was said to have remarked that Vivian looked like an immoral character, and in the presence of still other persons to have added, "You can't do anything with anyone so coarse and common as she is." Finally, during a telephone conversation, the evangelist was said to have accused Miss Denton of spreading a rumor that Sister McPherson took dope, supplied to her by one of the temple's electricians.

On February 22, a telegram arrived at the temple from Sister in New Orleans, firing Willedd Andrews as the temple attorney and canceling his retainer of two hundred dollars a month.

At the end of February, Miss Semple returned to the city alone, while her mother extended her holiday to Arizona and the Grand Canyon.

Then, on March 11, Miss Semple left Los Angeles for Phoenix, Arizona, and on March 12 Harriet Jordan followed. Also making the journey to Phoenix was the new temple attorney, Jacob Moidel.

In Phoenix, Mrs. McPherson met these three and signed important contracts embodying changes in the temple's administration.

By one contract, Roberta Semple was named assistant business manager at a salary of one hundred fifty dollars a month. Under a second, Jacob Moidel was retained as temple attorney at a stated fee of two hundred fifty dollars a month, plus twenty-five dollars for every day he spent in court. A third contract confirmed Harriet Jordan in her position as the temple's business manager. This was the first written agreement Jordie had ever had with her pastor during their fifteen years of association.

Miss Jordan, Miss Semple, and Moidel returned to Los Angeles, and there Moidel put out a statement that contained surprises. It read:

"Sister Aimee called Miss Jordan, Roberta, and myself to Phoenix Friday to discuss business and administrative problems affecting the welfare of the temple. We returned this morning. She authorized me to announce that Miss Jordan is to continue as business manager and that Miss Semple will be assistant business manager. . . .

"Sister McPherson is in no danger of losing control of Angelus Temple, in view of the fact that no effort is being made to oust her from that position, notwithstanding reports to the contrary. Sister McPherson continues to hold the presidency of the church and naturally will remain pastor as long as she lives, just as she has ever since it was founded. There are no members in Angelus Temple who seek to dislodge her from her positions in the corporations. The settled policies of the temple will continue to be as in the past, and no necessity exists for a change in personnel.

"Miss Semple is the only person authorized to issue any statements regarding the temple or its associated churches, outside of my office, on behalf of Mrs. McPherson."

This overvehement disclaimer of insurrection at the temple whetted the public's appetite for disclosures, and it was wondered why it had been deemed advisable to transact church business in Arizona, far from Echo Park. Explained Miss Semple:

"That is just the way Mamma does things. Mrs. McPherson wanted us to come over because there were some legal matters in connection with the branches and it was necessary that she sign the papers. We went there instead of her coming here."

Soon after this, the evangelist herself reappeared briefly in Los Angeles, and on April 8 the Phoenix contracts were entered in the minutes of the church corporation.

During this visit, Aimee took pains publicly to squelch the talk about a coolness between herself and Rheba Crawford. Emerging from a lawyer's office arm-in-arm with her associate pastor, Aimee said:

"There is no misunderstanding between Sister Rheba and myself. I will remain the temple's pastor for life. Sister Rheba will remain associate pastor for the length of her contract."

This reassurance still left much unsaid; and while probing for the truth, reporters came upon a report that Aimee's mother had been approached to resume the business administration of the church. Both Sister and Minnie issued denials.

"Mrs. Kennedy and I are on the most friendly terms," the evangelist said, disregarding the fact that they had hardly exchanged a word since 1929. "But I wouldn't dream of burdening her with the work of the temple."

Ma Kennedy, living in the peace she had fought for at Hermosa Beach, treated the rumor philosophically.

"There was a day when I was needed at the temple to help Sister Aimee in the harness, to rein her back when she was inclined to scamper," she recalled. "And if she ever needs me for that purpose again—well, what would any mother do?"

But as for taking over the business management—and especially as to lending the temple fifty thousand dollars—well, that brought a snort from still doughty Minnie.

"I got out of that temple because of three or four people who messed up its business affairs," she bobbed her head with spirit. "Those people are still there, and I'm not going to get mixed up with them again! Aimee and I once made a good team. We worked well together. After our first split I returned several times when she needed me. Several of my old friends have sent me word that they wished I was back, but there has been no official call. I'm not interested in managing that place again. I've served my time!"

Then the temple elders entered the picture by adopting a resolution calling on Sister Rheba Crawford to resign. She was not impressed.

"I was called to preach by God, not by any board of elders," she retorted. "The elders have no authority to ask for my resignation or to give me orders. I propose to sit tight and go ahead with my work. Of course, if they back me into a corner, I will kick, and if they start making charges against me, that sort of thing can reach both ways."

Denied the use of the temple radio facilities, she resumed over an independent station her vociferations against the city administration and named prominent citizens as implicated in vice protection. Moidel wrote to those whom she named, stressing that she was not speaking for Angelus Temple. Back in her pulpit, Aimee also issued a disclaimer:

"We are not in politics. Everybody talks too much. There is work to be done here. There is no time for bickering."

The confidence she reposed in her daughter she demonstrated by promoting her to be *associate* business manager, to exercise authority equally with Harriet Jordan. Succeeding Miss Semple as *assistant* manager was a temple worker who had risen through the ranks, the Reverend Giles N. Knight. Aimee announced these changes personally to all temple employees.

This occurred on July 10, and outward harmony prevailed for exactly seventeen days.

On July 27, while Aimee was aboard a train headed for Portland, Oregon, where she was to attend a church convention, word seeped out regarding a furious storm in the temple command involving Roberta Semple, Rheba Crawford, and Jacob Moidel. Roberta was said to have quarreled bitterly with her mother, Moidel was reported to be on the way out as temple counsel, and passersby were intrigued by the sight of a temple henchman unscrewing the electric light bulbs from the sign spelling Rheba Crawford's name across the facade of the building.

II

From Portland, Aimee, surrounded by reporters, telephoned to the temple and poured oil on the agitated waters. She authorized Roberta to state that Moidel still was the temple attorney. Then she hastened back to Los Angeles and moved into a new home not far from the temple, forsaking the parsonage. She seemed inexpressibly weary as she explained that her new residence was merely "a small cottage" where she hoped to find more quiet than was possible at the parsonage. The "small cottage," it developed, was a house of some pretentiousness in the Silver Lake district, in a fashionable development known as Moreno Heights. This was to be her home for the rest of her life.

The Vivian Denton suit was set for trial that month. Vivian had raised her claim for damages to an even five hundred thousand dollars, and it was bruited that Rheba Crawford would testify for the plaintiff. Rheba's own enigmatic words were:

"I will tell the truth on the witness stand as God is my judge."

Then suddenly the suit was settled. Vivian's friends said she had been paid five thousand dollars; temple sources put the amount at two hundred dollars. And Miss Crawford was ordered by Aimee to depart upon an evangelistic tour of the hinterlands. But Miss Crawford did not leave Los Angeles.

Then, on September 24, the lumbering volcano erupted.

In a letter to her mother, signed "lovingly and sincerely," Roberta Semple denounced what she described as an attempt to create a "dictatorship" at Angelus Temple, with Giles Knight, newly appointed assistant business manager, cast as the dictator. Jacob Moidel said he had been fired, and Mother Kennedy jumped into the fray with a bellicose:

"I refuse to tolerate any abuse of Roberta and will fully support any action taken by my granddaughter."

Roberta had issued her letter of protest to her mother from Jacob Moidel's office. Giles Knight, she asserted, was demanding unlimited power to deal with temple affairs, and "the powers he demands as necessary to his employment are unreasonable and illegal. Legal action will be taken to protect the corporation from those who wish to create a dictatorship at Angelus Temple. As you know, I have no personal quarrel with you."

Miss Semple's objections carried force, for she was a voting member of the church corporations, and vice-president and secretary of the Echo Park Evangelistic Association. Moidel gave his opinion that Mrs. McPherson, Miss Semple, and Rolf McPherson, the three trustees of the Echo Park Evangelistic Association, empowered under

California law to manage Angelus Temple, could not legally delegate their authority. As for his own discharge:

"I refused to resign as attorney for the organization, so Mrs. McPherson fired me. Miss Semple was there at the time."

Aimee's retort:

"With regard to this letter, I do not believe it is the language of my daughter, and there is nothing in my heart but love for her. It has been the fond wish of my heart that Miss Semple become president of the organization which I have built up, when she is ready to carry the burden."

She denied that Moidel had been dismissed, but criticized him for overmuch "anxiety for our church. He will be on safer ground if he confines his efforts to legal matters for which he is being paid."

Minnie Kennedy revealed that there had been a furious row at the parsonage, after which Roberta had telephoned tearfully to Hermosa Beach, and the next morning Minnie had driven into town and fetched her granddaughter to stay with her. She said she had telephoned to Aimee ("the first time I called her since we came to the parting of the ways in 1929") and told her that she did not approve of "giving Mr. Knight full authority to act without responsibility to the board of the Echo Park Evangelistic Association." And she said she had rung off with a final bit of advice for her daughter, to "stop treating Roberta like a child."

To reporters, Minnie outlined her stand:

"Angelus Temple was founded by Aimee and myself. It is only right that it should remain in the family. I have seen business managers come and go during the years of my retirement. There have been as many managers as years—and as many lawsuits as managers! Aimee can get her best counsel and management from her own children."

In the family crisis, Rolf McPherson, who seldom figured in the headlines, ranged himself beside his mother. He issued a formal statement, saying:

"My sister has absolutely no reasonable cause for objecting to the method or way in which the affairs of the temple have been run. I am sorry that Roberta has taken such an attitude, and I am sure that in this regard she stands alone around the temple. . . . There are three members of the board of trustees, and my vote will certainly be cast with that of my mother, the president."

Rheba Crawford, toward whom Roberta had not always shown partiality, came to Roberta's support, especially in regard to control of the temple radio facilities, which Rheba correctly termed "one of the most powerful forces at the temple." Aimee, Roberta, and Rheba were the trustees of KFSG, and Miss Crawford stated plainly:

"Miss Semple and I stand together as opposed to Sister's policy of allowing Giles Knight to become an autocrat in matters pertaining to the radio."

Knight professed to be mystified by the flare-up:

"I can't say what 'illegal powers' Miss Semple has in mind. This all comes as quite a surprise to me."

Sickened by the turmoil, Roberta collapsed and was put to bed by her grandmother. But Aimee remained immovable.

"I propose to direct the spiritual and temporal activities of the temple, which I built up," she stated with finality. "I will not allow anything or anybody to interfere with my work."

And she continued to rush headlong along a course that could lead only to humiliation and defeat. She seemed to have become a woman bent on destroying herself with her own extraordinary powers, now that the gage of battle had been flung down. Who should control Angelus Temple and its empire? Let her cling to that control, by no matter what means, and nothing else would matter.

On September 27, a letter typed on the stationery of the Echo Park Evangelistic Association was sent to Jacob Moidel, informing him that his contract with Mrs. McPherson had been terminated. This letter was signed by Aimee in her fourfold capacity as the president of four separate corporations. Moidel was ordered to turn over all records and files to Willedd Andrews.

To an enclosed second copy of this letter was attached a list of stipulations headed "My Terms." It laid down conditions for a peaceful settlement of the dispute. The demands included:

"Jacob Moidel and Aimee Semple McPherson will not speak disrespectfully of either in the future."

"Jacob Moidel will not be an attorney, either directly or indirectly, secretly or openly, against Aimee Semple McPherson, the board of elders or any one of the Angelus Temple organizations or any associated or affiliated organizations."

"Roberta Semple to present her written resignation as a member of all boards of directors . . . including the radio board."

"Trustees appoint Willedd Andrews."

"Mr. Moidel promises never to sue or to aid and abet my enemies."

Below these demands was another list of proposals, headed "In Return." They comprised:

"No derogatory statement shall be published by one party against the other."

"Roberta shall continue to assist me in publications, radio, platform, and any such reasonable church and social business as I may ask."

"A disagreement shall be kept confidential, that no one be embarrassed."

"Mr. Moidel, Roberta, and Mrs. Kennedy to promise to discourage all litigation as may be threatened against me from time to time."

"No apologies shall be deemed necessary by either party."

"A dignified statement shall be published mutually agreeable."

"Roberta shall have all rights to continue her residence at the parsonage."

"Her contract shall be held valid and her salary retained."

When Ma Kennedy saw these demands she snorted in disgust:

"Absolute surrender!"

And when Roberta Semple rejected them and engaged a lawyer, Minnie was delighted.

This letter had been dictated on a Tuesday. Late in the afternoon on Wednesday, Roberta and Moidel called at the parsonage. A violent scene ensued, culminating in Miss Semple's leaving the house for good. And Minnie Kennedy, her fighting spirit thoroughly aroused, proclaimed her intention of backing her granddaughter "with all my resources and my retentive memory."

Whereupon Aimee convened a meeting of the trustees of the Echo Park Evangelistic Association for Saturday evening. Roberta was notified. Her counsel protested in writing that she was too ill to attend, but nevertheless the meeting was called to order at the appointed time.

Seldom has corporate business been transacted in a more extraordinary setting. Immediately after conducting a divine healing service, Aimee went with Rolf McPherson to the temple offices in the parsonage next door. Giles Knight, Willedd Andrews, and a press representative were on hand in the capacity of observers.

Aimee and Rolf, meeting as directors of the Echo Park Evangelistic

Association, adopted a resolution appointing the president of the corporation (Mrs. McPherson) an executive committee of one to administer Angelus Temple, endowed with all the powers of the full board.

Then Jacob Moidel was discharged as the corporation's attorney, and Willedd Andrews was appointed in his stead.

Next, adjourning their meeting as directors, mother and son convened another meeting of themselves as the members of the association and voted a change in the bylaws that revoked the provision that two members should form a quorum; hereafter the president would be a quorum by herself.

Aimee and Rolf then adjourned a second time and retired to the private apartments upstairs.

An announcement was written out in longhand by the new corporation attorney, Andrews, in the presence of the reporter, to be given out for publication. As published, it contained the following passage:

"Mrs. McPherson has been intimidated, threatened, and blackmailed for the last time. This time she is prepared to fight to a finish. While she regrets that the war will be sanguinary—with her own child—the only course ahead of her is protection of the organization which has consumed the best years of her life."

Roberta read this statement in the newspaper and promptly sued Willedd Andrews for slander, charging that he had accused her of "blackmailing" her mother. She asked damages of one hundred fifty thousand dollars.

The shrieks of newsboys yelling this disruptive development outside Angelus Temple pierced the singing of the congregation inside, as they turned docile faces toward Sister on the platform. Willedd Andrews spoke briefly from the pulpit, denying that he had accused Miss Semple of blackmailing, threatening, or intimidating her mother, and Aimee demonstrated her confidence in her new legal adviser by publicly renewing his associate membership in the church.

But the uproar grew only shriller when a petition was lodged with the California State Bar requesting the disbarment of Jacob Moidel.

The complaint was signed by Giles N. Knight and William R. Black, secretary of the International Church of the Foursquare Gospel. It alleged, among other instances of asserted misconduct, that in Phoenix, Moidel had demanded that Mrs. McPherson discharge Willedd Andrews and engage Moidel as counsel; that Moidel had threatened that unless Sister signed the contracts with Miss Semple, Miss Jordan, and himself, he would bring court action to have her declared incompetent and insane and in Roberta's interest would demand an accounting of the temple, and would harass the temple's pastor with fifty quit-claim suits, filed one a day. When Mrs. McPherson yielded to these threats and signed the contracts, the complaint averred, Moidel had then forced her to sign a statement that her action was taken freely and without duress.

These supposed incidents in the hotel at Phoenix neither Knight nor Black claimed to have seen and heard; they were repeating what they had been told.

Furthermore, and still more startling, the complaint associated Jacob Moidel with a scene of violence at the parsonage, during which, it was said, he used abusive language to Mrs. McPherson and to Knight, and had seized Sister by the arms and shaken her until she screamed and Knight came to her rescue; that Moidel had threatened to "expose" the 1926 kidnaping case, and that he had raised so great a commotion in the alley between the temple and the Bible School that divine services were disturbed and Sister swooned.

Moidel's comment on this action was that it had been instituted simply to prevent him from suing for the balance of the salary due him under his voided contract. He challenged Mrs. McPherson to sign a complaint herself. She did not accept this challenge, and, after proper investigation, the State Bar threw the petition out as devoid of merit and absolved Jacob Moidel of any misconduct, without reservation.

Even then the storm had not reached its height. Rheba Crawford and Harriet Jordan were understood to be maintaining their status in the church precariously. Miss Crawford had not been near the temple or active in its behalf for months. Then, on the eve of Thanksgiving Day, Rheba—again ill and in the Glendale Hospital—received a special-delivery letter from Giles Knight terminating her contract and removing her as associate pastor in consequence of five alleged "offenses."

These, the letter said, were that she had conspired to take the temple away from Sister; that her business associations with underworld characters unfitted her for the ministry; that she had accepted money from a questionable source to pay for a holiday in Hawaii;

that she had demanded the removal of Willedd Andrews as counsel and the appointment of Jacob Moidel; and that she had constantly stirred up "unspeakable strife" in the temple organization and membership.

When reporters asked Mrs. McPherson about this letter, she seemed startled.

"What! You know about that!" she exclaimed. Then she set her lips tightly. "I have nothing to say about it or about Miss Crawford. There is a clause in our contract which prevents either of us from saying anything derogatory against the other."

Rheba remembered that clause, too. In reply, she denied the authority of Giles Knight to cancel her contract with Mrs. McPherson, demanded an accounting of all monies collected and spent since she had become associate pastor, and called for an investigation of "certain charges which have been discussed against me."

Then she sued Mrs. McPherson for slander, listing eighteen specific scurrilous and derogatory statements that she accused the evangelist of having made against her, and demanding damages of one million and eighty thousand dollars.

III

Aimee preached her Thanksgiving Day sermon, an annual festival, in a Priscilla Alden costume. She discharged her social duties, entertaining a group of the temple's elders at dinner in her Silver Lake home. Then she set about fighting Rheba's charges and her daughter's rebellion without quarter.

Sister McPherson's pulpit vocabulary and diction were well known. But the language that Miss Crawford, in her million-dollar action, asserted that Sister had employed when out of hearing of her congregation sounded like no utterance hitherto imputed, at least publicly, to the pastor of Angelus Temple, theological seminary president and God-ordained ordainer of doctors of divinity.

Rheba's eighteen citations of invidious and scandalous remarks that she attributed to Mrs. McPherson were buttressed by naming the times, the places, and the witnesses before whom the remarks allegedly were made. Among these purported statements were the following, according to Miss Crawford's complaint filed with the court:

"I'm going to do something about that Jezebel. I will never

Dressed as "Priscilla Alden," Sister Aimee preached her 1936 Thanksgiving Day sermon standing at the wheel of the good ship *Mayflower* in Angelus Temple.

forgive Jordie for making me sign that contract with Miss Crawford. She may have been good enough to have been a governor's mistress, but no woman of her kind is going to use my platform, my money, and wreck the temple and get away with it! This isn't Sacramento!"

"Mr. Andrews told me, didn't you, Mr. Andrews, that Rheba Crawford was in a conspiracy to murder me, and I will sign a complaint against her if it is the last thing I do. It is about time to put a stop to Rheba Crawford!"

"Our investigators have information that Rheba is having Miss Jordan manipulate the books so that it will look bad for me. I think that what Mr. Andrews says is true, that Rheba and Jordie are really stealing money from me. . . . She has stolen money from me just the way she did in the Salvation Army. It looks like 'once a crook always a crook.' "

"Talk about Capone and Dillinger! Miss Crawford is as bad as either of them! She has a gang here in the temple equal to either of theirs! She is a partner of the Devil!"

"I don't care how many detectives you hire, but get the goods on Rheba. Here she is trying to take the temple away from me and using my money to do it. If it is the last thing I do, I will show her up—the hypocrite! A fine associate pastor she has turned out to be!"

"Rheba had better look out, because if I told what I know about her Salvation Army life, she wouldn't keep her job here two minutes. Mr. Andrews has done fine work checking up on this Jezebel. . . . If she thinks I am so dumb that I don't know she has hypnotized Jordie, she is crazy!"

"Rheba hasn't any business hiring her spies to spy on the board of elders. What I do is my own business. I appointed them and they should be my friends, and I will fire every last one of them who double-crosses me or attempts to tell what he knows about me. It looks like our Jezebel has turned out to be a Judas, too!"

Minnie Kennedy's name was brought in when Aimee was alleged to have said:

"Rheba is just like Ma Kennedy was! She is trying to steal my temple away from me, but she isn't going to get away with it! Ma Kennedy embezzled plenty of money from the temple, and so did Rheba when I was away. She is playing the same game as Ma Kennedy did!"

An echo of the troubled period of Aimee's absence in Europe before her divorce from Hutton sounded in another purported statement:

"Miss Jordan tells me that they could bring in the letter that I sent to David Hutton when I was in Paris. That letter was strictly confidential between David and me, and if I want to write him any dirty stories, he is my husband and I am his wife. They can't tell me Rheba is not my enemy, when here she is circulating these letters to prove that I am an immoral woman!"

The Vivian Denton lawsuit was the subject of another alleged outburst, quoted as follows:

"I know that Rheba is back of Vivian's lawsuit against me, and if she takes the stand against me, as Miss Jordan says she will, and tells the truth about this affair, I will tell the truth about what I know of her love affairs with senators and officials in Sacramento. Even if I did say that Vivian looks like a madam in a whorehouse, she does, doesn't she? And if Rheba wants to associate with a person like that, or be her witness against me, all I have to say is that 'birds of a feather flock together,' and you know what Vivian is!"

And the temple's pastor was asserted to have harangued her board of elders, assembled to transact church business, in the words:

"This is the last time I am going to be blackmailed by Vivian Denton, Rheba Crawford, or anyone else! I have paid out my last huge money. I am going to fight this thing through to a finish! . . . Rheba testifying against your own pastor, who loves each and every one of you! Are you going to stand by me, or are you going to stand by that Crawford woman who is blackmailing me so Vivian will have some money to get treatments for her fatness? All she wants is to get money so she can reduce . . . I demand loyalty in the institution, and I will fire anyone who is not loyal to me!"

And so the charges ran, in terms bitter, denunciatory, and certainly in contravention of that ban against uttering remarks "derogatory" to either party to the Crawford-McPherson contract.

A process server handed the papers in Rheba's suit to Aimee as she was entering the Five Hundred Room to lead Thanksgiving worshipers in an hour of ardent prayer. Tossing back her head, Sister unloosed her best sarcasm:

"Our accounting department, which has paid Mrs. Splivalo six hundred dollars a month regularly, has netted her approximately thirty thousand dollars. I note that she still desires one million eighty thousand dollars. The lady in question told me that she is an ambitious person. Of this I am now thoroughly convinced."

During the Thanksgiving holiday interim, Aimee cleared decks for the coming battle by eliminating her daughter from all connection with the church or the family holding company, the Echo Park Evangelistic Association. Heretofore she had merely stripped Roberta of her positions of executive authority; now she prepared a total excommunication.

Miss Semple, encamped in her grandmother's house, was notified that a meeting of the directors of the Echo Park Evangelistic Association had been called, at which the question of her removal would be voted upon, inasmuch as she had absented herself from the parsonage more than sixty days and had failed to carry out her temple work assignments.

The meeting was called to order in the evangelist's parsonage quarters, with Willedd Andrews and Giles Knight present as observers. Roberta, who knew that her vote would be overruled by her mother and her brother and did not wish to provoke an unpleasant scene, did not attend. Aimee entered in the minutes that Roberta Semple had "refused to do any work whatsoever at Angelus Temple and has refused to perform her duties in connection with radio station KFSG." Then the president and her son voted away Roberta's rights as a director and expelled her from the corporation.

Later the same two met as directors of the Bible School and expunged Roberta from that corporation also, electing a new board composed of Aimee, Rolf McPherson, and Harriet Jordan, with Giles Knight as secretary.

The continued retention of Miss Jordan as dean of the Bible School (although she had been supplanted by Knight as temple business manager) occasioned surprise. But the fact was that Aimee was not yet of an assured mind about Jordie; their intimacy ran too far back, and there was a convincing air of sincerity and honesty about Harriet Jordan that caused the pastor to hesitate.

Roberta greeted her expulsion with a temperate, direct statement: "When I was a very small child, I was told that I must prepare myself for membership on the board of directors of the Echo Park

Minnie Kennedy rallies to the defense of her granddaughter, Roberta Semple, after the latter had left the Parsonage in a bitter row with her mother.

Evangelistic Association. I devoted my girlhood to the church and was elected to the board and became an official. Now my mother has seen fit to oust me from my lifework. I didn't believe she would allow herself to be so unfair. But if my own mother does not want me associated with her, I certainly do not intend to push myself into her affairs."

Minnie Kennedy, as usual, was more combative.

"I've managed to keep off the witness stand for nine years," she said grimly, "but it looks now as if I am going to be allowed to tell the truth at last—about everything! Roberta has been trained for that work since she was knee-high to a grasshopper—for years under my strict discipline. If for no other reason than in memory of Roberta's dead father, I intend to stand back of my granddaughter through this whole fight. I shall feel most comfortable in that witness chair!"

Then her mood changed, and she became reflective:

"Aimee has done the same thing to Roberta that she did to me ten years ago. Ever since she left home at the age of seventeen, she has never been able to hold anyone close to her. In casting out her own daughter, she has overturned her own lifework. We have the kindest feeling toward the temple and all its members. But if my daughter continues so recklessly to separate herself from her devoted family, I prophesy she will chart her own course to ruin. I am moved to pity for her now as never before."

The trial of Miss Semple's action against Willedd Andrews was delayed, by one maneuver or another, until the spring of 1937, and the route leading to it was, for all concerned, a *via dolorosa* of deposition-taking and painfully searching examinations. Two lawsuits were in progress simultaneously—Rheba Crawford suing Mrs. McPherson, and Roberta suing her mother's attorney—and it was generally accepted that really at stake in both actions was Aimee's reputation itself—her prestige, her supremacy, and her private happiness.

In Rheba's action, Aimee was examined before a court commissioner, and she stubbornly resisted answering many questions, particularly those bearing on her financial resources or the money affairs of Angelus Temple. Contending counsel wrangled heatedly, and Aimee sat composedly through the acrid debates, apparently unmindful of the disputing, absently fingering her taffy-colored hair or a spray of gardenias at her throat.

She produced a sensation by charging that Rheba Crawford had once planned to collect a payoff of one hundred thirty thousand dollars from the underworld and split it with her.

"I said, 'You are joking,' but she said, 'No, they paid off in other cities, why not here?' I asked her if she intended to continue her campaign against certain officials. She replied it was her policy to kick everyone in the shins . . . until they came through. . . . I told her I was sick and tired of it, and asked her why she did it. She said, 'I am fighting vice.' I said, 'It almost makes me laugh to think about it!' "

Among the persons who had protested to the temple against being vilified by Rheba's crusading, said Aimee, were the state's governor, the city's fire chief, the chief of police, members of the board of education, the board of supervisors, and other officials.

Asked whether she had ever alluded to Miss Crawford as a governor's mistress, Aimee snapped:

"No! But I said Rheba shouldn't get up before four thousand people at the temple, as she did, and say she had been accused of being the governor's mistress. She laughed heartily as she said it, I recall."

Nervously fingering her corsage, Mrs. McPherson testified that Rheba had refused to preach at the temple.

"The trouble started last February when Rheba said she wouldn't believe any of the elders on a stack of Bibles—that they were all liars. They all heard it. That made things difficult. I went to the board of elders and told them that I felt badly because she had refused to preach and help on the platform. She said it was because she felt only one star should be on the platform at a time. I said I thought the star should be Jesus. But she felt differently, though, and said she did not like to appear in a competitive light."

Letters written to David Hutton were produced, and when questioned about one of these, the evangelist waved her questioner aside with the reply that she never used profanity. Shown photostatic copies of several letters, she was asked whether they were in her handwriting.

"I have looked these letters over," she answered, drawing off her gold-trimmed black gloves, "and certain interjections have been made in them not in my writing."

It was proposed that she read aloud the passages that she believed were not in her hand, and she snapped:

"I won't read that filthy stuff!"

Time and again she begged her questioner not to shout, and frequently she (whose voice carried easily to the topmost seats in Angelus Temple's balcony) was admonished to speak up so as to be audible to the court reporter seated three feet away.

Questions regarding bank accounts and money matters she at first refused to answer at all, until warned by the commissioner that she might be held in contempt. In a continuation of her testimony the next day, she proved more responsive. She admitted that she was

Aimee displays chic and nonchalance while waiting to testify in a deposition hearing on her daughter's suit against Aimee's attorney, Willedd Andrews.

paid a salary by the church. Clasping and unclasping her hands and constantly touching the ever-present corsage (this time it was orchids, three large ones), she said hesitantly:

"My income is one hundred eighty dollars a week and is in return for the many things that I do, such as teaching in the Bible School, giving radio talks, publishing our weekly paper, preaching on the platform, praying for the sick, and being president of about four hundred branch churches. There is also a fund—we call it the tithe fund—which is available to me for trips, in case I should be called to some one of our foreign stations. All the churches contribute to the tithe fund."

She was unable to say how much this fund amounted to, explaining that the money was allowed to accumulate and the sum fluctuated.

She admitted ownership of a lot at Lake Elsinore valued at seventeen thousand dollars, and agreed that she controlled a corporation that owned a large lot on Glendale Boulevard close by the temple; also that she had received five thousand dollars recently for a five-week speaking tour. And she reverted to the quarter-of-a-million-dollar deed of trust that she held from the Echo Park Evangelistic Association, admitting that she had used the note as collateral for a fifteen-thousand-dollar loan. Sensing a subtle purpose in this line of questioning, however, she suddenly became tense and asked abruptly:

"Is the reason for this to learn if Rheba can take Angelus Temple from me if I lose this suit?"

"Just a minute," replied Miss Crawford's attorney. "Miss Crawford doesn't want your temple. If anybody else took over Angelus Temple it probably would be a skating rink the next week."

But the fear was ever-present to Aimee.

Miss Crawford flatly denied Aimee's accusations.

"The assertion made by Aimee Semple McPherson in her deposition, relative to a conversation with me, in which she says I told her an offer might come from the underworld of one hundred thirty thousand dollars, is manufactured from whole cloth and is false and untrue."

Thereupon the Church of the Foursquare Gospel added to the legal tangle by demanding from its former associate pastor the sum of four thousand and thirty-one dollars and ten cents, anticipated income from pledges to contribute, that had been revoked because of Rheba's alleged "misbehavior."

And Willedd Andrews tossed in a suit of his own, against Rheba Crawford and Jacob Moidel, charging them with having engineered his dismissal by Mrs. McPherson just when he was negotiating a new contract with the pastor, carrying a retainer of two hundred fifty dollars a month for the next ten years.

This action the court quickly quashed by sustaining the demurrers filed by both defendants.

But Andrews became the center of another storm when he was called for a deposition in Roberta Semple's suit against him. He contended that he had never used the words "blackmailed" or "coerced" in referring to the troubles between Mrs. McPherson and either her daughter or Miss Crawford. He had settled his contract with Sister,

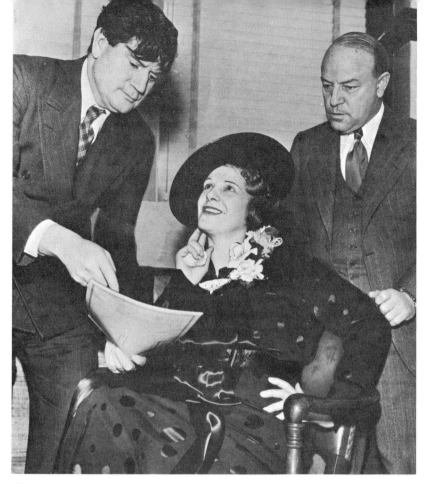

Questioning failed to shake Aimee's aplomb at deposition hearing when Joseph Fainer, left, counsel for Roberta Semple, showed her disputed document, while Willedd Andrews, who was being sued, kept watch.

when she discharged him, for eleven hundred dollars, he said. And under persistent questioning he at last confessed that his memory had erred in the matter of dates, when he had attributed his dismissal to the time of the reported drama in Phoenix; actually he had been dismissed nearly three weeks before that date. He insisted, however, that the asserted rowdy scenes in Phoenix had occurred and that Jacob Moidel had in fact threatened to have Mrs. McPherson declared insane unless she signed the contracts he had prepared.

Undeterred by the whirr of legal machinery, Aimee continued her church business with unabated zest. In February, 1937, she incorporated the Foursquare Gospel Press, Limited, to publish newspapers, magazines, books, and maps. The company was capitalized at twenty-five thousand dollars, and the directors were herself, Brother Knight and Brother Black.

On Washington's Birthday, Sister officiated at a military wedding before a standing-room-only crowd, uniting a veteran of Verdun with an army officer's daughter. The preacher's costume was dazzling: it combined a patriotic motif (cherry red, white, and blue, with appropriate stars), with hearts for St. Valentine's Day and true love, and was topped by the diadem of the Statue of Liberty—all irradiated by Sister's refulgent smile.

When Rheba Crawford was called to make her deposition, she discoursed liberally about Aimee and the temple, called Willedd Andrews a liar, slapped the face of an inoffensive man waiting for the elevator (she mistook him for somebody else), and alternately praised and pejorated Mrs. McPherson.

"Sister is a very skillful showman and a wonderful preacher," said Rheba, and in the same breath: "I tell you, she is the most tragic figure in America, living in mortal fear that the glories of her past will be taken away from her. That's why she thinks people are trying to take her temple. I have prayed the Lord to return her to what she was before the kidnaping. She could have been truly great, working for the poor and helping all mankind, but she has a money mania that has nearly wrecked her. Her downfall has been the love of money. She didn't want people to know how much she was getting from the church; she said the people wouldn't give as much if they knew."

She had made allowances, Rheba added, because Sister was suffering from thyroid trouble:

"I have pleaded with her to have an operation, but she never did."

As for the charge that she plotted to steal Angelus Temple, Miss Crawford entered a categorical denial.

"You know," she said, "Mrs. McPherson doesn't quarrel with you. She sticks knives in your back. She looks you in the face and says, 'Darling, I want you forever.' Then she asks someone to get me framed on a morals charge!"

Called back for further grilling, Aimee submitted meekly this time to most questions about money matters, although she was still defensive. Item by item, counsel extracted the information that when

Minnie Kennedy quit the temple she received one hundred and seven thousand dollars in cash and "some property" (just as Minnie had said); that Aimee's life insurance (twenty thousand dollars) was all that she was bequeathing directly to her children; that she owned nothing personally except the Lake Elsinore Moorish castle, everything else being owned by the Echo Park Evangelistic Association, of which she was president and whose note she held for a quarter of a million dollars.

"Even my gardenias are bought for me," she insisted smilingly. "Ella Nordin, my secretary, handles petty cash. I never sign a check." As for the deed of trust: "I have written into the minutes of the Echo Park Evangelistic Association that I will never exercise the mandate of the note. I will never demand the two hundred and fifty thousand dollars. Nor will I ask the ten thousand dollars a year interest due on the note until all the temple's other obligations have been met."

The questioning attorney tried to make her admit that the directors of the church were really herself.

"You named yourself, Harriet Jordan, and your daughter, Roberta Semple, to the board of directors?" she was asked.

"Yes."

"And you also dismissed them?"

Aimee twisted her tiny lace handkerchief nervously and murmured:

"I had hoped this would never be made public. It was Jacob Moidel. He grabbed Roberta by the hand and told her to get her clothes. Then he ordered her to leave and never come back. I begged my daughter to stay with me."

Under a volley of questions she denied that she had offered Roberta a free trip to England to witness the coronation of King George VI in order to get her daughter out of the way when Rheba Crawford's suit should come to trial. Such a trip had been discussed between them, she said, but it was not for that purpose.

But after this deposition sitting, Roberta said:

"Friends of Mother's have told me it would be nice if I were to leave the state for a while."

With this, the principals in Roberta's suit against Aimee's attorney settled down to await a decision in court. Aimee appeared determined but not embittered. At a final, brief deposition hearing, she came face

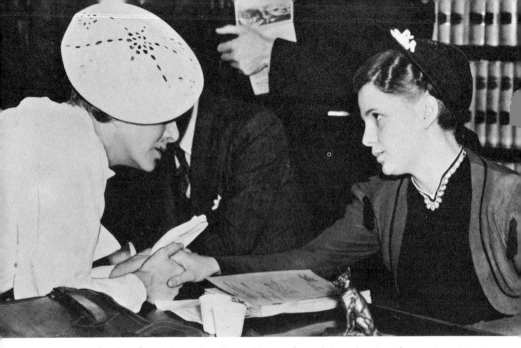

At the close of one hearing, Aimee clasped her daughter's hand and spoke in a low voice, but there was no reconciliation.

to face with her estranged mother and daughter—the first time Minnie had seen the evangelist since 1929. Aimee had already arrived when the two women entered the room; she waited for them to be seated, then smiled. They smiled back. At the close, Sister paused in passing Roberta and pressed her hand and whispered inaudibly; but Roberta and her grandmother marched out together, and Aimee was left pensive and alone.

A climactic worry was the low ebb of the temple's finances. A news service counted up forty-five lawsuits that had been brought against Mrs. McPherson within a few years, all demanding money in amounts ranging from more than a million dollars down to a claim by a discharged temple organist for two dollars and ninety-four cents. Strikingly, the record showed that two out of every three of these actions had never reached trial, indicating a settlement.

How long could the temple—and Aimee—stand such a drain? Again there was gossip that Sister might be deposed by the next convention of the church and Harriet Jordan be elected with a mandate to "save the temple." The rumor became so prevalent that Giles Knight published the wording of the church's charter regulating the presidency. Article VI of the incorporation agreement read:

"The office of president shall be held by Aimee Semple McPherson during her lifetime."

And Section 2 of the same Article:

"The first president of the corporation, Aimee Semple McPherson, may appoint her successor in office as president by depositing with a person or corporation, selected by her . . . a sealed envelope containing the name of the person whom she selects and decides upon to be, at her decease, or upon her retirement or physical disability, the president of the corporation in her stead . . . and upon the happening of such event the person thereby designated shall immediately become the president of the corporation."

So it was clear that only Aimee could nominate her successor, and all the talk about Harriet Jordan and an enforced change became pointless.

Sister did not seem to be worried. On the eve of the Roberta-Andrews trial, she invited the public's attention to the institution of which she was proudest—the Angelus Temple Prayer Tower. There, in a bare upper room for nearly fourteen years—one hundred and eighteen thousand two hundred and six hours—prayers had been offered uninterruptedly for the benefit of mankind. Ten thousand prayer requests were handled every month, Sister said. Prayer was offered in a dozen languages and dialects as devout of the yellow, white, and black races knelt elbow to elbow in amity. In an era of flagpole-sitters, marathon dancers, six-day bicycle races, sitdown strikes, and general church enfeeblement, the selfless dedication displayed by this group was impressive. Aimee credited all her achievements to the spiritual force thus generated.

"It is only through the strength provided by this earnest prayer to God that I am able to continue with the work of Angelus Temple and the Foursquare Gospel," she acknowledged humbly.

Then, on April 13, 1937, she took the witness stand in the last great courtroom drama of her career.

IV

The Sunday before the trial opened was Palm Sunday, and Aimee had preached under the eyes of two Los Angeles policemen, posted at the temple as a result of a rash of threatening letters; several film notables had received threats at the same time. The detectives sat stolidly on the platform while Sister, attired in a white gown with a cross of rosebuds on her breast, sang "In the Heart of a Rose."

When the trial was called in Department 19 of Superior Court, Aimee was on hand, but she left when informed that she would not be needed at once. Minnie Kennedy was in a front-row seat when Judge Kincaid opened the trial without a jury. Roberta Semple was the lead-off witness.

Alternately defiant and on the edge of tears, Aimee's daughter described her humiliation after the publication of the "blackmail" statement.

"Quite a few people stopped me on the street and asked me if it was true that I tried to blackmail my mother. I said, 'No,' but they said it must be true or my mother wouldn't let Mr. Andrews say it. I knew the only way my mother could help me was to stand up and say to the public she had never been blackmailed by me."

This, of course, Aimee had pointedly failed to do.

After their rupture, Roberta continued:

"I went back to get my clothes. I found the lock on the door had been changed and I couldn't enter. She [Aimee] laid down ten conditions on which I might return to my work and the parsonage. She said if I didn't accept those conditions, she would have my friend, Mr. Moidel, disbarred."

As next witness, Jacob Moidel recounted the protest he had made to Willedd Andrews, after the appearance of the "blackmail" statement:

"I told him if he had any blackmail information to take it before the grand jury. Another thing I told him was, 'This is one time you have shot off your mouth too often.' He then replied that Miss Semple had blackmailed her mother and that Mrs. McPherson had told him so. I asked him when Roberta had ever blackmailed or threatened her mother. He said, 'In Phoenix, Arizona.'"

The truth of what had happened in Phoenix thereby became a pivotal issue.

A newspaper reporter swore that Andrews had made the "blackmail" statement to him, for publication. A reporter for a rival newspaper testified that over the telephone Andrews had disavowed using the word "blackmail."

All this was fairly tepid, but with Sister Aimee scheduled to take the stand on the second day, the courtroom and adjoining corridors became a bedlam of pushing, yelling would-be spectators.

"You are breaking my ribs!" screamed one woman caught in the crush.

"You're here of your own accord," grunted the bailiff who, with half a dozen deputies, was struggling to hold back the mob.

Two women came to blows over who was standing on whose feet.

Aimee, as star of this drama of mother love spurned—a radio soap opera come to life—obviously relished every instant. Hardly was she seated in the witness chair before she complained of thirst. She was handed a paper cup filled with water.

"I can't drink out of a paper cup!" she protested, handing it back gingerly.

A few minutes later two spectators who had squeezed their way out, squeezed their way in again bringing a large sodawater glass procured from a drugstore. Someone else produced a pitcher of ice water, and Aimee quaffed deeply. Throughout the day she continued to consume water at such a rate that the newspapers called obliging court attendants mere "water boys for Aimee." At one time three pitchers and several glasses were lined up beside her, and her intake so shocked the white-haired counsel who was appearing for Andrews that he warned her solemnly against the perils of such indulgence.

Sometimes weeping, and again nodding and smiling to friends on both sides of the railing, Sister traced her legal and domestic woes. She got into the record that she had been held a virtual prisoner in her hotel room at Phoenix for almost an entire night while being subjected to a "regular third degree," and that by this duress she had been coerced into signing the contracts for Roberta, Moidel, Harriet Jordan, and also one for Rheba Crawford. Rheba's name wove like a shuttle in and out of the testimony.

Speaking in a low voice, dabbing at her eyes with a lace handkerchief, Aimee described that night of torment and how she had prayed for guidance.

"No sooner had we deposited our bags than Roberta turned to me and said, 'Mother, there has been a blowup at home.' She said, 'I have four contracts—or options on contracts—which must be signed,

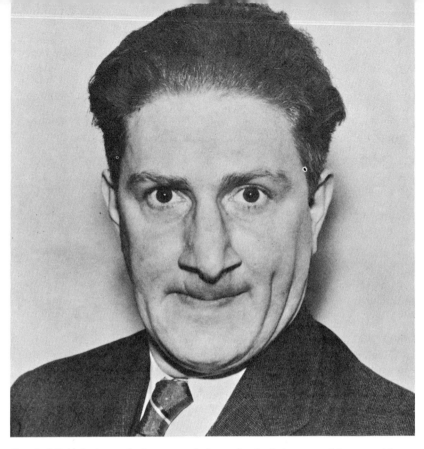

Jacob Moidel showed the sort of faces he had been making at Aimee McPherson on the witness stand in the Willedd Andrews slander suit, when she appealed to the judge and made the same faces at him.

or you will be plunged into a million-dollar lawsuit by Miss Crawford and forty or fifty other lawsuits, to be filed one a day, until you end up by probably losing the temple.' "

At several points during this testimony, Ma Kennedy was seen to hold her nose.

Jacob Moidel was seated with Roberta's counsel, and suddenly Aimee protested that he was "making faces" at her—"like this," she said, making the same faces at the judge. Moidel was ordered to observe decorum or he would be put out of the room, and Aimee, brushing tears from her eyes, thanked the judge profusely.

At the noon break she was assisted from the stand, apparently exhausted. But she rapidly regained strength and during the afternoon's questioning was in even better fettle. She was by turns so apt in her answers, and then so baffling, dilatory, and evasive, that Roberta's attorney, Joseph L. Fainer, finally asked:

"Mrs. McPherson, are you telling the truth?"

"What!" she recoiled.

"I mean, do you testify with a mental reservation?"

"I testify to the very best of memory!" she snapped. But even then she did not get down to the basic facts.

Fainer did succeed in getting her to recollect that she had sent for Moidel to come to Phoenix, that he had not shown up uninvited.

"Yes, I was waiting for Mr. Moidel to tell him about the situation at the temple," she conceded.

But she seemed unable to grasp the import of many questions, and refused to answer until they were explained. Fainer repeated such questions patiently, but objected when he caught her making notes on a slip of paper. However, the judge ruled that it was permissible for her to make notes for reference. Thereafter Aimee scribbled industriously.

She admitted that at the time of the Phoenix conference she had been worried about a threatened "blowup" at Angelus Temple, and that her discussions with Moidel and Roberta in Phoenix had concerned temple affairs generally, not just contracts. But when Fainer tried to show that she had been in an "emotional disequilibrium" as a result of worry and had misinterpreted the words and actions of her visitors, Aimee would not concede it. Frequently her memory wandered, and she sobbed when she said her daughter was in love with Moidel. And continually she brought in Rheba Crawford's name.

A diversion had been provided by Minnie Kennedy just before the afternoon session. Walking up to Aimee, who was standing by the counsel table, Ma said in a loud voice:

"Well, Aimee, this is some different from ten years ago in your kidnap case. Then I was nailed to the cross for you. Now you are doing your best to crucify Roberta."

"No, I am not!" gasped Sister.

"Yes, you are—daring to say she *was* a good girl!"

"I'll explain that she *is* a good girl," Aimee offered hastily.

"You'd better straighten that out," retorted Ma, thrusting forward her pugnacious nose. "Because if you don't, I'll do it for you! I want you to tell the truth!"

"I am!" cried Aimee, backing around the table apprehensively.

Aimee appeared in court wearing a cross-shaped corsage of flowers nobody could identify. "They were given to me by a reformed bandit," she said airily.

"Well, don't tell any more things that aren't true!" Minnie flung out. Then marching toward her daughter, she brandished her fist and shouted, "Mrs. McPherson, I want you to stop telling lies about Roberta!"

Aimee flushed through her makeup, and Ma marched back to her seat with satisfaction.

The dress, the accoutrements, and especially the corsages of the famous evangelist fascinated the observant press and public. The first morning Sister appeared adorned with a cruciform ornament, a spray of white flowers that no one could identify. Aimee didn't know their name, either.

"They were given to me by a reformed bandit," she said.

That afternoon a dozen Talisman roses—a bunch large enough to serve as a funeral bouquet—replaced this anonymous corsage, and thereafter Aimee wore orchids, gardenias, and sweet peas. The floral profusion spread to the women spectators, so many showing up with horticultural effects on their shoulders that the courtroom was smothered in blossoms and perfume. Succumbing to the influence, Roberta's attorney sported a yellow ranunculus in his buttonhole, set off by a McPherson plaid necktie.

Sticking to the issues proved difficult for Aimee, and she wound up her testimony (she was on the stand two and a half days) with a hint of forgery. The minutes of temple meetings were shown to her, and with a dramatic flourish she turned to the judge and asserted:

"At a few places in the temple records my name has been copied!"

Fainer demanded a handwriting expert be called, but after another glance Aimee reluctantly conceded that the scribbled signatures might be hers. The minutes in question showed that the Phoenix contracts had been entered in the church records without objection considerably after the time of the supposed intimidation.

Aimee's concluding shot as a witness was:

"Mr. Moidel and Roberta put me in fear when I signed those contracts. I was willing to do anything."

The testimony continued to echo with Rheba's name. Brother Black described a meeting at the parsonage, attended, he said, by Roberta and Moidel among others, during which Miss Crawford "stormed up and down and nobody could get a word in edgewise." This meeting, he was positive, had occurred on March 12.

"Well, didn't you know that Roberta left Los Angeles for Phoenix on March 11?" interrupted Fainer.

"No, I didn't," said Black, flustered.

Giles Knight enlivened the hearing with his account of a catch-as-catch-can bout in the parsonage at the time Roberta walked out. The disturbance occurred while services were going on in the temple next door, he said.

"Mrs. McPherson demanded the minute books of the temple. Mr. Moidel brought them to the parsonage, in which were grouped Mrs. McPherson, Miss Semple, Miss Jordan, and myself. Mrs. McPherson went to Mr. Moidel and shook him. Moidel dropped the books and shook her, and I rescued her."

But in starting toward Moidel, Knight said, he slipped on a throw rug and slid, baseball fashion, into Moidel's legs. Moidel squared off, and so did Knight, until Moidel exclaimed, "Here, we mustn't lose our tempers!"

"His red hair turned yellow right there," sneered Knight in a loud voice. "I told him he was no gentleman and no attorney either, and he ordered Miss Semple to leave with him. He also told her never to enter the temple again. As they left, Miss Semple called to her mother, who was pleading with her to stay, that she would be back. Mrs. McPherson swooned then and we placed her on a divan."

"And where was her nurse, Ella Nordin, all this time?" asked Fainer. "Wasn't she in the patio with five thousand curling irons in her hair?"

Knight made no answer.

Plump Ella added her version of the scuffle:

"I heard Sister scream, and came into the room just in time to see Mr. Knight slide across the floor on a carpet. Mr. Moidel was standing there red as a beet. Sister said she wanted her record books, which Mr. Moidel was holding."

"What was his attitude?"

"He was very excited and red in the face. Poor Roberta was standing there getting paler and paler. Mr. Moidel just kept getting redder and redder. Finally Roberta walked over to her mother and said, 'Don't you worry, you know I love you,' and Sister said, 'I love you, too, but I must have my minute books!'"

Then, said Ella, Moidel ordered Roberta to leave with him and come back later for her clothing.

Asked whether Sister and she had prayed for guidance in Phoenix before Mrs. McPherson signed the contracts, Miss Nordin nodded:

"Yes, we did."

"Did you get an answer?"

"It sure wasn't a good answer!" she replied, making a face.

In rebuttal of this testimony, Roberta gave her version of the parsonage scrimmage and said her mother had begged her to stay only after she had put on her hat and coat to leave.

"I turned to her and said, 'I'll be back as soon as you calm down and behave yourself,' and I left, leaving Mother still screaming."

She testified that she had repeatedly remonstrated with her mother about Andrews's work.

After a long ordeal on the witness stand, Aimee was led away exhausted by her son, Rolf McPherson, left, and the Rev. Giles Knight, Angelus Temple manager.

"I pointed out that he had lost a number of temple suits totaling twenty-five thousand dollars, and that his work was sloppy."

And in direct refutation of her mother's assertion that she had been coerced at Phoenix, kept a prisoner in her room until she signed the contracts, Roberta brought out that the contracts had been signed only the next morning, after everybody had slept on the matter.

Miss Semple also described her mother's overpowering belief in a secret society that was scheming to wrest Angelus Temple from her.

"Who did she say told her all this?" she was asked.

"Mr. Andrews."

"Did you ever talk to your mother about coming back?"

"Yes, I talked to her on the telephone, but she refused to see me. She said she was too busy, that she was having her hair curled."

There were titters when a letter of Roberta's was read, containing the phrase:

"You needn't worry, Mother; everything is 'jake' now."

Jacob Moidel was recalled and described the strife at the temple. After Miss Semple had refused to take orders from Giles Knight, said Moidel, "there was some discussion about Miss Jordan, and I said to Mrs. McPherson, 'Don't go kicking Miss Jordan around just because you are in love with Mr. Knight.'"

This had precipitated a hectic scene, Moidel said. Roberta started to cry, her mother told her to "shut up," and at last Roberta said, "Mother, you have to choose now. Do you want Mr. Knight or do you want me?" Moidel quoted Aimee as saying, "I want Mr. Knight!" Then she had started screaming and had ordered them both to get out of the house and never come back.

"I said to her, 'That's certainly a fine thing to do, just because you are in love with Giles Knight—to throw your daughter out in the street because you see a new face!'"

Moidel confirmed that the Phoenix contracts had been signed not on March 14, but on the morning of March 15, after everybody had had the benefit of a night's sleep. He was histrionic on the stand, mimicking Aimee's voice in falsetto, standing up and throwing back his coat to show how Knight had charged at him, punctuating his words with fierce gestures. In the front row of spectators, Minnie Kennedy and Rheba Crawford took in the scene with interest.

Knight was recalled to deny emphatically that there was any romantic inclination on his part toward his pastor. He was, he said in a voice that defied contradiction, married happily.

In the midst of the testimony, Ma Kennedy created a momentary flurry when she entered carrying a large cardboard box tied with string. This she plopped down in Roberta's lap and panted that the box held the archives of the 1926 kidnaping case—letters, notes, affidavits, depositions, telegrams—and they were all for Roberta to use, if necessary. While successive grand juries had ransacked Southern California for these "secret documents," they had been reposing snugly under Minnie's bed.

Support for Miss Semple came from a police sergeant and a fire inspector, who swore that Willedd Andrews had spoken to them about Mrs. McPherson's being "blackmailed," and had implicated her daughter.

The defense received another setback from the testimony of Harriet

Jordan, who took the stand as a witness against Sister for the first time in their long, intimate association.

Aimee eyed her Bible School dean coldly, nervously tapping a pencil against her lips, while Miss Jordan gave a straightforward account of the happenings at Phoenix.

"I told Sister the only contract I wanted with her was love and confidence," she stated. "At no time while I was there did Sister McPherson complain of being intimidated."

"Was there any reference to a 'powder keg' about to blow up at home, or how she had signed under protest?" asked Fainer.

"No. They kidded some about the contracts, Mrs. McPherson saying they were the last she would ever sign."

Miss Jordan also fixed the time of the contract signing as March 15, the day she arrived in Phoenix, because she had left Los Angeles a day behind Roberta and Moidel.

At this point Judge Kincaid became keenly interested and took over the examination.

"Did you see Mrs. McPherson signing any documents in Phoenix?" he asked.

"Yes, I did."

"Was the contract prepared for you, or did you see it prepared in the hotel room?"

"Sister McPherson dictated them to Mr. Moidel."

"Do you know whether she dictated yours?"

"This one of mine? I know it was."

Here Aimee leaned over and whispered something to Andrews's counsel, who sprang to his feet and objected:

"Your honor, I want Mrs. McPherson to keep her tongue! She just said, 'That's a lie!'"

"I didn't hear any remarks," observed the judge, and Aimee leaned back with a tight smile.

Miss Jordan was asked whether she still felt well disposed toward the evangelist.

"I certainly do!" she replied fervently. "I shall always love and hope to serve her."

Then she stepped down.

As she passed Mrs. McPherson's chair, the evangelist muttered audibly:

"I'm glad they smoked the badgers out! I know who will be the new dean of the Bible School tomorrow!"

Later, when challenged to repeat this remark before several attorneys, Aimee merely laughed:

"Did I say that? Oh, I never did!"

Willedd Andrews then took the stand and stoutly repeated his denial of having used the word "blackmail." Then in a spirited finale Rheba Crawford gave a dramatic performance that almost equaled Sister's.

Aimee, seated at the counsel table, gave no sign of recognition as Rheba tripped past. And Rheba ignored Aimee. The trial was the first occasion on which the two had seen each other for a year.

"I don't want to tell you this," the witness began, speaking so rapidly her words at times became indistinct, "but Mr. Andrews said I was the mistress of a man in town and that he would produce affidavits to prove it, but he never did. I told him I resented his efforts to destroy my reputation."

Questioned about a conversation with Mrs. McPherson, Rheba replied:

"She expressed the hope that I would remain with her forever, but I said, 'Not if I am going to be ruined in the pulpit!' "

Another time, she said, she told Sister that she had been informed that Willedd Andrews was going to "frame" her.

"I told her I wasn't going to take that!" she cried, flailing her arms with evangelistic fire.

Lawyers were rebuffed by her harangues, and the judge was obliged to scold her three times for not sticking to the questions. Andrews's counsel, terming her a "revengeful and spiteful woman," waived his right of cross-examination, exclaiming as he pointed toward Aimee:

"I've got enough to handle there!"

The summing up by the attorneys unleashed forensics that were spiced with quotations from the Bible, Shakespeare, and legal tomes. Andrews's lawyer improvised on the theme of mother love, only to be reminded by Roberta's attorney that a few days before he had called the pastor of Angelus Temple "a female Neptune straddling the equator."

The judge, who had steered a steady course through the outbursts and contradictions, then ruled—in Roberta's favor.

Roberta Semple, Minnie Kennedy, and Rheba Crawford hugged each other for joy after judge decided in Roberta's favor in the suit against Aimee's lawyer.

"The court feels that judgment for the plaintiff vindicates her position," he concluded. Rheba Crawford he absolved of having had any part in the Phoenix doings, or of using her influence to harm Angelus Temple. Mrs. McPherson's testimony about the contracts and the scene in the Phoenix hotel the judge said he simply did not believe. He awarded Miss Semple two thousand dollars' damages and ordered Andrews to pay counsel fees and costs.

Aimee was not in the courtroom when the judge gave his decision. The oratory of the summations had overcome her, and weeping hysterically she had been half-carried to an anteroom. Lying on a couch while Rolf swabbed her brow, she sobbed steadily.

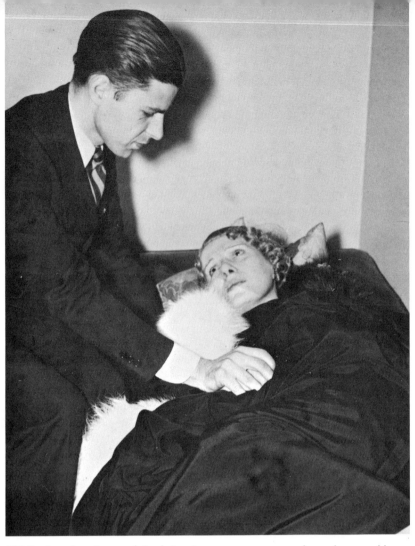

While her daughter rejoiced in the courtroom over her victory, Aimee wept in an anteroom, comforted by her son, Rolf McPherson.

In the adjoining courtroom, Roberta was receiving congratulations.

"I'm terribly happy that my name has been cleared, terribly, terribly happy!" Aimee's daughter repeated over and over, as she, Ma Kennedy, and Rheba Crawford hugged each other. Their triple alliance had scored a smashing victory.

Still sobbing, surrounded by her coterie—Ella Nordin, Giles Knight, and solicitous Rolf—Aimee was led to an elevator and quietly escorted home.

Weary Finale

*"And if thou tell'st the heavy story right,
Upon my soul, the hearers will shed tears."*
—*Henry VI, Part 3*

Rheba Crawford's lawsuit still loomed in the legal foreground, and Aimee had no heart for it. She had been rebuffed, publicly humiliated, her dignity as a woman sullied, by the outcome of her daughter's action. Photographs of the exulting Roberta, Minnie, and Rheba were splashed in the newspapers, bringing home to Aimee that now, except for Rolf, she was alone. Mother—husband—daughter—all alienated. She had not planned it that way. True, she still had the temple—yet even Angelus Temple was in jeopardy. After all the years of effort, Angelus Temple was mortgaged, and the mortgages were falling due.

Even before the close of the Andrews trial the public had been given an insight into Sister's need of funds. At a Sunday morning service, Brother Knight had made an extraordinary appeal for cash. It was needed, he said, to defend Sister and the church against Rheba Crawford's million-dollar suit.

"Last Sunday Rheba Crawford said over the radio that she still loved Sister," Knight told the faithful. "I guess she does—to the tune of one million and eighty thousand dollars."

He told why money was urgently needed.

"When I assumed the management of the temple nine months ago," he said, "it was practically insolvent. Bills totaling $66,005.25 were being pressed for payment by creditors. During the last nine months, $21,000 of these bills has been paid, and in addition, more than $10,000 worth of repairs has been made on the temple."

Now Sister's supporters must show their faith in her by giving,

Angelus Temple Melting Po

Aimee Semple McPherson
DEFENSE FUND

"We Will Defend Our Pastor"—with our

Cash	Chains	Gold Coins	Platinum	Silv
	Gold Watches	Diamond Rings	Gold Rings	
Wedding Rings		Bracelets	Gold Teeth	Pir

***"Blessed Are They That Protect the Priests
of The Lord"***

Name ....

Address .... Church No................

Knight exhorted—they must give their houses, their real estate, their automobiles, rings from their fingers, the watches from their wrists and vests, even gold teeth and bridgework from their mouths. Special contribution envelopes were distributed, on which was printed:

We will defend our pastor with our cash, gold coins, platinum, silver, gold watches, wedding rings, bracelets, gold teeth, pins. *"Blessed Are They That Protect the Priests of the Lord."*

The Scriptural-like quotation was not from the Bible.

A large nickel-plated bowl on a tripod was placed on the platform, and into this the donations were dropped. One man promised to sign over his automobile. A couple gave two hundred and sixty-five dollars they had saved for their summer vacation. Jewelry, currency, coins, eighteen-karat molars were tossed into the pot, to be refined into cash for Sister. And that evening Knight repeated the call for cash, cash, cash.

At this service Sister appeared, making the usual triumphant entrance. The story was the same: the temple crowded and hundreds shut out. During her sermon, Sister wept, and sinking to her knees told her congregation how she hoped that her "divided house" might become united. On her feet again, she encouraged the procession of contributors past her melting pot, rewarding each with a smile, a hand-shake, a pat on the back, as the line was herded along by the ushers. Knight said it took three men to carry the motley collection off the platform. Reporters who had haunted the temple for years had seen many bizarre performances there, but nothing as bizarre as this.

Rheba Crawford was moved to pity.

"I am deeply humiliated that I should be the means used by Mrs. McPherson and Giles Knight to separate the faithful Angelus Temple flock from their few pitiful remaining possessions. It is easy to understand why Mrs. McPherson and I quite obviously could not agree."

Several times during the Andrews trial, Aimee had expressed willingness to be reconciled with her mother. When she left the witness stand, she had come over and sat beside Minnie, and they conversed. But the breach was too wide to be filled in. Said Minnie later:

"We quarreled. Aimee came to me in that courtroom. She came to my side. A few minutes later I went to her side. I talked harshly with her, I know, but that is the way I always did in the past, as a first step in a reconciliation. Now? . . ."

She shook her head doubtfully.

Aimee's eyes misted with tears in telling her forlorn hope that peace might be restored in the family.

"That is what I want more than anyone will ever understand," she said, and wept softly.

In the temple she told her people:

"The last two weeks have been trying, but I want to assure my daughter that my love is unchanged. Someday I hope to pass my work on to her hands. When she was born I named her in my heart, 'My Star of Hope,' and that she remains."

Sister Aimee posed for photograph advertising that she will preach on the Rheba Crawford suit in a "vividly illustrated" sermon.

Sister Aimee and her elders kept the line of contributors moving as they dropped donations into her "melting pot" on Angelus Temple platform.

Yet this olive branch seemed drawn back immediately by Sister's coincidental announcement that Rolf McPherson had stepped into Roberta Semple's place and was doing the work satisfactorily.

Roberta was skeptical of her mother's intentions.

"Mother has made so many charges against me in open court that I would find it necessary for her to make a complete retraction," she said. "She would have to come to me and show me her real sincerity."

Retraction was not in Aimee's nature. For a while Roberta Semple was active with a competitive Los Angeles religious center, then she moved to New York, and there at last she found escape from the shadow of the temple.

Harriet Jordan, of course, was thrown out as dean of the Bible School, and another link with the bright days of the temple's beginnings was snapped. Four assistant workers resigned in indignation over this "unjust and unrighteous" expulsion, but Jordie allowed her contract to be terminated without scandal.

Jacob Moidel roiled the waters again when he sued to collect salary due under his canceled contract. He won the case, but only after another reenactment of the parsonage brawl.

All this led to a public revulsion. In the Andrews trial, the judge had lectured all the litigants on the necessity of their working in harmony for the good of their church.

"It is not for the court to point out any moral lessons to be derived from the facts and circumstances of this case, or to preach any sermon thereon," Judge Kincaid had said. "There are those directly involved better able, and with greater propriety, to do this. I have only this to say: a repetition or continuation of the internecine warfare between those responsible for the building, maintenance, and future well-being of Angelus Temple can only result in its eventual collapse and disintegration."

In the Moidel case, a second judge added his rebuke:

"It is a sad state of affairs when a family brings its disagreements into court, with the mother arrayed against the daughter, and a brother arrayed against his sister—especially when that family is connected with religious organizations. It seems to me that no amount of money could be involved to justify this action."

The feeling of the public generally was well caught by the *Los Angeles Times,* which said in an editorial:

"A news moratorium on the McPhersons et al. is the crying need of the day. Many families have quarrels. Few of them, with the intense ardor of three generations, succeeded in becoming what might be listed as court perennials, regular customers. The first time it was a sensation. The second time it was still good. But now it is like the ninth life of a cat, about worn out."

So decided was the reaction, a delegation of churchmen waited on both Mrs. McPherson and Miss Crawford and urged that for the good of the community and the cause of religion they compose their differences. Civic officials and business leaders also applied pressure, contending that the publicity generated by the wrangling was giving Los Angeles a bad name around the world.

In the face of this opposition, Rheba and Aimee gave in, and an agreement was reached through their attorneys by which the quarrel was "amicably adjusted, in deference to the earnest solicitation of the Christian ministry." Rheba agreed to dismiss her slander suit "with prejudice," meaning that it could not be revived, and in return she received a financial settlement of an undisclosed amount. The two women released each other mutually from all claims and litigation

Sister Aimee opened a new term of her Bible School by addressing the students from a balcony—just like the Pope or Mussolini. The new freshmen wore dunce caps.

of every character, and three days after the pact was ratified Rheba withdrew her action.

For Aimee, 1937 ended bleakly.

II

During the decade 1926–1937 it was estimated that Aimee Semple McPherson's name had appeared on the front pages of the Los Angeles newspapers an average of three times a week and in the national press only a little less frequently. Whenever a situation had called for a scene, Aimee had provided one, and had played it with all stops out. But by 1937 her position and her appeal to people generally had deteriorated, although her own communicants remained devotedly loyal.

Fortunately in Giles Knight she had found that firm supervisory hand that she had always needed, and he was able to arrest the downward trend. He threw a protective screen around the temple's pastor, cutting her off from all extraneous publicity or promotional ventures. Reporters who had been accustomed to call Sister Aimee at almost any hour found themselves unable to reach her. She accepted no calls from the press, and all inquiries were routed to uncommunicative intermediaries. It was the sort of regime that Mother Kennedy had tried to get her daughter to adhere to years before.

The Lake Elsinore showplace was disposed of, two Los Angeles men buying the castle as a speculation. It was understood that they paid much less than the one hundred nineteen thousand dollars it was said to have cost.

Aimee continued to preach, travel, and multiply the number of her adherents at home and afield. Somewhat subdued, sometimes straining a bit to bring off her sure-fire effects, but bringing them off, she narrowed her activities to the closed circuit of temple routine. The world outside the temple's "crystal doors" no longer invited her. The temple was her reality. For it she had sacrificed friends, family, happiness, health, and even, for one perilous moment, almost her reason; now it had her securely, and it would absorb the rest of her life.

She retracted none of her claims, and never acted as though aware that her position had been weakened. But it had been. Aimee had become a tourist attraction, like Catalina Island or Hollywood's film studios, and with the patronage of tourists she managed to keep the temple's insatiable maw fed. Her gaudy banners were flaunted along its walls like circus heraldry, and though her platform mannerisms might become stereotyped and the harsh Canadian accents of her voice take on stridency, she never gave less than her best before a throng.

Birthdays and holidays were gala occasions. On her forty-eighth birthday she appeared in the pulpit wearing a gingham dress and beribboned sunbonnet, carrying a milkpail full of milk. She served her elders a cupful apiece and then used the bucket to take the collection in. Nearly six thousand persons were on hand, including newcomers from every state in the union except Maine. When Sister asked all who had formerly lived on farms to stand, hundreds arose, as a wag in the gallery shouted, "Hay-men!"

Thanksgiving Day was another annual milestone, and whether ill or well, Sister managed to appear. After one bout of fever, she came to the platform on Thanksgiving Day shielded by bodyguards who turned back all persons approaching her. The temple was festooned with quilts and clothing prepared for distribution to the needy, and Sister gave a short talk on the blessings of liberty in the U.S.A., apologizing for her brevity, but promising to be back Sunday with a full-length sermon on "Who's Afraid of the Big, Bad Wolf?"

Illness troubled her intermittently, and she traveled restlessly. Upon each return from a trip she was welcomed home with the usual fanfares—flowers and flag-waving and singing of hymns—and the newspapers marveled that these did not become perfunctory. In the summer of 1938 Sister came back from a tour of the Eastern branches of the church and addressed more than two thousand admiring welcomers at the railroad station, speaking from a decorated baggage truck. The next year she received a welcome that the papers said resembled the receptions accorded movie stars in the gaudy days of the silent screen. While the temple band played "California, Here I Come," Sister marched under an arch of crossed flags (United States and Foursquare Gospel), carrying an armful of six dozen American Beauty roses and holding high her souvenir—a bird in a gilded cage.

After a year of strict church economy, the new administration's policy bore fruit, and on New Year's Day, 1939, Sister climbed to the top of the temple dome, and in the glare of huge floodlights ("one million candlepower") publicly burned the mortgages on the church— notes for sixty-six thousand five hundred and five dollars going into a blazing brazier. Across the street in Echo Park ten thousand spectators cheered, while girls in white robes, with angel wings attached to their shoulders, sounded trumpets and flitted about the roof in an allegory representing "the triumph of faith over gold."

Once during this period of retrenchment, the curtain of silence surrounding the affairs of the church and its pastor parted long enough to indicate the possibility of another family conflict. The incident occurred during the annual convention of the church. Aimee was endeavoring to push through a change in the bylaws, which would exclude from the ministry of the church any divorced person who married again. She spoke vigorously in support of the change, and Rolf McPherson, her son, was reported to have spoken as vigorously against it. The resolution was carried by a small margin; and

Thanksgiving Day service brought display of work done by the members —quilts and children's clothing for distribution to the needy. Aimee, in 1938, glowed upon her congregation, backed by her Temple elders, substantial citizens proud of their glamorous pastor.

as if to counteract the gossip about a serious disagreement, Aimee called in reporters and posed for their cameras with her arm around her son.

"Since Rolf was born, there has never been a quarrel between us," she assured all. "We have always agreed perfectly on everything."

This occurred in January, 1941. In December of that year, Roberta Semple was married in New York to Harry Salter, a radio musician. Under the new bylaw, Aimee's daughter thus became automatically disqualified from ever occupying the temple pulpit. Whether the evangelist had been aware of her daughter's intention to remarry at the time the bylaw was passed was never made clear. Thenceforward Roberta would make her home permanently in the East.

During World War II Aimee McPherson preached to thousands of servicemen, and here prays with converts in Angelus Temple.

World War II curtailed Aimee's travels, but still she roved "wherever there are no torpedoes." Her church continued to expand. She distributed Testaments to servicemen in gross lots (in two world wars she handed out nearly two million Bibles, by her count; she called it her "hobby"), and in sermons of brimstone invoked gruesome curses on Hitler and Tojo.

"How many of you would like to see Hitler covered with boils from head to foot?" she cried. "Well, I would!"

In 1942 she staged a war bond rally in Pershing Square, in downtown Los Angeles, wearing a red, white, and blue costume, and in one hour sold one hundred fifty thousand dollars' worth of bonds.

A "Holy Ghost revival" at that year's church convention brought a faint echo of her rousing "Holy Roller" beginnings: for fourteen hours delegates leaped and shouted, clapped hands, danced in the aisles, spoke in tongues, and fell prostrate in ecstasies. Attending reporters were flabbergasted, but Aimee answered their startled inquiries good-naturedly:

"What makes people jump out of their seats? Well, if there's a

At the 1941 convention of her church, fires fell, delegates shouted, swooned, and spoke in tongues in an old-fashioned "Holy Ghost" revival, an echo to Aimee of her early days.

fire under you, you just can't sit still. Did you ever try sitting on a hot stove?"

All this made news spasmodically, although little of it came directly from Sister. The restrictions that hedged her, the virtual abdication from sensationalism, she appeared to accept with relief after so many years of strife. Her magnetism and her charm remained indestructible. On her fifty-second birthday, a Los Angeles newspaper columnist saluted her on behalf of a group of men and women who had seen her in all seasons, under all conditions, and who knew her about as well as anyone could—the members of the city's working press. They had been at times her remorseless antagonists; they had also been her collaborators; and their admiration of her was unbounded. Remarking on her age, the columnist said:

"No one would guess it—not by a jugful of years! She certainly doesn't look it. And a world war is the only thing that could have reduced Mrs. McPherson to an inside page. . . . She will live forever in the affection of every newspaperman who journeyed with her along life's rugged highway, when she established a world's record for sustained, countrywide news interest. A birthday toast, then, to the most original, exciting, and newsworthy space-getter in the land!"

Mother Kennedy dropped out of the news during this period, except for brief mention now and then. She did attract some attention when she petitioned the court to drop the name Hudson and be legally restored to Minnie Kennedy again. The court granted the request. Ma's attorney in this action, it was noted, was Jacob Moidel. But Mother was content to remain in obscurity.

The year 1943 was trying for Aimee. On a visit to Mexico she contracted tropical fever, and in August, while in British Columbia, she suffered a relapse. From then on she often was absent from her pulpit. In January, 1944, a rumor spread that Rolf McPherson was to take over the church direction from Giles Knight, and it was deduced that Aimee was planning to retire.

Knight did resign his executive positions in the church—vice-president and secretary-treasurer of Angelus Temple, of L.I.F.E. Bible Training College, and of the Echo Park Evangelistic Association, as well as Sister's personal manager; most of these posts he had held for six years. Then on February 1, 1944, Aimee once more summoned reporters to her hilltop home and introduced them to her son at the close of his first full day as vice-president of the church.

"Rolf," she said proudly, "is vice-president permanently."

Her health, she went on, was better:

"I feel magnificent—good for the next fifty years!"

Joking with these ancient friends and foemen, she reproached them playfully for having neglected her.

"Aimee good—that's no news," she pouted. "But Aimee bad—oh, boy!"

That summer illness again beset her. In the autumn a new branch church was to be dedicated in Oakland, in the northern part of the state, and appeals came that Sister preside at the ceremonies. Aimee consented, and on Monday, September 25, flew north with Rolf. In her party also were the temple's music director, a press agent-pastor, a tenor soloist, an assistant evangelist, and Aimee's personal maid and companion.

On Tuesday, Sister heralded her arrival by driving a horse and buggy in a parade to Oakland Auditorium, where she preached on

Age failed to dim Aimee McPherson's magnetism and charm. This un-retouched press photograph was taken in 1941, on the eve of her fifty-first birthday. She was wearing her Temple uniform, with her hallmark corsage. She had long given up wearing a wedding ring.

"The Foursquare Gospel." Ten thousand persons filled the hall, and newspapers said the response was warm. The next evening, she announced, her topic would be "The Story of My Life"—a sermon in which she never failed to thrill.

Back at her hotel, she chatted with Rolf for a while in her darkened room (the wartime blackout was in force), still keyed up and tense from the excitement of the evening. Standing at the open window, she listened to the drone of airplanes overhead, and mused:

"I wonder, when we die, if we will be riding around in airplanes."

Rolf kissed his mother good night and went to his room.

The next day—Wednesday, September 27—the world's newspapers were taken up with accounts of Armageddon battles—Arnheim, and the whole European theater of the war in flames.

On February 1, 1944, Aimee called in the press and announced the appointment of her son, Rolf McPherson, as vice-president and general manager of her church. Reporters loved her, and she always had a smile for them.

Amid these reports of convulsions of nations, there appeared—on the front pages—a headline eloquent in its brevity:

AIMEE IS DEAD.

At ten o'clock, that Wednesday morning, Rolf McPherson had gone to his mother's room and found her lying in bed, breathing stertorously. On the pillow and spilled on the floor beside the bed were several capsules. Telephone calls brought medical assistance, but at 11:45 A.M. the evangelist was pronounced dead.

Immediately it was rumored that Aimee had committed suicide. The doctors tentatively attributed death to a heart attack, but the discovery in her purse of a phial containing a powerful sedative of the same kind contained in the capsules scattered on her pillow caused the coroner to order an autopsy and pathological tests.

Her physician in Los Angeles denied having prescribed the drug found in her purse, and the State Board of Pharmacy became curious about the lack of a druggist's label on the bottle. The medicine, a comparatively new barbiturate classified as a hypnotic sedative, could be dispensed legally only by prescription.

Rolf described his mother's mood and behavior on her last evening as wholly normal; he had seen no indication of despondency or depression. She had professed to be delighted with her reception at the auditorium, he said; and while he knew she had been taking sedatives, it had been to induce sleep during her illness and to ease the pain in her throat after a recent attack of laryngitis. Talk of suicide seemed preposterous to him.

The temple's attorney, Joseph Fainer (the same who had won a victory for Sister's daughter in the Andrews slander trial), had flown north at the first word, and with him Rolf hastened back to Los Angeles, where they found the temple in disarray. The whole building pulsed with wailing and lamentation. Women sobbed, shrieked; they crawled on their knees to the pulpit, moaning, "Oh, Lord, send Sister Aimee back to us!" Others jumped up and down in uncontrollable spasms, and still others crouched with heads bowed to the floor, motionless, stunned by their grief. Children watched in amazement their mothers imploring Heaven's pity: "Please send her back! Lord, she hasn't gone! Amen-amen-amen!" One middle-aged woman danced across the foyer, tears trickling down her cheeks, as she chanted, "Oh, Lord, please don't! Please don't! Please don't!" From

Word of Aimee's death in 1944 plunged Angelus Temple into frantic mourning. Here the grief-stricken pray in the "500 Room."

prostrate forms arose a groaning: "Please, God, have mercy on her!" A plump housewife, hat askew, shook clenched fists above her head and shrieked, "Lord, it cannot be!" In the Bible School a preacher sobbed that Sister had left this world, and there was nothing he could do for her now. "No, no, no! Brother, don't say it!" wailed the crowd.

Outside the temple, workmen were covering the forty-foot-high photograph of Sister above the entrance canopy with hastily printed announcements of future services. From the marquee a Bible College student disconsolately removed the sign announcing the subject of the sermon Sister was to have preached the coming Sunday: "Going My Way?"

Time was needed to assemble the hosts of the church for a fitting farewell to its founder and inspiration, and Rolf McPherson announced that the funeral would be held on October 9. The body was to lie in state under the temple dome for three days before that.

Across the city in Hermosa Beach, Mother Kennedy was reported to be near collapse. Mother, who lived, like Aimee, with a paid companion, was said to have had a presentiment the day before her daughter died—a strange dread, just like the feeling she had had on

the day Robert Semple died in China. The seventy-three-year-old
woman sent word:

"I don't want to talk about it, I just want to pray."

Everywhere tributes appeared, with column-long obituaries in the
newspapers. The *London Daily Mail*, although reduced by wartime
newsprint scarcity to four pages daily, ordered a thousand words
cabled on the event. Everywhere the uniqueness of Aimee's genius
was signaled out for comment. "A legendary figure"—"put hallelujah
in the headlines"—"dynamism that galvanized millions who heard
her preach"—"a voice that cast a hypnotic spell"—"she took revivalism
from the gaslighted tent circuit into a glamorous temple and drew
millions of followers to her cause"—"the world's acknowledged
mistress of hallelujah revivalism"—"an incredible capacity for living"
—supernacular eulogies—the clear outline of her personality streaked
but not obliterated by the contrast of controversies and human failings
that had so checkered her life.

The funeral was on a scale commensurate with the achievements
of Sister. For three days her body lay in state on the platform where
she had made herself a legend in her time. Fifty thousand mourners
passed the bier, the lines extending for a block along both sides of
the temple, four and six abreast. Despite the wartime gas rationing,
automobiles stood double-parked for half a mile around. Seventy-five
city policemen controlled the throng, and inside the temple uniformed
police officers stood guard at the head and foot of the coffin.

Aimee lay in a bronze casket lined with quilted white satin. (Its
weight was twelve hundred pounds and it cost ten thousand dollars,
the news-greedy public was told.) She was dressed in the uniform
of her church, white gown with shield and cross on the bosom and
long blue cape. Her hands clasped a Bible bound in white satin, and
on her shoulder were gardenias and roses. The platform, the orchestra
pit, the choir loft, the aisles were filled with flowers; five carloads
were not even taken into the temple because of lack of space. Florists
declared nothing like the display had ever been seen in Los Angeles,
and the cost was estimated at more than fifty thousand dollars; the
orchids alone were appraised at ten thousand dollars conservatively.

While the lines shuffled past the embowered casket, organists in
relays played revival tunes and Sister's own lively or lachrymose
compositions. The temple chimes, which had broken down almost at
the moment of Sister's death, had been repaired and rang dolefully

The line waiting to view Sister Aimee lying in state in Angelus Temple stretched for blocks for three days.

every hour. On the last day the crowd still was so large the elders permitted the doors to remain open until ten o'clock in the evening, and even then many were shut out.

The next morning, before dawn, the lines formed again, and when the funeral ceremonies got under way not only was the temple jammed as it used to be when Sister preached, but the Bible School auditorium and subsidiary chapels and meeting rooms also, while two thousand persons stood on the sidewalk. The eulogies and music continued for three hours. Although not programed to speak, Rolf,

The funeral, with full band and massed choirs, in the Temple where she had made herself a legend.

in an impromptu outburst, passionately called for a rededication to carry on Sister's work.

"Mother is not sorrowing," he cried. "She is rejoicing with our Savior!"

The entire audience surged to their feet and raised their hands in the gesture Sister had taught them, the gesture of joy and affirmation.

The official eulogists ranked Aimee Semple McPherson with a host of Christian leaders and reformers—Zwingli, Knox, Wesley—Huss, Wycliffe, Savonarola—Whitefield, Luther, Moody. But perhaps the words she would have liked best were one pastor's affirmation:

"Today we are here to commemorate the stepping up of a country girl to God's Hall of Fame."

Mother Kennedy did not attend the temple rites; she would not trust herself to enter that building under the harrowing circumstances. Nor was Roberta Salter present. She had not arrived from New York; messages to Rolf said that she could not obtain an airplane reservation.

Dressed in black and seated among the faithful was one unlooked-for figure—Rheba Crawford Splivalo.

A funeral motorcade of six hundred cars escorted Aimee along Los Angeles streets rendered almost deserted by wartime gasoline rationing.

Another face that drew curious glances was that of an elderly man who strikingly resembled Rolf McPherson—his father, Harold S. McPherson, who had traveled across the country from Florida by bus, he said, since that was the only transportation he could procure with wartime "priority" travelers taking all airline space. He had wished, he said, "to be with Rolf and comfort him in his sorrow."

It was the first meeting between father and son in fifteen years. The slight, graying man met the press in the temple office, and recalled Sister's early struggles, when she had preached to knots of listeners in vacant lots and on street corners. Rolf escorted his father on a tour of Angelus Temple—the first sight Harold McPherson had had of the famous structure upon which his name had so long blazed in electric lights.

The motorcade that whisked through traffic-empty streets to Forest Lawn Memorial-Park added up to six hundred cars—a turnout that would have delighted Aimee. The cemetery had been closed to the public for fear of a demonstration, and only about two thousand persons were admitted—the family and church officials, including seventeen hundred Foursquare Gospel ministers whom Sister had ordained personally. These flanked an Avenue of Sorrow to the tomb, on one side holding American flags, on the other the flags of their church. Twelve ministers staggered under the tug of the coffin; several times they were forced to put it down and rest.

A supercolossal floral tribute had been planned for the cemetery—a cross of white roses measuring six hundred feet from top to bottom, with the arms projecting two hundred and fifty feet on either side, and twenty-five feet in breadth. Two carloads of white roses had been shipped, but sheer lack of space forced abandonment of this project.

At the tomb, Minnie Kennedy, weeping silently, was joined by Rolf and Lorna Dee McPherson, their own daughters, Kay and Marlene, and Harold McPherson—the family complete, except for Roberta. Aimee had purchased the imposing tomb ten years before, at Depression prices, when her Blessed Hope cemetery scheme back-

The family at the graveside. From left: Minnie Kennedy, between a woman companion and Joseph Fainer, Temple lawyer; Harold S. Mc-Pherson, Rolf McPherson's father, with hand on the shoulder of Marlene, Rolf McPherson's younger daughter; Kay McPherson, the older daughter; Mr. and Mrs. Rolf McPherson. Roberta, Aimee's daughter, was absent.

fired; it stood on Sunrise Slope, topped by a slab of polished Italian marble lettered in bronze "McPherson." (Later the legend was altered to read "Aimee Semple McPherson," rendering the tomb unmistakably her own.) On either side, on pedestals, knelt guardian angels; a third statuary ornament, the figure of a kneeling woman, Aimee had ordered removed. A screen of pines formed the backdrop, and checkering the level greensward before the sarcophagus were the gravestones of Sister's followers, in position to "go up with Aimee" at the last trump.

The sun was setting as the ceremonies concluded and the mourners dispersed, shivering a little in the evening chill. Aimee was left alone—on October 9, 1944, her fifty-fourth birthday. Her funeral had been her last birthday party.

Aimee Semple McPherson's tomb on Sunrise Slope in Forest Lawn Memorial-Park. Later the inscription was changed to her full name.

Afterpiece

As in the old-time theater, where the melodrama was followed by an afterpiece, in death Aimee did not short-change her audience. Minnie Kennedy, for one thing, survived. And there were questions, many questions, respecting both Angelus Temple and its lost leader. There was, immediately, the question of how Sister had died—whether naturally, or by voluntary choice. This question had not been answered when Aimee was placed at rest amid the evening shadows at Forest Lawn.

Three surgeons conducted an autopsy. They reported finding the evangelist's heart perfectly sound. Tests were run on vital organs, and five days after the funeral the conclusions were presented at an inquest in Oakland.

The examining pathologist reported that traces had been found indicating that Mrs. McPherson had taken a heavy dose of the same barbital sedative that was in the capsules scattered on the pillow. Also, the evangelist had been suffering from a serious kidney ailment. One of the first effects of the drug in question, it was brought out, was to numb or depress the memory.

"Could death have been accidental?" the coroner asked.

"It could," answered the pathologist. "A person could get in such a state of forgetfulness that he might not remember how many he had taken of these pills."

Supporting evidence was seen in the circumstance that the capsules on the pillow were moist, as if they had fallen from her mouth after she had already reached drowsiness from a previous dose.

The coroner's jury returned a verdict that "death was caused by shock and respiratory failure from an accidental overdose of barbital compound and a kidney ailment."

Said Roberta Salter:

"It is a relief to know that it was accidental and that she went quietly and without pain."

Aimee's daughter had arrived in Los Angeles on the day of the inquest. At the airport, she was met by her grandmother and, surprisingly, Willedd Andrews. No explanation of Andrews's presence was given.

Rolf McPherson already had been announced as Sister's successor and president of the interlocking church corporations, by virtue of his mother's will and also of the church's charter. And the day before Roberta's arrival, Lorna Dee McPherson had been introduced to a temple audience as the new vice-president of the Echo Park Evangelistic Association.

At the airport, Roberta gave no enlightening information; in fact, she was almost prevented from speaking at all: every time a question was put, Minnie Kennedy dug an elbow into her ribs and told her not to answer. After an unproductive interview, so far as the press was concerned, Roberta went to stay with her grandmother at Hermosa Beach.

The next day, Aimee's mother, daughter, and son gathered at the evangelist's grave. And that day her will was filed for probate. Her estate was described as small, her attorney, Fainer, being quoted as saying that she had died possessing less than four thousand dollars—"she poured it all back into the church."

The will, dated March 27, 1944, left Roberta Salter twenty-five hundred dollars. The entire residue, including personal effects, the parsonage, and its contents, was left to Rolf McPherson. To Mother Kennedy her daughter bequeathed ten dollars, with the proviso that should she contest the will, she should receive five dollars. Rolf McPherson was named executor without the necessity of posting bond, inasmuch as the cash value of the estate was less than ten thousand dollars.

Told of her legacy, Roberta said:

"That was very nice of Mother. She did not need to do it, but it shows she was thinking of me."

Minnie was less appreciative of her ten dollars.

"It must be a mistake, or one of her practical jokes!" she exclaimed. "Why, just a few weeks ago I sent Aimee eleven hundred dollars from the sale of some property of mine in Canada. However, she didn't need to mention me at all."

Contest the will? Ma laughed. Her elastic spirit had rebounded, and she had regained her sparkle.

"I'll just smile," said she.

Roberta Salter soon returned to New York. When Rolf's final accounting as executor was accepted by the court, it showed that the evangelist had left a personal estate of thirty-three thousand six hundred and three dollars. Out of this the executor had paid approximately twenty-one thousand dollars, and the net inheritance was some twelve thousand dollars—all that remained to the woman through whose hands had flowed millions.

After her daughter's death, Minnie Kennedy withdrew from public notice almost entirely. Her congenial employment was the management of her properties and the periodic rewriting of her will. Her regard for the Salvation Army remained warm; at one time she bequeathed the organization a considerable sum of money, then in a codicil took part of it back because she said she couldn't afford it.

Early in 1947, while riding in a brand-new automobile, she was in a collision with a truck. The side of her car was ripped away, and though she escaped with bruises, the shock aged her. Neighbors at Hermosa Beach, where she was living with three cats and two dogs, noticed that she was failing, and one day in November she asked the man next door if he would take care of her pets should anything happen to her.

A few days after that she was found dead, sprawled on the kitchen floor. To her, as to her daughter, death had come suddenly and alone.

An autopsy showed that she had succumbed to the infirmities of age: she was worn out, she had not surrendered. At her funeral, the Reverend J. G. Gay, the friend who had married her to Guy Edward ("Whataman") Hudson, officiated, with a Salvation Army colonel. And she was buried—"promoted to glory"—in her Salvation Army uniform.

Mother's will (it had been drawn in 1940 and amended later) left one thousand dollars apiece to her great-grandchildren, Rolf McPherson's daughters. Her interest in the land on which Angelus Temple stood she bequeathed to Rolf McPherson. Most of the rest went to Roberta Salter. The final inventory disclosed bank accounts totaling one hundred and fifty thousand dollars, and property held in joint tenancy with Roberta valued at one hundred twenty-six thousand dollars more. After all charges were paid, the net inheritance amounted to some two hundred thousand dollars—proof that a tambourine, in the right hands, may be a remunerative instrument.

In her earthly farewell, Minnie Kennedy ringingly recited her allegiance, devotion, and debt to the Salvation Army—"as a soldier who loved it, lived in it, and went to glory from its ranks. All that I have been humbly able to accomplish for God and others is due to my early Salvation Army training, its discipline, honor, integrity, loyalty, and goodness."

To Aimee, living when the will was written, her mother had bequeathed nothing except two hundred dollars in cash, with a sealed letter of instructions as to how it should be spent.

Thus died Minnie Kennedy, no longer sprightly but undaunted. She was buried in a different cemetery, on the opposite side of town from Aimee.

The church that Minnie Kennedy and Aimee Semple McPherson had created and that Sister Aimee haltingly had carried to maturity did not wither and crumble after their passing, in spite of predictions to that effect. Under the direction of Rolf McPherson, it rallied from the shock of Sister's removal and thereafter progressed steadily in size and affluence.

Two years after Aimee McPherson's death, the report made to the church's annual convention showed that the Church of the Foursquare Gospel possessed property valued at $4,225,000. At the end of 1947 this had risen to $5,525,000; in 1952, to $12,350,000; in 1954, to $17,609,000; and at the close of 1958 it stood at more than $21,000,000—exclusive of Angelus Temple and its dependencies, valued at another $1,500,000. Since then it has increased steadily, and at the end of 1969 stood at $59,000,000.

The membership in the quarter of a century since Aimee's death has kept pace with the material increase, reaching 78,500 in 1951, 122,907 in 1958, and in 1969 it was more than 193,000.

By 1969 the Foursquare Gospel banner was said to hang in 776 churches in the United States and Canada, and in more than 2,000 overseas mission stations and "meeting places" in twenty-seven countries.

In Los Angeles, dormitories for students of the Bible College had been built as a memorial to Sister McPherson, together with a youth center and gymnasium, and a missionary rest home.

Fundamentalist and Pentecostal in its tenets and practices, Angelus Temple retained none of the flamboyance that marked it during Sister's time. The great auditorium, in the succeeding years, seldom was filled except during a church convention, and there were no standees around loudspeakers on the sidewalks. The star of the production having moved on, a road-show company was left to continue the familiar observances. Though there is subdued vitality, no shivers of excitement await the visitor to Angelus Temple today. The little door, high up in the balcony, through which Sister made her entrances, opens upon no comparable glamour under the rule of the epigone. The name of Minnie Kennedy is seldom mentioned there.

Yet these two women together achieved something that is given to few men or women ever to accomplish—they founded a church, which survives and prospers long after their departure from the earthly scene. United or divided, this is their story. It is, of course, not the whole story. That will have to wait.

NOTE ON SOURCES
AND READING LIST

It is perhaps needless to point out at this stage that this account has been drawn scrupulously from the record of Aimee Semple Mc-Pherson's activities and those of her mother and that nothing has been imagined, no incident invented, and nothing altered in the recorded word or fact.

Any work that has been twelve years in preparation, as has this book, necessarily becomes based on an accumulation of information derived from both published and unpublished sources. In this instance the published sources far outweigh those of a private nature. This is because few careers have been as copiously and variously chronicled as those of Minnie Kennedy and Mrs. McPherson. The incessant prying by the press into every aspect of their lives (most of the time with Aimee's exuberant cooperation) merely reflected the long-continued interest of the public in them and their affairs. In consequence, few secrets that Aimee wished to preserve stayed inviolate long. Sooner or later, through some personal disagreement, a change of command at the temple, a breach of confidence committed by a discarded or disgruntled associate, or through testimony given in a lawsuit, a revealing light would be thrown on incidents or events that had occurred perhaps years before and had remained dark and inscrutable since then. For a peculiarity of Aimee's private life was that, whether with her hearty consent or willy-nilly, it was lived in public.

The prime source of day-by-day information about Mrs. Mc-Pherson and her fortunes, therefore, remains the daily newspaper press. Running to millions of words, this press record is almost inexhaustible. Newspapers principally drawn upon in preparing this study include:

> *Los Angeles Times*—(The complete file, from 1920, when Aimee
> received her first few lines of notice, until her death.)
> *Los Angeles Examiner*

Los Angeles Herald and *Los Angeles Express*—(Later combined
    as the *Herald-Express*.)
Los Angeles Record
Los Angeles News
San Francisco Examiner
San Francisco Chronicle
San Francisco Bulletin
San Francisco Call
Oakland Tribune
Sacramento Bee
Sacramento Union
Seattle Post-Intelligencer
Seattle Times
Portland Oregonian
Montreal Star
Detroit Times
New York Times
New York World
New York American
New York Journal
New York Daily News
New York Graphic
Chicago Tribune
Chicago Herald & Examiner
London Daily Mail
London Mirror
Variety
Billboard

Also, less intensively, various other daily and weekly newspapers
published in the United States and Canada.

An additional source of much verbatim material has been the
transcripts of testimony, depositions, briefs, complaints, and other
evidence contained in the voluminous record of Aimee Semple
McPherson's litigation.

The only published biographies are Aimee's own. These are to be
approached with caution. They provide some factual information
regarding the early years, mingled with a jumble of verbal trash and
misinformation, some apparently intentional and more unintentional,

and they abound in eloquent omissions. Mrs. McPherson's numerous other publications also have been to some extent serviceable in reflecting her mental traits, and occasionally giving clues to her preoccupations and purposes at different times. Her own writings, or those credited to her, that have been consulted, are:

> *This Is That*—Personal Experiences, Sermons, and Writings, by Aimee Semple McPherson. Published privately 1919, 1921, 1923, Los Angeles; reissued by the Echo Park Evangelistic Association, Los Angeles, 1958.
>
> *In the Service of the King*—The Story of My Life—(Ghost-written but signed by Aimee Semple McPherson.) Boni & Liveright, New York, 1927.
>
> *The Holy Spirit*—Challpin Publishing Co., Los Angeles, 1931.
>
> *Give Me My Own God*—H. C. Kinsey & Co., Los Angeles, 1936.
>
> *The Story of My Life*—(A hagiographic collection of extracts crudely lifted from Mrs. McPherson's writings, issued posthumously over her signature.) Published by International Correspondents, Hollywood, California, 1951.

Numerous sermons, pamphlets, and recordings made by Aimee Semple McPherson, including:

> "Divine Healing in the Word of God"—(Recorded sermon.)
> "Three Little Pigs"—(Recorded sermon.)
> "From Milkpail to Pulpit"—(Recorded sermon.)
> What's the Matter?
> America, Awake!
> Lost and Restored
> Behold! The King Cometh
> The Scarlet Thread
> The Temple of the Word
> "Thus It Becometh Us"
> There Is A God!—Debate Between Aimee Semple McPherson, Fundamentalist, and Charles Lee Smith, Atheist.
> Divine Healing Sermons

Of contemporary fugitive writings about the evangelist and her mother, pamphlets, etc., the following:

> *The Disappearance of Aimee Semple McPherson*—John J. Kershner, Los Angeles, 1926

"McPhersonism"—Rev. R. P. (Bob) Shuler, Los Angeles, 1924, reissue of 1926

Antics of Aimee—Charles H. Magee, Los Angeles, 1926

"Aimee"—The Gospel Gold-Digger!—Rev. John D. Goben, Los Angeles, 1932

Books dealing with Mrs. McPherson and Mrs. Kennedy:

Sister Aimee—Nancy Barr Mavity, Doubleday, Doran & Co., New York, 1931

Conquistador, American Fantasia—Philip Guadella, Ernest Benn, Ltd., London, 1927

The Vanishing Evangelist: The Aimee Semple McPherson Kidnaping Affair—Lately Thomas, Viking Press, New York, 1959

The Aspirin Age—Edited by Isabel Leighton. Chapter entitled "Aimee Semple McPherson: 'Sunshine in My Soul,'" by Carey McWilliams, Simon & Schuster, New York, 1949

Mrs. Astor's Horse—Stanley Walker, Stokes, New York, 1935

Magazine articles consulted include several by H. L. Mencken, and the perceptive appraisal by Sarah Comstock published in *Harper's Magazine*, December, 1927.

A book containing some interesting information regarding revivalists and revivals in America during the nineteenth century, although deficient in insight and dully written, is Bernard A. Weisberger's *They Gathered at the River*, published by Little, Brown & Co., Boston, 1958.

Aimee Semple McPherson has inspired characters in a number of novels of varying merit, none of which are distinguished by a close adherence to the facts.

A source of constructive assistance has been the thousands of photographs of Aimee and her circle, as well as her antagonists, reposing in newspaper files and private collections. Many of these photographs have never been published. They have served to verify, and in some instances to correct, published statements made both for and against the evangelist.

Finally there have been reminiscences by contemporaries of Mrs. McPherson and her mother, which have been passed along by letter and in confidential conversations. For these confidences, and for the generous cooperation of all the thoughtful, earnest contributors to the undertaking, a debt of gratitude is acknowledged.

INDEX